blue
moon
rising

andy **buckley**

richard **burgess**

andy **buckley**

Andy Buckley has been a journalist for 25 years. He started on the *Sale Guardian* as a news reporter before moving to the *Bolton Evening News* to work as a sports reporter. In 1990, he became the Manchester City reporter at BBC *GMR*, where he has now been the sports editor for the past seven years.

richard **burgess**

A Manchester City supporter all his life, **Richard Burgess** started his journalistic career as a news reporter on the *Grimsby Evening Telegraph*. He moved to the *Manchester Evening News* to work on the sports desk and covered Manchester City. In July 1999, he joined BBC *GMR* as a sports producer.

blue moon rising

First published 2000 by Milo Books

Copyright © Andy Buckley and Richard Burgess

The moral right of the authors has been asserted

ISBN 0 9530847 4 4

Typography and layout by
Barron Hatchett Design, Manchester

Printed and bound in Great Britain by
Guernsey Press Co Ltd, Guernsey

MILO BOOKS
P.O. Box 153
Bury
Lancs BL0 9FX

Contents

ACKNOWLEDGEMENTS

THIS BOOK would not have possible without the help and co-operation of players and staff at Manchester City FC, both past and present. The club is renowned for its honesty and friendliness, a reputation which is richly deserved. In particular, we would like to thank the people who have agreed to be interviewed for *Blue Moon Rising*.

Many people have given us their perspective on the last decade in extended interviews and we thank them for their frankness, trust and time. In particular, we would like to personally extend our gratitude to Joe Royle, David Bernstein, Francis Lee, Brenda Swales, Chris Muir, Frank Clark, Brian Horton, Howard Kendall, David White, Tony Coton, Georgi Kinkladze, Michael Brown, Eddie McGoldrick, Mike Turner, John Dunkerley, John Maddock, Mike McDonald and Paul Hince. We should also like to thank Ashley Lewis, Willie Donachie, Gary Tipper, Lee Bradbury, Paul Lake, Steve Coppell, Dave Wallace and Ian Niven.

There are many other people who have given us their support and co-operation. We extend a sincere thank you to Chris Bird, Sara Billington, Julia McCrindle, Peter Spencer, Ian Cheeseman, Stephen Wood, Joyce Burgess, Louise Deeks, Julie Buckley, Chris Buckley and Rob Buckley.

Material from the BBC *GMR* and *Manchester Evening News* archives has also proved invaluable in our research for this book.

INTRODUCTION

FRANK CLARK'S REACTION said it all. The former Manchester City manager chuckled merrily as he contemplated a book about the last ten seasons at Maine Road. His familiar warm laugh, sounding more like Father Christmas than a football manager, began to die down. "You're not going to be short of things to write about, are you?"

The story of City's recent history is one of the most extraordinary tales in modern English football – a compelling journey from the heights of the Premiership to the depths of despair in Division Two, and then back again. No other club has witnessed so much drama and upheaval in such a short space of time. No other club's support has remained so unceasingly loyal under such duress. No other club is quite like Manchester City.

The aim of this book is to present an independent, authoritative and accurate account of the last decade at City. We felt it was important to chronicle the events because it is such a great story. There are so many personalities involved, so many memorable incidents and so much you can easily forget. As journalists who have covered City on a full-time basis throughout that period, we have had a unique insight into the club's affairs. It is a great job and there has hardly been a dull moment. With this book, we are hoping to recount the story behind the headlines.

We have spoken at length to dozens of people who have been intimately associated with City over recent years. It has been an enriching experience for us and we have learned so much we did not know before. Obviously, without the co-operation of the interviewees, this book would not have been possible. To be honest, you can sometimes forget how many people have been touched by City in such a short period of time – fans, players, managers, employees and chairmen.

The two men at the heart of the club's recent revival, Joe Royle and David Bernstein, have spoken honestly about the problems of the past and the climb back to the top. They have disclosed information which has never been public knowledge before. The City chairman talks about his pivotal role at the club over the past six years, starting with his participation in Francis Lee's takeover bid. Royle reveals his true thoughts about Georgi Kinkladze and a transfer deal which almost brought one of Europe's top players to Maine Road.

Francis Lee speaks openly for the first time about his controversial four-year reign and delivers a passionate defence of his record as chairman. He offers a frank opinion of the managers he appointed and the players they bought.

His predecessor as chairman, Peter Swales, never spoke out after his resignation from the board in 1994. He died two years later but now the person who knew him best, his widow Brenda, has broken her silence in an exclusive and emotional interview about the man who led City for 20 years. She talks about the takeover campaign and the pressures it inflicted on her family life.

Throughout six months of research and writing, we have tracked down managers, players and directors from every era to ensure the story was as complete as possible. We have been struck by the huge level of interest in the Blues from all walks of life. Their fascination with City has been a source of inspiration in our work.

Some people have decided not to speak publicly about their time at the club, but the vast majority have been encouraging and helpful. We have always believed strongly in our impartiality, preferring to leave it up to the readers to make their own conclusion.

Last season was a wonderful experience for any fan of the Blues with the club's return to the Premiership. This book documents every step of the way in a match-by-match diary of the season. Hopefully, it will bring back some happy memories. The final match at Blackburn Rovers was an unforgettable afternoon and a fitting climax to the engaging story of Manchester City over the last decade.

Andy Buckley and Richard Burgess

OVER**VIEW**

THE VINYL FLOORING was coated in champagne. It lapped around the players' feet as they sat and pondered their triumph. The air was still dripping with emotion, but the words had dried up. After everything, there was suddenly nothing. Manchester City were back in the Premiership but, like the bubbly, it had not yet sunk in.

Tucked in a corner of the Ewood Park dressing room, alone with his thoughts, Joe Royle stared into nowhere. Drained and dishevelled, every ounce of energy had been squeezed out of him. The broad shoulders, which had carried such a weight of expectation, were now slumped forward. His hair was untidy, his suit crumpled and his tie needed straightening. Amid the chaotic scenes of celebration earlier on, somebody had clearly got hold of him by the scruff of the neck. Not that he minded – he had done the same to City over the past two seasons.

A club which had claimed so many victims over recent years, had at last discovered a saviour. Royle, the man who bridged a decade at Maine Road, could have taken over as manager in 1989, but turned the job down. Now, as the new Millennium dawned, he had guided them back to the big time after a dramatic finale at Blackburn Rovers. The wheel had turned full circle.

Maybe the Manchester City story was always meant to unfold this way. Maybe it was just a matter of fate. Maine Road has seen it all over ten intoxicating seasons, from the devastating decline to the dizzying ascent back to the top. And on that sunny afternoon in East Lancashire, it seemed as if a guiding force was on City's side.

Blackburn were rampant for 60 minutes. They had scarcely played as well all season. Matt Jansen's goal had given them the lead, but it was the near misses which defied belief. Nicky Weaver's woodwork had been struck four times as his team-mates seemed locked in a state of paralysis. All they needed was a point, but they could – and perhaps should – have been four or five goals down. As promotion rivals Ipswich held the lead at Portman Road, City's fans held their breath. They had been there before: the familiar feeling of dreaded anticipation was starting to overcome them.

The rest, as they say, is history. For no obvious reason, Royle's men suddenly aroused from their slumber and began to play again. True to form, they had kept everyone waiting, but it was worth it. Shaun Goater's equaliser, Christian Dailly's own goal, Mark Kennedy's clincher and Paul Dickov's finishing touch – they were four goals which turned the air blue.

Hundreds of City fans had gathered on a nearby hill. Even though they could see only a small portion of the pitch, it made no difference. They had to experience the conclusion of their club's great adventure. By the end, the gates had been unlocked and the ticketless fans had joined the party inside Ewood Park.

As the final whistle sounded, supporters streamed on to the pitch and spilled on to the streets of Manchester to celebrate. After all the heartache, this was their day. The players sprinted off the field to escape the onrushing hordes and, once shielded from the pandemonium outside, sprayed bottles of champagne around their dressing room as the paparazzi and television cameras recorded their every move. After a few exhilarating minutes, it was suddenly quiet again. The flash bulbs had gone out, the cameras were turned off.

The men who had represented City so proudly over the past nine months were allowed time to reflect. Richard Jobson, just two days short of his thirty-seventh birthday, had played his forty-eighth consecutive game. A little over a year before, his career had been written off as he laboured to overcome an incessant ankle injury. Now he was back in the top flight and it hardly seemed credible. The university-educated player, his greying hair plastered to his head, looked down at his boots and appeared almost unable to summon up the energy to untie his laces. He glanced up to ask if he could keep his sweat-stained red and black striped shirt... for proof, perhaps, that it had all really happened.

Ian Bishop sat bare-chested a few spaces away. His eyes were blood-shot and his voice trembled with emotion as he struggled to sum up his feelings. The Scouse midfielder, who had played in City's last victory over Manchester United eleven years ago, contemplated the return of the Manchester derby. His body might have been exhausted, but his mind was still sharp as he thought back to that remarkable day in September 1989 when the Blues beat their neighbours 5-1 at Maine Road.

Paul Dickov, meanwhile, was still wearing his kit as he stood in Blackburn's crowded reception area. He was talking to his father, who had travelled down from the family home in Scotland. The irrepressible striker, whose introduction as a second-half substitute had stirred his team-mates to life, talked passionately about the game. His energy seemed boundless, his will to win having once again proved priceless to Manchester City.

Twelve months before, it was his injury-time equaliser which salvaged the season and restored the confidence to City's battle-weary supporters. Thousands had trudged out of Wembley Stadium in despair and resignation as their side trailed 2-0 to Gillingham with only seconds remaining in the Second Division play-off final. But fate was preparing another twist as Royle's side fought back into the game and clinched promotion through a penalty shoot-out. At long last, it seemed as if somebody up there *did* like City after all.

Joe Royle had always believed it would come right. From his first press conference as boss, the "ego in him" said he would succeed. Even when Robert Taylor's second goal for Gillingham hit the back of the net, Royle "did not give up hope." And now, as he surveyed the scenes of celebration at Blackburn, his thoughts must have been trained already on the next stage of his masterplan. Whatever the future held, Royle at least knew one thing – he had put back the pride in the blue shirt.

A little over two years earlier, in Royle's third game in charge, the fans had shouted that the players were not even fit to wear the jersey. The club had become the laughing stock of English football, riddled with division and on the brink of bankruptcy. After their relegation from the Premiership under Alan Ball, City turned into a graveyard for managers. Five tried their luck in a crazy and humiliating four-month spell at the end of the 1996. Finally, Frank Clark offered the prospect of stability but his reign would last a little over a year before ending in acrimony and embarrassment again.

The worst was yet to come, though. Even with Royle in charge "fighting the fires," City could not avoid the unthinkable. They were relegated to English football's third tier for the first time in their 104-year history. In the following season, their derby would be against Macclesfield. Yet, as the team went further and further down, the crowds went up. Wearing their laser blue shirts as a badge of honour, supporters were determined not to abandon their club in its hour of greatest need.

The fact that City survived is a marvel in itself. The fact that the club was reborn is a phenomenon. Its story over the past decade takes some believing. Yet there are at least 30,000 witnesses who have watched the soap opera unfold in front of their eyes every week. And perhaps that is why the club has maintained such an enduring appeal. Even in their darkest days, the Blues have never been boring. In the past five years, only one final game of the season has been meaningless – the 3-2 win over Reading in May 1997. Without the heartbreak, the cynical humour and blind faith, City would not be City. Life is not all about winning and Manchester's Maine Road club has proved it time and time again.

It could all have been so different if former chairman Peter Swales had got his way in November 1989. Mel Machin's sacking had followed a familiar pattern at a club where managers had an infamously short life-span. Back in 1974, Ron Saunders lasted just five months before being dismissed by Swales. The new chairman chose Tony Book to replace him and the former club captain enjoyed a relatively successful time in charge – leading the Blues to victory in the 1976 League Cup Final. By the end of the decade, Book had been joined by Malcolm Allison, who was in his second spell at the club. But the chemistry which had brought Allison so much success with Joe Mercer a decade earlier was now sadly lacking.

After Allison was sacked in 1980, the Norwich City manager John Bond took over. He led the club to the 1981 FA Cup Final, before resigning and leaving his assistant, John Benson, in charge for a brief spell. It was then the turn of two Scots, Billy McNeill and later Jimmy Frizzell, ahead of Machin's appointment in the summer of 1987.

He survived two years before the axe fell and Swales offered the job to Oldham Athletic's ambitious manager. Joe Royle, a former City player, initially intended to accept the offer but changed his mind overnight after heeding the pleas of his club's fans. Oldham went on to reach the final of the League Cup and the FA Cup semi-final in that season.

"Peter Swales said to me many times afterwards that if I'd gone to City at that time, they wouldn't have had all the problems that

they did have with managers," says Royle. "My answer might have
been different had Oldham not been doing so well. People ask me
if I regret not coming the first time around and I don't. I've wondered
but I've never regretted it. You can't live and look back in anger."

It was hard, though, for supporters not to dwell on the past
after such a tempestuous period in their club's history. They had
witnessed eight managers, three chairmen, two relegations and two
promotions in the space of ten seasons. In an era when their deadliest
rivals won every honour in the game, City's fans spent much of their
time searching for a hero. Whether it was Clive Allen, Garry Flitcroft,
Uwe Rosler, Francis Lee, Georgi Kinkladze or Terry Cooke, it did
not matter. The fans just needed someone to champion their cause.
The problem is that footballers, and football chairmen, are human
and fallible. Heroes are not.

More than eight years after turning down the job, Joe Royle
returned to take over as manager. He is the latest to be entrusted
with the great expectations of the Maine Road masses. But he remains
acutely aware that football is intrinsically fickle. As he relaxed in his
Platt Lane office, just days after his side's promotion back into the
Premiership, he was quick to point out the pitfalls of popularity.

"I always felt that sooner or later, somebody was going to get it
right at this club. But, look here, I don't think I've done that yet. We
have just got back to base and we have to go forward from here. The
fans won't forgive me if we don't. I know I'm probably more popular
at Maine Road now than I have ever been. But, equally, I know
football changes and it can happen very quickly."

Royle accepted the so-called job from hell in February 1998
after the sacking of Frank Clark. The departing manager spoke
bitterly of a malicious "vendetta" within the club. He labelled it the
"fifth column" and claimed it was becoming almost impossible to
manage City. Royle knew there was only one way to silence the
whispering campaign.

"The only way to shut people up is through success," says Royle.
"You get it at every club when it's in trouble or turmoil. When Alex
Ferguson went to Old Trafford, for the first three years every ex-
player and ex-manager was sniping. But it all stopped when he won
that first cup. "It's all blown away by success and, quite honestly,
that's the only way to handle it. I never came in and said I need to
stamp my authority on the club, because it makes no difference if
you are losing."

By the end of the 1999-2000 season, City had only lost 11 times in their last 73 League games. Royle had conquered their losing mentality and obliterated any voices of dissent. His record spoke for itself with back-to-back promotions in the job which nobody else dared to take. After being hounded out of Goodison Park three years earlier, Royle must have felt a surge of satisfaction at his side's achievements. "Proving people wrong," he says, "is still one of the greatest feelings in life." Yet the man who has led City out of the wilderness insists he has nothing to prove. His reign in charge at Everton ended in acrimony when he walked out, following a "vitriolic" campaign by the local newspaper. But he remains proud of his record at the club, which included an FA Cup triumph in 1995.

"I was a success at Everton, but a number of factors conspired against me," he asserts. "A major influence was the *Liverpool Echo*, which waged a vendetta against me. It wasn't just criticism – it was personal. But that is history now and I honestly don't let it bother me."

The proud Liverpudlian, whose boyhood dream was to play for Everton, has a new spiritual home. His calm authority permeates throughout Maine Road as the club attempts to recover from the most divisive era in its history. Royle's task has been to heal the wounds.

"I have strong ideas about the way things should be done and stick to them. Of course, I can be tough. I wouldn't be where I am today if I wasn't. There's this image of genial Joe, but that's all it is – an image. My wife and close friends would probably say that I am very stubborn. Ultimately, I just hope that I'm fair with people.

"I still have a great bond with my former clubs, like Oldham and Everton. In fact, I have nothing but fond memories of the places. But I am City now; they are my club. They are my present and my future."

CHAPTER ONE

The Swales **empire**

THE REVOLUTION had begun. English football was changing and would never be the same again. After an era of stagnation, the game was about to be turned on its head in the space of a few years. Looking back, the seeds of change seem all the more obvious: the disaster at Hillsborough, Arsenal's last-minute title winner on live television, Gazza's Italia 90 tears, Lord Taylor's report and Sky Television's ubiquitous satellite dishes.

The whiff of revolution was certainly in the air as the country's elite convened for another season in the summer of 1990. Yet one of English football's traditional patriarchs had more than enough reason to feel optimistic. Peter Swales was at the height of his powers. Chairman of Manchester City and of the FA's international committee, Swales had steered an unsteady course through the 1980s. Relegation had twice threatened to dethrone Maine Road's warrior king, but he had survived. Buoyed by a growing sense of invincibility, Swales was now looking forward to the new decade with confidence.

Born in 1932, the son of an Ardwick fishmonger, Swales had always possessed a strong will to succeed. He became the first pupil from Ardwick Municipal School to win a scholarship to Hulme Grammar. After leaving school, he was ordered by his father to work in an accountancy office, but hated it. His National Service spared him from the boredom of pen pushing and number crunching. After two years in the Royal Army Service Corps, he was demobbed in the rank of sergeant. He had already met his wife-to-be, Brenda, at Sunday School.

"I always thought he was very special," she remembers. "I met him when I was sixteen and I thought he was wonderful. We were separated for around four or five years when I went to college and he joined the army, but we got back together and in 1955, we married."

The marriage, which produced three daughters, would last steadfastly until Swales's death in 1996. It was undeniably the pillar of unstinting strength and security within his life. Without Brenda, it is unlikely Swales could have launched so successfully into a life full of risks and uncertainty. He branched into the world of business in the 1950s with his friend Noel White, who would later become the chairman of Liverpool. They began their partnership in a tiny 12ft by 10ft shop selling sheet music in Altrincham. Each put up £50 as working capital and shared the £6 a week rent.

Business boomed and in 1960 the two friends widened their interests into television and radio. In 1968, Thorn EMI bought the business for £500,000 and Swales stayed on to control the 130 outlets across the North West. Meanwhile, he was beginning to dip his toe in the football world. Along with White, he funded Altrincham's rise up the ranks of amateur and then semi-professional football. By the early 1970s, they had turned the club's fortunes around and Swales was desperate to break into the professional game. In 1971, he overheard two Manchester City directors in a pub talking about the problems the club was facing as its board became riddled with factions. Swales, never shy, simply broke into the conversation and convinced them that he was the man to solve their problems. Initially, he was co-opted in a peacemaking capacity and successfully brought the warring factions together. Two years later, he was appointed chairman by a unanimous vote and promised to make City the most successful club in the country.

It was a typically bold claim from a man whose unconventional outward appearance masked a deeply complex character. Swales, whose combed-over haircut, broad Manchester accent and Cuban-heeled shoes would attract much ridicule during his time in the public eye, could be a ruthless and uncompromising leader. At the same time, the lad from inner-city Ardwick was a sensitive, flawed and emotional human being. His public pronouncements came from the heart and, as such, could rebound in spectacular fashion. In 1976, he wrote in the club's matchday programme: "If we've not hit the high spots in two years, I will consider that a failure. My personal ambition is to see City as the number one club in the country. Anything other than that and I have failed, and I hope I am big enough to accept it if the ambitions are not fulfilled."

Fourteen years later and the Maine Road trophy cabinet had received only one addition – the 1976 League Cup. Nevertheless, Swales's power at the club remained undiminished. Chris Muir was a member of the City board from 1967 to 1970, and then from 1972 to 1996 before later taking on a similar role at Blackpool. A blunt Scotsman and close friend of Swales, Muir had no qualms about his place in the club's pecking order.

"I was Peter Swales's lackey," he remembers. "I would do all his hatchet jobs, but there was no question who was pulling the strings. Peter basically owned the club. Everyone was there by his grace. He was the chairman-cum-managing director, and made all the decisions. The brewery, Greenalls, owned 20 per cent, but they never flexed their muscle and the other major shareholder, Stephen Boler, would always back Peter."

John Maddock, formerly the northern sports editor of the *Sunday People*, was another close friend of Swales and would later become City's general manager. "Peter was very much a dictatorial figure and could create enemies quite easily," says Maddock. "He ran the board with an iron fist and was very much a power broker."

Yet, to Brenda, her husband was neither a dictator nor a figure of fun. He was her life. He was her Peter and she saw a very different side to the man. "He was unassuming. He didn't like anything flash and wasn't materialistic. In fact, he was very quiet in that respect, not pushy at all. If there was a crowd of people, we would be at the back of the room, not at the front. Whenever we met anybody he would treat them all exactly the same. If you met the dustbin man or anybody he spoke to them exactly the same as he spoke to the Queen Mother or any royalty. He was always the same. He wasn't one for holidays because he just enjoyed life, he enjoyed his work and he loved football. He just wanted to make City great really."

The club very soon began to dominate his life. At his large detached house in Bowdon, in the heart of Cheshire's stockbroker belt, Swales's growing obsession was obvious. He named one of his rooms the Blue Room and it became his sanctuary from the outside world. Painted a light 'City' blue, it housed an addict's collection of Maine Road memorabilia and videos. Yet, famously, Swales could not bring himself to watch any re-runs of City defeats. "It just hurts too much," he said. The man who ran his club with an "iron fist" had a soft core.

"He was a complete enigma," says Muir. "One minute he was rollicking you and the next, he could be extremely compassionate. He was very loyal, in fact."

Swales, the man who dreamed of bringing glory to Maine Road, also loved the make-believe world of Hollywood. He adored Doris Day movies and, according to Brenda, would have "loved to have been a film director." But, as in the world of football, dreams could so easily be shattered by cruel reality. On a trip to America, Swales excitedly asked a cab driver to take a detour past Doris Day's house. "What do you want to go and see that drunken old cow for?" came the reply.

"He was crushed," says John Maddock. "I remember he said to me that you should never shatter an illusion."

Any illusions he had about running Manchester City had long since been destroyed by 1990. Relegation from Division One in 1983, and again in 1987, had prompted hostility from some sections of the crowd. Swales kept a picture on his wall of himself surrounded by a police escort at the height of his troubles. It was intended to keep him humble, but possibly only reinforced his sense of infallibility. Whatever the supporters demanded, it seemed Swales could brazen it out. He had seen off the bad times and surely now the tide was beginning to turn.

Howard Kendall had taken over from Mel Machin as the club's manager late in 1989. The former Everton player and boss had an impressive pedigree, having won two Championships, the FA Cup and the European Cup Winners Cup during a six-year tenure as manager at Goodison Park. Yet, in 1987, he turned his back on Merseyside for the fresh challenge of managing abroad – in Spain with Athletico Bilbao. Ironically, he could have moved to City instead. Kendall met with Swales and vice chairman Freddie Pye about the possibility of taking over from Jimmy Frizzell but they could not agree terms. Two years later, he was back in England and City needed a manager yet again.

Machin had been sacked as the Blues lurched back towards the First Division's abyss, with Swales claiming the former Norwich coach had never seen "eye to eye" with the fans. Kendall was immediately targeted as the man to take over but once again his contract demands were too much for City. They turned their attention instead to another former Evertonian, Joe Royle, who was fast earning an impressive reputation as Oldham's manager. Although intending to accept the job, Royle changed his mind at the last moment and opted to stay at Boundary Park. The way was open for Kendall again and Swales had no choice but to meet his asking price.

It was a gamble which came dangerously close to backfiring. Two months after taking over, Kendall looked on grimly as his rebuilt City side slumped nearer the foot of Division One and aroused recriminations from the terraces. "Everton Third Team", was the acrimonious cry from the Kippax Stand as Kendall's collection of ex-Goodison Park favourites struggled to reclaim their former glories. Peter Reid, Alan Harper, Mark Ward, Adrian Heath and Wayne Clarke, all ex-Everton players, had been signed, while crowd favourites Ian Bishop and Trevor Morley had been sold.

"I made the decision very quickly that the squad wasn't good enough," recalls Kendall. "I know there was a lot of criticism about the players I brought in, but they were people I trusted. The sale of Ian Bishop, who's done extremely well since, was not popular but I felt it was right at the time because of the position we were in."

Kendall's judgement was ultimately vindicated as City climbed to safety, led by a player who would very quickly become a talisman at Maine Road. Niall Quinn was signed from Arsenal in a £700,000 deal just days before the transfer deadline. It was a masterstroke by Kendall, who had patently not lost his ability to unearth a footballing gem.

"Niall was the icing on the cake for us because if you were struggling in a game you could always pick him out and he was always a threat and a target," says Kendall. "He was a good one-touch finisher as well and had served a good apprenticeship at Arsenal. His contribution for us was priceless."

With City's First Division status assured, Swales's gamble had paid off, but there was still another hurdle to negotiate in the summer. Bobby Robson was ready to step down as England manager after the World Cup and Kendall was on the shortlist to take over.

"Peter Swales, who was on the FA's International Committee, called me into his office one morning and said, 'You're on a shortlist of three for the England job. You don't want it, do you?'" remembers Kendall. "I said, no I don't. I felt Graham Taylor was going to get it anyway and I didn't want to leave the day-to-day involvement at club level."

Taylor got the job after another front-runner, none other than Joe Royle, also dropped out of the race. It left Kendall clear to continue his overhaul of City's playing staff. After saving the club from relegation, he was in a position of strength and looked to stamp his authority. Tony Coton, the Watford goalkeeper, was bought for £1 million, along with Mark Brennan from Ipswich. Another ex-Everton player, Neil Pointon, was also signed in a £1.5 million part-exchange deal for Andy Hinchcliffe. Hinchcliffe was the first of the club's "famous five" youngsters from the 1986 FA Youth Cup-winning side to leave. It was another defining moment for the club as they moved into a new era.

"There was a nucleus of some very good young players at the club," says Kendall. "I didn't go in and think, well, they're not good enough, let's get them out. I brought in experience to help them and I think it did."

Swales, meanwhile, was content to back Kendall's judgement. He openly described him as "the best manager I have ever worked with." Little wonder then that City's chairman felt a warm, if somewhat unfamiliar, glow of confidence as the 1990-91 season began.

City opened their campaign on a balmy August day at White Hart Lane. The ground was basking in the late summer sunshine, and there was a mood of excitement in the air after England's valiant failure in the World Cup semi-finals. Paul Gascoigne and Gary Lineker, national heroes after Italia 90, lined up against a City side which had changed out of all recognition in the 11 months since its famous 5-1 victory over Manchester United at Maine Road. Just three players remained from Mel Machin's side of September 1989: Ian Brightwell, David White and, most notably, Paul Lake, who was named as Kendall's new captain.

While others in City's homegrown alliance were shipped out, Lake was on a verge of becoming one of the most eminent players of his generation. He had been picked in Bobby Robson's preliminary squad ahead of the World Cup and it seemed only a matter of time before he stepped up into international football. Also, at the age of 21 Lake had become City's youngest-ever skipper for the match against Tottenham. He would wear the coveted armband only twice more.

It was Lake's mistake which led to the opening goal at White Hart Lane. His wayward back-header was the ideal invitation for Lineker to race clear and power a shot past Coton. Niall Quinn equalised before half-time, but the day was always going to belong to Spurs and their World Cup heroes. Lineker restored their lead and then the stage was left to the nation's chosen son, Gascoigne, to wrap up proceedings with a 65th minute strike. "Here endeth the first lesson," declared Kendall afterwards. "If we persist defending like that, then trouble looms." He need not have worried. It would be his last defeat as City manager.

Following a victory over Everton at Maine Road, City took on an Aston Villa side which was still recovering after finishing second in the previous season's Championship race and losing its manager, Graham Taylor, to England. Kendall's efficient if unremarkable, team chalked up another win but it was an incident early in the second half which would haunt the club for years to come – and change one young man's life forever. After gracefully intercepting a through ball, Paul Lake collapsed to the ground in agony, clutching the injured knee which would end his career. In an innocuous instant, Lake had ruptured his cruciate ligaments and shattered his chances of playing football again. Commentating for *Granada Television*, Clive Tyldesley noted that "at least Lake has time on his side." Unfortunately, all the time in the world could not cure the injury curse which befell City's most promising young player that night. Five and a half years later and after several aborted comebacks, the Denton-born player abandoned his battle for fitness and retired from the game.

"It was a tragedy. I cannot believe what happened to the lad," continues Kendall, who has little doubt about Lake's unfulfilled potential. "I had found a position for him and I felt he was going to be a great, great centre back. He had a very good spring in the air, he was quick and was never afraid to come out of defence. He would have been playing for England now without any shadow of a doubt. He was a footballing centre half like Alan Hansen. Top class, really top class."

Lake, who went on to become a physiotherapist for Burnley and Altrincham, is still haunted by the night when his football world caved in. "I still get angry when I think about what happened. The whole episode left me feeling numb and I didn't know what to do with myself. When I look at players like Richard Edghill, Roy Keane and Niall Quinn, who've had similar injuries, and are still playing, it makes me wonder what went wrong for me. I have to admit I'm envious when I look at those players, but it just wasn't meant to be.

"I've hardly got any mobility nowadays. All I can do is trot around a football field. The hardest thing is that I used to love going for a run and keeping fit, but I just can't do that any more. It is getting worse and worse as well. I've been to see the PFA to see if I cannot have more correction to the knee joint. I want to enjoy the rest of my life, but it is painful most of the time. I go to the pictures and I have to sit on an aisle seat so that I can keep my leg stretched out.

"I've heard people say my problem was that I couldn't take the pain but that is outrageous. I had eighteen operations, my leg was straightened in 1996 because my legs had got so bowed. A triangular piece of my shin bone was cut out and titanium screws were put into my knee. I have chronic arthritis now and need medication every day just to compensate for the pain."

Nevertheless, Lake's absence did not disrupt City's uncharacteristically solid start to the season. Two victories and four draws later, the two sides of Manchester convened at Maine Road for their 113th derby. With 12 minutes of the game left, it seemed the Blues were heading for a second successive home victory over their rivals. Two David White goals and a beautifully-worked third from Colin Hendry had given them a 3-1 lead. Kendall thought the game was won and replaced his influential player-coach, Peter Reid, with Ian Brightwell. It proved a costly decision as United went on to salvage a draw through two Brian McClair goals in the space of three minutes. City would never come as close to a derby victory again during the rest of the decade.

"We are experimenting for life without Peter Reid, but it's not working at the moment," explained Kendall afterwards.

Eleven days later, it was City who were left to contemplate life without Kendall. Colin Harvey's sacking had created a vacancy in the manager's office at Everton. The word from the "wise" was that Joe Royle, still with Oldham, would take over back on his native Merseyside. City's manager was not even mentioned, never even considered – except by the Goodison Park board. They wanted their old mentor back, the man who had led them to almost every domestic honour in a golden age in the 1980s, and they had an ace up their sleeve: Kendall's contract.

"Out of courtesy, I told Howard this morning that Everton had made an enquiry about him," explained Swales at the time. "And it soon became apparent that he wanted to go and there was nothing I could say to stop him. I'm not bitter, just very disappointed and a little bit upset."

In truth, Swales was shattered by his manager's decision to enforce a "get-out" clause in his contract. It allowed Kendall to leave, so long as Everton were prepared to pay a set amount of compensation. "It was a massive blow for us," recalls Chris Muir. "He'd brought this Everton mafia with him and now we were stuck with them. Swales pleaded with Howard to stay, but it was no good."

Kendall had made up his mind. He could not resist the lure of returning to his old kingdom, memorably describing his relationship with Everton as a "marriage" as opposed to his "affair" with City. It was an ill-judged remark which only served to heighten the anger felt in Manchester. If Swales chose to suppress his bitterness, there was no disguising the feeling among City's supporters. They felt betrayed, particularly in the light of a recent newspaper article in which Kendall had claimed he wished to spend the rest of his career at Maine Road. He was labelled a "Judas" and accused of having mercenary motives, a charge he still strongly denies.

"The only thing that changed was the name at the top of the contract and that is a fact. I did not go back to Everton for one penny more than I was earning at Manchester City. My contract gave me freedom of choice and the pull of coming back to Everton was too great. I know I upset a lot of people and I'm genuinely sorry about that, but it was a decision I felt I had to make.

"Maybe people were hurt or felt hard done by that I'd gone when things were starting to pick up and go well and they felt, 'How can Everton be a bigger club than we are?' But I wasn't saying that, I was just going back to somewhere where I'd had so many happy times. Maybe it was the heart rather than the head which was ruling me, but that was a decision I made.

"I still feel very proud of the job I did at City in that space of time. It set them on the road. A lot happened in such a short period because it needed shaking up and I certainly did that. When you talk about being successful at clubs, it's not always about winning cups or leagues or promotions."

For the players, it was yet more upheaval at a club which had finally found a semblance of stability. Kendall's smooth man-management skills had cultivated a new spirit of optimism and belief in the dressing room. David White, one of the few remaining players from the Machin era, has no doubt about the impact Kendall made.

"We were going down under Mel, there's no question about that. Howard Kendall was just brilliant. He was a very clever man and had turned the football club around. I know some of the supporters were unhappy about the ex-Everton connection, but that was just nonsense. None of the players ever felt like that. The likes of Alan Harper, Adrian Heath, Mark Ward and Peter Reid were all great players, and they improved the team dramatically. When Howard went, we were all just bitterly disappointed."

City's next League game, at home to Leeds, was live on television and the supporters were intent on displaying their anger. "Even our cat hates Howard Kendall" and "Kendall robbed Mavis and Derek" were just two of the banners placed conspicuously around the ground, the latter referring to a topical storyline on *Coronation Street*. But it was the Maine Road soap opera which was now taking a familiar turn. Not for the first time, the club was searching for a new manager. The majority of fans, though, had no doubt who should take over: Peter Reid.

At 34, his playing days were nearing an end but his influence on the pitch – and off it – was showing no signs of diminishing. So much so that Kendall begged his midfield general to join him at Everton, where their partnership had begun. Reid refused. He had his eye on the manager's job at City and took over in a caretaker capacity for the visit of Leeds.

"I'm not going to apply for the job, the chairman knows all about me anyway," said Liverpool born and bred Reid. "I'd like the job but if Mr Swales opts to bring in someone else then I'll stay on as a player; it's not a problem for me."

Significantly, Reid also insisted that he would remain as caretaker boss for only one game, thus neatly heaping all the pressure on to Swales. City's previous search for a manager had ended in humiliation as Joe Royle performed a public U-turn at the last minute. Swales did not dare make the same mistake again. Reid was a safe choice, supported by fans and readily available for the job. Swales, the notorious gambler, knew that on this occasion he could not afford to chance his arm.

"The feeling was that Reid was very streetwise and would be able to control this group of desperadoes which Kendall had left us with," says Chris Muir, Swales's most trusted lieutenant.

And, according to David White, it was the players who swung the balance in favour of Reid. "We all thought that the club needed continuity after Howard had left. I don't think Swales wanted Reid as manager. I think he could foresee a personality clash, but the players forced his hand. Everyone stood up and said, 'We want Reidy to get the job,' and I think that was highly significant." City lost 3-2 to Leeds in only their second defeat of the season, but three days later, Reid was named as the club's eighteenth post-war manager and the eleventh during Swales's chairmanship.

"Peter's popularity was a significant reason we took into account when reaching a decision," announced Swales. "He has got the personality and the charisma, we just need to see if he's got that spark which separates the Cloughies, the Dalglishes and the Kendalls from the ordinary run-of-the-mill manager."

Reid was the club's first player-manager, a role which Dalglish and Kendall had already served with distinction at Liverpool and Blackburn respectively. But while Reid's motivational skills on the pitch were never in doubt, his tactical ability in the dressing room was unproven. The experience of others was clearly going to be crucial if he was to succeed.

"I had no doubt he could do the job," recalls Kendall. "He always had Tony Book there to help him along as well. Looking back, I am sure he would say he made some mistakes, but who doesn't? He then had to stand up on his own two feet and be his own man. He had to bring in people he felt were right for the job. He was now the decision maker. We spoke fairly often, but you find when people take over they tend to want to do it for themselves, with their own people, rather than going back to someone they've worked for in the past."

And there was little doubt that the new manager was determined to be very much his own boss. On his first day in charge, Reid declared that he had no intention of appointing anybody else to his backroom staff. "I am confident I can fulfil both roles (playing and managing) without bringing anyone else in from outside. Mick Heaton (Kendall's assistant) and Tony Book provided valuable assistance to Howard Kendall and I am convinced the same system will work for me. This is a great opportunity and I don't intend on wasting it," declared Reid.

Less than four weeks later, though, reality hit home and Reid appointed a new number two. It was a decision which would colour his entire reign as City manager. Sam Ellis, the former Bury and Blackpool boss, was the chosen man. A tough operator who had spent almost all his life in football, Audenshaw-born Ellis had always dreamed of joining City as a player – and had now got his chance as a coach. If there was any sentiment involved in his move to Maine Road, you would scarcely have known it. Ellis, renowned as a long-ball specialist, set about his new job in typically uncompromising style.

As a managerial pairing, they formed a redoubtable partnership. Reid was the tough yet charismatic leader whose career had been marked throughout by a tenacious will to succeed; Ellis was his henchman, a street fighter whose gnarled complexion seemed to characterise perfectly his rugged approach to life. Yet, the public image belied a deeper, more intelligent side to Ellis. He knew football and he knew sometimes you needed to be tough to survive in the game. Sure, they had inherited a sweet legacy from Kendall, but the task ahead was fraught with difficulties. City's fans had been starved of genuine success for almost two decades and they demanded change. They wanted a team to feel proud of, they wanted a trophy but, perhaps most of all, they desperately wanted to overhaul United and become Manchester's footballing aristocrats.

The new regime certainly enjoyed an encouraging start. After two draws and a victory under Reid, City again faced their opening day opponents, Spurs. The conditions could scarcely have been more different from their first encounter of the season. A deep fog descended upon Moss Side, forcing Reid's side to wear their more distinctive maroon away strip just to be seen. But the weather could not cloud the game: it was a classic, described most memorably by *The Guardian* as "great tub-thumping stuff."

Paul Gascoigne put the visitors ahead in the first half with a wonderful virtuoso goal, dancing through the heart of City's defence before slotting the ball past Tony Coton. But it was Reid, 11 years his senior, who stole the show with an awesome display of his enduring midfield ability. The old campaigner, who had begun his professional career with Bolton back in 1972, drove his side to new heights as they battered Spurs for the entire second half. With a quarter of an hour left, the North London resistance was finally breached. Steve Redmond scuffed in an equaliser and moments later, Mark Ward's penalty put the home side ahead. It was a rousing fightback, but the abiding image of the day seemed to transcend football. It came early in the second half when Gascoigne, once more playing the clown, patted Reid on the head in a playful, yet blatantly condescending, gesture. City's new manager stood bolt upright and stared menacingly back at his young opponent. "Don't mess with me, son," was the message and Gazza got it loud and clear. From then on, there was only ever going to be one winner in their battle of wills.

Reid's influence over his side had never been greater. He was leading from the front and continuing to play some of the best football of his career. Any fears about his lack of managerial experience seemed irrelevant, Reid, the pocket powerhouse, was taking on all-comers. Born in the tough Liverpool suburb of Huyton in 1956, he was quickly hardened to the realities of life in the industrial north. Football was his escape route and he battled through an endless stream of crippling injuries to become one of the country's top players. After an apprenticeship under Ian Greaves at Bolton, Reid became a key figure in Everton's successful side of the 1980s. He went on to play football at the highest level, representing England in the 1986 World Cup in Mexico. He signed for City late in 1989 on a free transfer from Queens Park Rangers.

Yet as he adapted to life as a football manager, he would soon face one of his sternest tests: a return to Goodison Park and a head-to-head with his mentor, Howard Kendall. The travelling fans took the opportunity to bait their former manager with a ferocity usually reserved for those from the Red side of Manchester. The City team, though, could not match the passion of their supporters as Everton ran out comfortable 2-0 winners. It was obvious that Kendall knew City better than they knew him. The *Manchester Evening News* wrote that Kendall had enjoyed the last laugh. But as one City fanzine, *King of the Kippax*, more astutely put it: "He had the first, second and third laugh as well."

Ultimately, though, Kendall's Goodison Park return would not leave him smiling. Three years later, he departed – only to return again for an unlikely third spell in charge in 1997 – and could never rekindle the glory days. Perhaps, when he looks back at his managerial career, Kendall might regret walking out on his "love affair" at Maine Road, although it is doubtful that he would admit it.

"There's no point looking back and wondering, I made the decision which I believed was right at the time," he concludes.

Despite City's demoralising defeat at Everton, they quickly recovered their self-belief. With Niall Quinn beginning to thrive up front and David White proving a worthy soul mate, City were rapidly becoming a more intimidating proposition for their opponents. Victory at Crystal Palace, courtesy of a Quinn hat-trick, propelled them into the top six and provided the chance to finish ahead of United for the first time in 13 years. It was a dizzying prospect.

"It was so important to the fans, and particularly Peter Swales, to out-do United," recalls Chris Muir. "He was almost obsessed with them. He was fanatical that City should be on a par with United, and he would lose all rationality about it. I think it was one of his great weaknesses. There were others on the board as well who had this obsession. Ian Niven (a fellow director) wouldn't even refer to United by name – he always called them Stretford Rangers. It was a bizarre way for a professional company to behave."

Yet, on the pitch, the Blues were beginning to get things right. A team which had become renowned for its "cock-ups" could suddenly do no wrong. Never was that more apparent than the home match against Derby towards the end of April. Niall Quinn opened the scoring with a low half-volley from the edge of the area, but it was his heroics at the other end of the pitch which would prove decisive. Before half-time, Coton brought down Dean Saunders in the area and referee Ken Lupton had no doubt it was a penalty and a clear sending-off offence. Out came the red card, accompanied by the proverbial red mist as Coton flung his gloves at the referee in a show of temper. But it was Quinn who picked up the gloves and proceeded to save Saunders' spot-kick, diving low to his left and palming the ball behind.

As if that was not enough, City went on to double their lead through David White's solo run and shot, while Mark Ward began penning his own Maine Road obituary. Substituted for Reid, the

Scouse winger refused to shake hands with his manager and kicked over a bucket of water which splashed over a policeman. He escaped with a £1,000 club fine but the incident was duly logged in the memory banks and Ward was sold as soon as the summer arrived.

City's impressive run continued, claiming 17 points from a possible 21 as they geared up for the second Manchester derby of the season. With Tony Coton suspended and Andy Dibble out injured, City's teenage Welsh goalkeeper Martyn Margetson was chosen to make his League debut in front of a full house at Old Trafford. It was a truly daunting prospect. Nevertheless, it was another young Welshman who stole centre stage – United's latest prodigy, Ryan Giggs. Hailed, rather predictably, as the new George Best, 17-year-old Giggs carried a burden of expectation before he had even kicked a ball. Yet the youngster was not about to disappoint and was credited with the game's decisive goal, although in reality it deflected off Colin Hendry and past Margetson. It was a suitably tame way to decide a distinctly uninspiring game.

Nevertheless, the dream of finishing ahead of United was still realised after a last-day victory over Sunderland, which sent the Wearsiders down. Reid's side had not won anything but had ended the season with local pride restored. But while the Blues savoured their admittedly minor triumph, the Reds were chasing glory in Europe. Just days after their derby victory, Alex Ferguson's side lifted the Cup Winners' Cup, beating Barcelona 2-1 in the final. They were beginning to show a glimpse of the form which would turn them into the dominant force of English football in the 1990s; a dominance which would have a devastating effect on their neighbours.

CHAPTER TWO

Ellis the **enforcer**

PETER SWALES was not exactly the last of the big spenders; more accurately, he was one of the first. In the late 1970s and early 1980s, the City chairman sanctioned a succession of big-money transfers into the club. Steve Daley, Michael Robinson, Trevor Francis and Kevin Reeves all came and went, with varying degrees of failure.

After the chastening experience of relegation in 1983 and 1987, Swales vowed never to be dragged into football's money pit again. At the start of the 1991-92 season, though, it was clear his temperance would be tested to the limit. A new Premier League was looming for English football and Swales knew his club simply couldn't afford to miss out. His new young manager was equally convinced that only an injection of cash could assure City's place in the top flight. Over the summer, a series of articles appeared in the *Manchester Evening News* demanding that Peter Reid be given the necessary financial resources to significantly strengthen his squad. Although written by the paper's City reporter, Peter Gardner, the suspicion remained that Reid was using the local press to influence his chairman.

The tactic seemed to work as Swales provided enough funds to break the transfer record for an English defender. Keith Curle was signed for £2.5 million from Wimbledon only weeks before the start of the new season. The 26-year-old had served a long apprenticeship in the lower reaches of English football and was now determined to make the most of his elevation in status. After spells with Bristol Rovers, Bristol City, Torquay United and Reading, Curle joined Wimbledon, becoming a permanent fixture in their starting line-up. His effortless speed and skilfully-smooth ability immediately attracted a host of top clubs but Reid was always at the head of the queue. He and Sam Ellis knew that pace was a prerequisite in the modern game, and Curle provided just that. He was immediately made club captain, taking over from Steve Redmond and became a mainstay of City's defence for the next five years.

As the new season approached, Reid also tabled a £1.7 million bid for the former City striker Paul Stewart, now with Tottenham Hotspur but reportedly keen on a move back to the North. The deal could not be agreed and Stewart eventually signed a new contract with the Londoners. Although the purse strings were loosened, Swales still demanded that money was recouped. Mark Ward and Alan Harper rejoined their former manager, Howard Kendall, in a £1.3 million deal. But perhaps even more significant was a transfer which barely merited a mention in the media. Young striker Ashley Ward was sold to Leicester for £80,000. Seven years later and after a number of expensive moves, he joined Blackburn Rovers for £4.75 million. Ironically, Reid would spend the rest of his managerial career at Maine Road searching for a striker to partner Niall Quinn. He never found one.

One man definitely out of the equation was Clive Allen. Never a favourite with Reid and Sam Ellis, the former Spurs striker seemed destined to leave Maine Road but had rejected a £300,000 move to Luton in the summer. It was a decision which would taint the rest of his career at City.

Signed for £1.1 million from Bordeaux, Allen was a renowned goalscorer from his days at Tottenham Hotspur. He arrived in the summer of 1989 as Mel Machin added the finishing touches to his newly-promoted side. With five England caps to his name, Allen was the star in Machin's modest outfit. But, although his reputation had not waned, his prolific powers in front of goal had diminished. A return of ten League goals (including three penalties) from his first season at Maine Road was not a disaster, but it was hardly earth-shattering either. By the time Reid had taken over, Allen was very much a bit-part player, making only occasional cameo appearances from the substitute's bench.

His frustration at the lack of first-team opportunities finally boiled over in October 1991. After failing to figure at all – even as a substitute – in the new season, he was recalled to the bench for the trip to Notts County. Injuries to Keith Curle, Andy Hill and Niall Quinn had left Reid no choice but to extend the olive branch to his exiled star. The pair had not spoken since the summer when Allen's decision to reject a move to Luton had infuriated his bosses. Ellis and Reid had banked on the £300,000 from Kenilworth Road to fund their bid for Paul Stewart. When their plans were scuppered, they retaliated by banishing Allen to the reserves. The 30-year-old former England international was ordered to train with the club's youngsters, an indignity which cut deep for a proud and decent man.

Allen's opportunity to hit back came early in the second half at Meadow Lane. With the game poised at 1-1, he burst into the action to hammer home his message to Reid and Ellis. Within minutes of replacing Mark Brennan, Allen made and scored a penalty, then moments later slammed a volley into the roof of the net. Months of pent-up frustration exploded as he celebrated extravagantly in front of the travelling fans, pointedly kissing the club badge on his shirt. His post-match outburst was no less dramatic.

"Peter Reid and Sam Ellis are trying to ruin my career," he raged. "I have been treated with no respect and made to train with the kids. I cannot believe what has been happening to me. I have kept my counsel up until now, but I can be silent no longer. All I want to do is play football and help Manchester City climb the table."

Reid was left suitably chastened, but unmoved, as he defended his corner. "These things happen in football clubs," was his somewhat unconvincing response. It failed to satisfy the fans, who had made clear their sympathies lay with Allen. Peter Swales, meanwhile, publicly instructed Reid to make peace. Reluctantly, he agreed and Allen was selected to play in their next match, a League Cup game against Chester. Yet it only delayed the inevitable. The former Spurs striker was on his way out.

"Clive Allen just wasn't a Peter Reid-type player," says Tony Coton. "He was a good pro, and had a great manner about him, but his style of play didn't suit Reidy. He would swap a Kinkladze for a Bracewell every time. "Different managers want different things and some managers only want their strikers to come alive in the box and will forsake the rest. Reidy probably wanted his strikers to push out wide and close the full-backs down. But Clive would not do that."

For the fans, it seemed a simple choice between Allen and Adrian Heath, the former Everton striker who was booed on his City debut and had not scored for 14 months. There appeared to be no contest. Heath's case was hardly helped a little over a month later when he fluffed an elementary chance to settle the Manchester derby at Maine Road in City's favour. His howling miss prompted the *Manchester Evening News* to comment that Heath had a mental block in front of goal "as big as the North Stand." But as the diminutive forward continued to keep out Allen, it seemed to supporters an obvious case of "jobs for the boys." They vented their frustration on Heath, who became a target for crowd abuse.

"I couldn't believe it," recollects David White. "It used to drive the players mad to hear the stick which Inchy (Heath) was getting. Alright, he didn't score many goals, but the team did and he was creating most of them. In my opinion, his name should have been on the team sheet every week. Let's face it, Clive Allen only became popular when he was left out of the team. Suddenly, he became this cult hero. But to be fair to Clive and Adrian, there was never any friction between them. They were both good pros who didn't let the situation affect their working relationship."

Heath's barren spell – 14 months and 46 games – finally came to an end four days after his glaring miss against United. He scored the first and claimed another (in fact an own goal by Ray Wilkins) as City beat QPR 3-1 in the Rumbelows League Cup. Afterwards, the former Everton man was even prepared to laugh at himself. "At least that should end the joke about the first thing Terry Waite is supposed to have said on his release: 'Has Adrian Heath managed to score yet?'"

The breakthrough did not herald a change in fortune, though, and Heath was sold to Stoke on transfer deadline day after adding only one more goal to his City tally. Allen, meanwhile, could not change the fixed mindset at Maine Road either. He scored again in the match following his sensational reintroduction at Notts County. A typically clinical finish against Chester in the League Cup prompted a piercing chorus of 'Are you watching Peter Reid?' from the travelling City fans. But the manager's obvious embarrassment was lifted when Allen picked up an injury and was forced to sit out the next game at Spurs. He never started for City again and was sold to Chelsea a month later in a £300,000 transfer.

Also on his way out was City's wholehearted Scottish centre-half Colin Hendry. Another never to find favour under Reid and Ellis, the 24-year-old powerhouse defender had been displaced from the team after Keith Curle's arrival. His natural attacking instincts and occasional lapses were used to justify the decision to sell him to Blackburn for £750,000. Yet, in reality, City's manager needed the money. His efforts to strengthen his squad were being consistently thwarted by a lack of cash in the boardroom. "I would dearly have liked to keep Colin, but I needed to generate funds," Reid has since admitted. "You have to make judgements and I felt there were other areas in the squad which were more deserving."

Without a win in six League games at the start of December, plus defeat in the League Cup at Middlesbrough, City's season was beginning to sink fast. Reid needed to act and turned his attention to Arsenal's unsettled midfielder Michael Thomas. It soon became clear, though, that Thomas favoured a move to Liverpool, a club still adjusting to life under its new manager, Graeme Souness. One man not enjoying the changing times at Anfield was Steve McMahon, a high-octane midfield general in the mould of Reid. The 30-year-old Scouser was looking for a fresh challenge in the fading years of his highly-successful career. Capped 17 times with Liverpool, McMahon won three League Championship medals and played in two FA Cup finals, winning one of them, during his time at Anfield. His duels with Reid in the heat of Merseyside derbies during the 1980s were renowned for their ferocity. Now Reid saw his former adversary as the ideal man to lift City's flagging fortunes. After weeks of protracted negotiations, Liverpool eventually agreed to part with their midfielder and he signed for £900,000 on Christmas Eve.

With McMahon on board, Reid had found his natural successor and could hasten his own retirement from playing – or so the theory went. The City boss was eager to wind up his on-the-field commitments as he concentrated on building a squad fit to challenge for honours. Yet even after McMahon's arrival, Reid played in all but five of the remaining fixtures. His involvement meant that more and more responsibility was heaped on to the considerable shoulders of his assistant, Sam Ellis. The suspicion among supporters was that Sam called the shots. And, as the team's style of football became more direct, it was he who was blamed.

Was the red-haired assistant a malign influence on his impressionable boss or was Sam simply misunderstood? Opinion, as ever, is divided. Clive Allen's rhetoric after Notts County notably pointed the finger at Ellis, whose strict regime seemed to allow no room for free spirits.

Chris Muir, a key director at the time, remembers: "Sam was a very tough disciplinarian. To be honest, his treatment of some of the players was terrible. He could be very cruel. He would leave people waiting outside the manager's office for hours and wouldn't speak to them. "The board had a lot of sympathy with the players – but perhaps that was wrong. You need to let a manager manage, don't you? Sam was an unusual character. On the one hand, he was one of the most intelligent persons I have ever met. He is very interested in world affairs and even architecture. Yet he likes to give off this different image to the public and it backfired badly at City."

Nevertheless, not all the players had an aversion to Ellis's style of man-management. David White, who thrived under the Reid-Ellis regime, is adamant that the assistant boss brought many assets to the job.

"I heard this rumour that Sam and I hated each other, but it couldn't be more wrong. Sure, he was a fiery character who was likely to bawl you out from time to time. But there was another side to him. I wouldn't say he was an emotional person, but he was the most genuine giver of praise that I have ever worked with. If you were playing well and doing the right things, he was just so happy and would quite often just fling his arms around you to hug you," says White.

"To be honest, I regarded him as a real old-fashioned type of manager. He had basic ideas about the game and he got them across to the players without complicating matters. I know some of the players didn't get on with him – the likes of Clive Allen, Colin Hendry and Mark Brennan – but Sam was very good for me."

Tony Coton was another player whose career was beginning to flourish under the tutelage of Ellis. Yet the City keeper admits it was often a volatile mix within the City dressing room. "You either liked Sam or you couldn't stand him. As it was, I'd met him a few times, through Graham Taylor, when I was at Watford. I knew his background and I knew if you were weak with Sam from the start, he'd tread all over you. On the other hand, if you stood up to him, he'd be as nice as pie to you. So, I knew straight away how to play him and to be honest, he was fine with the senior players like me, Curle and Quinny."

The top order players were creating a powerful clique, something which subsequent managers would find difficult to handle. Ellis, though, had few difficulties. His strength of character pervaded the club and, as Reid himself acknowledged, "You don't argue with Sam." Supporters, meanwhile, distrusted a man whose managerial roots lay in lower league football and whose tactical sensibilities were notoriously crude. As the results went City's way, there were rarely dissenting voices. But as cracks began to appear, it was Ellis who came under fire. Despite occupying fourth place in the table, a 4-0 defeat at Queens Park Rangers prompted calls of "Ellis Out" from the visiting fans. It was a graphic indication of his deteriorating reputation at the club. As ever, the club's fanzines were quick to communicate those concerns to a wider audience. Ellis was depicted as an evil Svengali-like figure in a series of brilliantly satirical pieces by Colin Nicholls in *King of the Kippax*.

The inference was obvious, if hardly subtle: while Reid cheerfully acted as the front man, Ellis was pulling the strings behind the scenes. The City manager did little to dispel the image, writing in the club's programme: "You can't sort things out while you are on the pitch. This has to be left to one man. If we need to change anything, it's Sam who has the say. It's difficult enough thinking about my own game. At half-time, Sam does the talking to the players from what he has seen from the sidelines, but I might chip in with a few words after he's finished."

There was patently a dichotomy of power at the top at Maine Road. Ellis's advice was vital to a young manager still acclimatising to life in the hot-seat. But, according to David White, the fans' image bore little relation to reality. "There was never any doubt that Reidy was in charge. He picked the team and would always have the final say. But I suppose it goes without saying that Sam was definitely not a 'yes man'. They used to argue about things and certainly weren't afraid to have disagreements in front of the players. To me, though, that's inevitable. In all working relationships, people have disagreements, and it's healthy to talk them through. Ultimately, I just saw Reidy and Sam as a good partnership."

Ellis was not the only source of wisdom within Reid's regime. Remarkably, there were eight former managers employed at Maine Road during the 1991-92 season. As well as Ellis, Reid could turn to the club's general manager, Jimmy Frizzell, previously in charge at Oldham and City. Another ex-City boss, Tony Book, was first-team coach while Ken Barnes, once manager at Wrexham, had been made the youth development officer. Taking his place as chief scout was Bobby Saxton, formerly in the hot-seat at Blackburn, Exeter, Plymouth and York. The club's reserve team coach, Les Chapman, had enjoyed stints in charge at Preston and Stockport. Swelling the managerial contingent were two "consultants" to Reid. John Neal, the former Chelsea, Middlesbrough and Wrexham manager, and Ian Greaves, Reid's mentor at Bolton.

Greaves was brought in during the summer of 1991 as Reid added yet more experience to his ever-increasing backroom staff. The man who had shaped his early career at Burnden Park was now helping to hone his managerial qualities at City. In fact, if there was one person in football who Reid trusted above all others, it was Greaves. His influence at Maine Road cannot be underestimated but ill health prevented him from taking a more active role.

The City manager was receiving "wise words" from all around and it must have been increasingly difficult to formulate one cohesive strategy. Evidently fearful of his lack of experience in management, Reid was surrounding himself with a cabal of "sagacious" old heads. Nothing was decided without copious consultation, and committee approval. The idea was sound but in practice Reid knew he needed to strike out alone and take control. He has since admitted that if he could change anything about his time at Maine Road, he would "be more my own man."

As well as Greaves and Saxton, there was another addition to the backroom team in the close season. Terry Darracott was appointed youth team coach, nominally to work alongside Glyn Pardoe and Colin Bell. His arrival coincided with the emergence of Mike Sheron, Michael Hughes, Mike Quigley and David Brightwell from the club's floundering youth development programme. A production line which had spawned the country's most exciting batch of young players in the late 1980s, was now being left in the shade – most notably by near neighbours Manchester United. The ultimate insult for the Blues was the maturing and prodigious talent of Ryan Giggs. The young Welshman was spearheading a revival of fortune at Old Trafford, but had begun his career at City's school of excellence. At a club renowned for its ability to self-destruct, it was another blunder which had backfired badly.

The appointment of Darracott did little to alleviate the fears of City's supporters, who suspected it was merely another example of Reid's cronyism. The former Everton man had never coached youngsters before in his career and he faced a daunting introduction at City. "This is probably the only job in football which I haven't done," admitted Darracott on his first day.

One of his first actions was to recommend the signing of a young left-back from Doncaster. Nick Limber impressed Darracott in an FA Youth Cup tie against City, and the 18-year-old was duly signed in a £75,000 deal, rising to £300,000. Two and a half years later, and without making a first-team appearance, Limber rejoined Doncaster on a free transfer. Clearly, the more things changed, the more they stayed the same.

Of the current crop of youngsters, Sheron was the first to force his way into City's first-team squad. But at the start of the 1991-92 season, Reid opted instead for a front pairing of David White and Niall Quinn. After three matches, it was looking a shrewd decision as City sat at the top of Division One with a 100 per cent record. But it would not take long for the shine to wear off. Six games and four defeats later, City had slipped to tenth in the table and Reid knew he had to act.

Michael Hughes was brought in at the expense of Mark Brennan, who had fallen out of favour with the City management. Hughes, a precocious 20-year-old winger from Northern Ireland, was already being compared to – yes, you've guessed it – George Best. Although his introduction was hardly auspicious (missing a penalty against Everton), the youngster went on to establish himself as a regular in Reid's side. At a time when perspiration most definitely ruled over inspiration, Hughes was like a breath of fresh air. His intricate skills and bravado on the ball made him an instant hit with the supporters, who yearned to be entertained. By the middle of December, Hughes was beginning to thrive on the left wing, with the *Manchester Evening News* lauding his "dazzling wing wizardry."

Yet after 28 consecutive appearances, the youngster from Larne was dropped without any satisfactory explanation. Supporters were bewildered by the decision, especially as it coincided with City's worst run of the season (four League defeats in the space of five games). Hughes, who was out of contract at the end of the campaign, had fallen out with Reid and Ellis and neither party was showing any inclination to agree a new deal. It seemed as if there was simply no room within Reid's hard-working side for a touch of artistry. At the end of the season, Hughes was sold to Strasbourg for £450,000 and the club would struggle to find a suitable replacement to fill their creativity chasm.

While some faltered and fell out of favour, others in Reid's squad seemed almost invincible. In goal, Tony Coton was enjoying one of the best spells of his eventful career. The Tamworth-born keeper made his League debut as a 19-year-old for Birmingham City and within 50 seconds had saved a penalty. It was a typically colourful introduction for a young man who had no shortage of confidence.

"I had a bad boy image back then and used to mix in the wrong circles," admits Coton. "To be honest, if it had not been for football, I would have almost certainly have ended up doing time."

After six years at Birmingham, he moved on to Watford where he forged a reputation as one of the country's most promising goalkeepers. Now, as City continued to challenge near the top of the table, it was Coton who was earning most plaudits for his outstanding performances. With his former manager at Watford, Graham Taylor, now in charge of England, it seemed only a matter of time before Coton would receive his international call-up. But it never came.

"I was winning all these personal awards and travelling all over the world with England but I'd never get a game," he recalls. "All I've got to show for it all is half a match in the B team."

If Taylor was reluctant to reward Coton, there was no disguising how the City supporters felt. They voted him City's Player of the Year and chanted "England's Number One" at him throughout the length and breadth of the country. By the end of the season, his fellow professionals had also endorsed that view, voting him on to the PFA's Division One select side. It was all very different from his early days at Maine Road when the reaction of fans threatened to curtail his stay in Manchester. Coton received a distinctly frosty welcome from the rank and file, who still felt a great deal of affection for the man he replaced, Andy Dibble.

Coton remembers: "I was all for packing up and going back down south. But I had that belief, inner strength or stubbornness, or whatever you want to call it, and decided to stay. I was determined to stick it out and win over the fans and I did just that."

While Coton was a tower of strength at the back, it was Niall Quinn who was leading from the front. With 13 goals and a host of good reviews to his name, the rangy Irishman was beginning to attract interest from a number of Italian clubs. One report suggested he could even be sold for £1 million. Reid was horrified: "It's absolute rubbish. And even if it was true and they offered five times that amount, they wouldn't get him. As far as I'm concerned, the big fella is priceless."

Still, even if Reid was not looking abroad for lira, he was increasingly scanning the Continent for new players. Danny Hoekmann joined on a one-month loan from Den Haag and was quickly despatched home again, while Soviet strikers Igor Kolivanov and Igor Korneev both had spells on trial. Perhaps the most intriguing arrival was Oyvind Leonhardsen, Norway's young Player of the Year. A midfielder with great skill, he was photographed on the back page of the *Manchester Evening News*, holding aloft a City scarf. But Reid could never agree a fee for the 21-year-old from Molde, who was represented by the notorious Norwegian agent Rune Hauge, the man who was at the centre of the "bung" scandal involving George Graham. Leonhardsen would go on to sign for Wimbledon, Liverpool and Tottenham Hotspur in multi-million pound deals. City, meanwhile, signed the distinctly less successful Kare Ingebrigtsen the following season in another deal brokered by Hauge.

Reid did have some success in his overseas dealings. Michel Vonk joined the Blues on trial in early April 1992 from SVV Dordrecht. The powerful centre-half complimented the more subtle approach of Keith Curle in the heart of defence. In his second full match, Vonk commanded the back-line as City demolished a Leeds side fighting tooth and nail with Manchester United for the League Championship. As the Blues crashed four goals past Howard Wilkinson's side, thair fans literally did not know whether to laugh or cry. Their most comprehensive and exciting display of the season so far appeared to have handed the title to their deadly rivals.

But in their next match, Reid's side managed to curtail United's bid for the Championship. Despite trailing 1-0 and having Neil Pointon sent off at Old Trafford, City fought back and clinched a point through Keith Curle's 62nd minute penalty. With five games left, there was still a faint chance of the Blues qualifying for Europe. But defeat in their next game at Sheffield Wednesday put paid to those hopes.

As for United, they never truly recovered from the morale-sapping derby game against City. Despite appearing to be the Champions-elect throughout the season, Ferguson's men threw away the opportunity of their first League title in 25 years. Their demise was met with delight at Maine Road. City might have missed out on Europe, eventually finishing fifth, but their neighbours had forsaken a far greater prize.

Peter Swales, who perhaps should have kept his counsel, could not resist a gloat. "We're going to beat them (United) to the Championship. While sympathising with the way they missed out, it was good for us, giving us the chance to get there first. We've achieved a level of consistency over the last two seasons, yet without ever being in the title picture. We could be a lot closer next time. Peter Reid is doing a magnificent job. I'm confident he'll prove to be a top manager. We have re-established ourselves as one of the best five clubs in the country. And I think we will take a bit of shifting from that group now."

CHAPTER THREE

The **split**

PETER SWALES simply could not bring himself to look at the newspapers that morning. The man who once admitted he would stand on his head for the cameras "so long as they mention City in the caption," was inconsolable. He would hardly have cared if his club was never mentioned again. Yet, that morning, the Blues were plastered over every paper – headline-makers for all the wrong reasons.

On 7 March 1993, Maine Road hosted an FA Cup sixth round tie which descended from outrageous expectation to public humiliation within the space of a few chaotic hours. A sense of fevered anticipation filled the air as City's supporters gathered for the showdown with Spurs. After years of missing out, the Blues were just two games away from Wembley. With Manchester United striding inexorably towards the title, their rivals felt it was almost ordained that they too should sample some success. At long last, *this* was going to be their year.

In his programme notes, Peter Reid alluded to the demands bearing down on his team. "The buzz around Maine Road and the feedback from supporters in the build-up to today's match has been fantastic," he wrote. The overwrought atmosphere was further heightened by the presence of BBC television cameras to transmit the match live on terrestrial TV. For the first time in years, the eyes of the nation would be on City.

They made the perfect start, with Mike Sheron heading them into a tenth-minute lead. But Spurs, who had earlier in the season knocked City out of the League Cup, hit back. Goals from Nayim and Steve Sedgeley put them ahead at half-time and it was clear the home side were going to face an almighty struggle to go through. When Nayim scored again almost immediately after the break, the air of belief evaporated. A pall of desperation fell over the ground as Tottenham strolled into the semi-finals. Nayim completed his hat-trick and put the game beyond any doubt with five minutes left. But the day's real drama had not even begun.

The club's new Umbro (Platt Lane) Stand had been opened to coincide with the quarter-final tie. It was, according to the programme, "an auspicious date in the recent history of the club." Yet, with three minutes left, it would become memorable for very different reasons. The unlikely figure of Terry Phelan, a £2.5 million signing from Wimbledon, embarked on a mazy run towards goal. Before he could even think about it, Phelan found himself one-on-one with the Spurs keeper, Erik Thorstvedt, and calmly slotted the ball past him into the net. It was too little, too late, but as Phelan celebrated in front of the new stand, fans began spilling on to the pitch. On an afternoon when reality seemed to have slipped away, a sudden and spontaneous eruption of madness took hold of Maine Road. More and more supporters began piling on to the playing surface in a child-like act of defiance. As the silent majority just stood and watched, more than 150 City fans ran aimlessly around with little or no intent.

The players were withdrawn, but not before Thorstvedt scuffled with one of the more pernicious pitch invaders. Within minutes, mounted police arrived to restore order and prevent a possible clash with the away fans. All Swales and Reid could do was watch from the sidelines as their season of hope fell apart in front of their eyes. Both were furious, but, more acutely, both felt deeply hurt.

"I woke up this morning thinking it was going to be a great day for Manchester City," said Swales. "But now I will go to bed after what was probably the worst day I have had in football. The pitch invasion was terrible. Nauseating. Obnoxious. I can take defeat and like to think our supporters can. And the best team won on Sunday, no question. What I can't take is that kind of exhibition by people who call themselves supporters of Manchester City. We don't want them here at Maine Road. I have to admit that I feel betrayed after what we have done to try to provide a safe ground without fencing people in."

The Football Association launched an inquiry and found City guilty of failing to control their crowd, but the Blues escaped with a suspended sentence. Swales conducted a hunt to track down the guilty parties and vowed to ban them from Maine Road forever.

Dozens of grainy head shots were published in the programme, with fellow supporters urged to come forward and name names.

As for Reid, he even considered his future as manager. The cumulative effect of defeat and disgrace had taken its toll on the demonstrative Scouser. In his programme notes for the next match, he revealed how much events had left him anguished and confused: "There was a moment or two after the Spurs game and the pitch invasion when my gut reaction was whether it was worth carrying on or not. But then I thought about the thousands of genuine City fans who have been magnificent home and away this season."

While Reid opted to carry on, the defeat by Spurs would nevertheless prove to be a turning point in his managerial career. The season had started out full of hope and expectation as City looked to build on their recent rehabilitation in the top flight. The long-awaited Premier League had finally dawned, with its attendant financial benefits for the leading clubs. Satellite television was promising to pump millions of pounds into the game, in return for near blanket coverage. The Blues were first to sample the new glitz and razzamatazz of *Monday Night Football* on a clear August evening in 1992. Dancing girls, fireworks and deafeningly loud speakers greeted Reid's men as they took on QPR at Maine Road. In an idea pioneered in the United States, BSkyB was seeking to establish a new culture within English football. It was no longer just a game, it was supposed to be an occasion.

For Peter Swales, the Premier League offered an unmissable opportunity to secure City's place in the upper echelons of the game. If its advent also meant the rich clubs siphoning off more and more money while the rest struggled to survive, then so be it.

"This is the age of the £3 million player, top players earning £7,000 a week and of vast sums from television and sponsorship," said the City chairman. "Obviously, the Premier League will generate more money for the top clubs but that is the only way to compete with the big clubs on the Continent, like Inter Milan and Marseilles. Old systems don't last forever. You can't stop progress because of what might happen to the ninety-second or ninety-third club."

And Swales was determined that City would not be one of the unfortunates left behind by the financial revolution in English football. Over the summer, three of the club's most senior players – Tony Coton, David White and Niall Quinn – signed long-term contracts. Quinn, who signed a five-year deal, commented, "I've committed myself to City for the bulk of my career, if not the entirety. I aim to make it a very successful time and my big aim is to win a Championship medal with City." It seemed a reasonable, if optimistic, ambition.

Reid's ventures into the Continental transfer market continued, but once again with little success. A three-month chase for Twente Enschede winger Arthur Numan ended in humiliation in a Dutch courtroom. City had identified the youngster as a perfect replacement for Michael Hughes, who had moved to Strasbourg. The Blues agreed to pay more than £1 million for the Dutch under-21 international, but he favoured a move to PSV Eindhoven, believing it would boost his chances of a full call-up to the Holland national side. With PSV offering £600,000 less than City, Numan's club refused to sanction the transfer. Reid believed he had got his man but Numan was not to be denied his dream move. His case went to a tribunal, which City's manager and chairman attended. Despite their impassioned arguments, the court ruled in favour of Numan, who duly signed for PSV.

"To say I'm amazed is an understatement," said Reid, who had openly admitted that Numan was his number one transfer target. "I've been after him for three months and it's all been for nothing."

With the Numan deal over, City found themselves with a glaring vacuum on their left-hand side. Chief scout Bobby Saxton suggested a move for Oldham's unconventional winger Rick Holden. A swap deal involving Neil Pointon and Steve Redmond was agreed just prior to City's pre-season tour of Italy. Redmond, an honest and industrious defender, moved reluctantly after a City career spanning eight years and including 235 League appearances. He was not the only stalwart to leave the club during a turbulent close season.

Without any warning or real explanation, Glyn Pardoe and Roy Bailey were sacked. Pardoe, a member of City's Championship-winning side in 1968, was the club's youngest debutant at the age of 15 in 1962. His career was effectively ended in 1970 when a tackle from George Best broke his leg. After his retirement a few years later, Pardoe joined City's coaching staff, working most notably with the club's youngsters. He nurtured the all-conquering FA Youth Cup-winning side of 1986 and had brought through the likes of Earl Barrett, Paul Warhurst and Gerry Taggart. However, City's fountain of youth had dried up in the late 1980s and early 1990s. Reid had clearly decided it was time for change.

Pardoe commented at the time, "I think the manager wants to bring in his own men, but I have not lost my enthusiasm or anything. To be honest, I don't know why he did it and I don't know why Peter Swales allowed him so much power."

Bailey, who had worked as the club's senior physiotherapist since the late 1970s, was equally bewildered by his treatment. A familiar figure on the bench at Maine Road, he was not a fully-qualified physiotherapist. Eamonn Salmon, Plymouth's physio and formerly the head of a North East clinic, took over. Meanwhile, Terry Farrell, the club's assistant chief scout and a former fire officer, was appointed youth development officer. Later on in the season, he was joined by Jack Chapman, a friend of Sam Ellis from their days working together at Blackpool. While the changes in personnel did little to revive City's wilting youth programme, they undoubtedly diminished Reid's reputation among supporters. Pardoe and Bailey were popular figures at Maine Road and their abrupt sackings were seen as a betrayal of the club's past.

Reid's search for summer reinforcements continued with the almost seasonal chase for Paul Stewart. The Tottenham striker was once again pining for his native north and it was thought he might favour a return to Maine Road. But the lure of joining Liverpool proved too great and City were left to contemplate another failure in the transfer market. As the season approached, Reid made bids for Andy Sinton, Kevin Gallacher, John Barnes and even Alan Shearer – but to no avail. He would have to begin with only one new signing, Rick Holden.

There was another more welcome addition in the starting line-up for their Monday night extravaganza against Queens Park Rangers. Paul Lake had successfully negotiated three games in City's tour of Italy and was now finally ready to make his long-awaited return to first-team action. "It's like having a new £2 million player," wrote Reid, enthusiastically. The Maine Road faithful welcomed back their returning hero with a mixture of joy, relief and a touch of trepidation. Their fears seemed unfounded as he emerged wholeheartedly back into the action. In fact, it was his intervention in the 37th minute which set up an opportunity for David White to open the scoring against Rangers. Andy Sinton equalised in the second half, but it was a more than satisfactory start to the campaign for City. Two days later, their early-season optimism was shattered.

On a cold evening in Middlesbrough, City were looking to bury their jinx against the Teesiders. After exiting both cup competitions at Ayresome Park in the previous season, Reid's side owed their opponents one. Yet City's luck was not about to turn – in fact, things got worse. Within a few minutes, Lake collapsed to the ground in anguish as his patched-up knee joints gave way again. His dreams of a return to the big time had been cruelly snuffed out.

Despite many fruitless attempts, there was to be no way back this time. The only hope seemed to be revolutionary surgery developed in the United States. In an operation pioneered by American specialist Dominic Cisto, the damaged cruciate ligament was replaced by the Achilles tendon of a recently-deceased donor. It had worked for Crystal Palace's John Salako and Iain Durrant of Rangers, but Lake was different. His knee had suffered such devastating damage that even a new tendon could not support it. Reid, though, was determined that the club should do everything possible to help their injured star even if his own public statements were beginning to sound distinctly gloomy.

"As long as Paul is prepared to battle on, he can count on the support of everyone at Maine Road," said Reid. "Anything which can be done will be done, even if it means expensive treatment in America."

In September 1992, Lake flew to Los Angeles to undergo the three and a half hour operation. It was declared a success, but as the 23-year-old Mancunian sat alone in an empty hospital room 8,000 miles away from home, he began to question whether it was all worth it. "My knee was strapped together and I was in such pain," he commented. I felt so low and began to wonder why this had happened to me. But there's no point in feeling sorry for yourself, you just have to get on with your life.

"The surgeon said it was the most lax knee he had seen come over from Britain – and he had dealt with Iain Durrant from Rangers who had a terrible injury. There was so much movement in the joints. The surgeon did his best, but there was nothing he could do. To be honest, I knew before the start of the season that the knee wasn't right. It felt like a bag of bones, but you just hope don't you?"

The other players, aware of Lake's torment, arranged a whip-round and raised enough money for their team-mate's girlfriend to travel out to America to be by his bed-side. It was a magnanimous gesture but only served to illustrate the inadequacy of City's provision for their player's rehabilitation. After his operation, Lake flew back to England alone. It was an agonising journey. He was the forgotten man of Maine Road again; City, meanwhile, had to rebuild without their favourite son.

With the Premier League's millions beckoning, Swales knew he had to dig deep again to ensure City's survival. Reid had been chasing another express-heeled defender from Wimbledon throughout the summer of 1992. Terry Phelan, a 5ft 8ins left-back, had begun his career at Leeds United, but it was only after his move to Wimbledon in 1987 that his true potential was realised. Another renowned member of the so-called Crazy Gang, Phelan's pace and neat skills had attracted the attention of a number of top clubs. Born in Salford, the 25-year-old was a boyhood Manchester United fan and had been linked with a move to the Reds but it was City who cherished the diminutive defender's talents. They faced stiff opposition from Crystal Palace, whose interest ensured Phelan's valuation rocketed. The fact that Palace and Wimbledon shared their headquarters at Selhurst Park was dismissed as merely a coincidence. Whatever the truth, City eventually agreed a fee of £2.5 million for Phelan, who arrived seven days into the season.

"He's a quality player, with tremendous pace and should be a great asset to the side," said Reid. "Although, I have to admit he cost us a good deal more than we wanted to spend."

Phelan joined his former Wimbledon team-mate Keith Curle as Reid fashioned one of the quickest defences in the top flight. Curle had made an impressive start to his City career and had caught the eye of England's new manager, Graham Taylor. When Taylor needed a replacement right-back for Euro 92, he called for Curle. The City captain played in the opening fixture – a 0-0 draw against Denmark – but struggled in an unfamiliar position. His elevation to international status was short-lived and suddenly it seemed his stay in Manchester might be similarly truncated. A story in the *Sunday Express* claimed Curle wanted to leave City after a training ground bust-up. "It has nothing to do with football," he was quoted as saying. Yet, just days later, he flatly denied the suggestions, responding in

The Pink: "My ambitions lie at City. I want to set the record straight, I've had no trouble with Peter Reid and Sam Ellis and cannot recall a cross word, let alone trading punches, with any team-mates." The suspicion remained, though, that City's skipper was far from happy.

Curle was not the only City player to scratch the surface of the England side. Late in September, David White won his one and only cap for a friendly against Spain in Santander. After a run of seven goals in seven League games, White was the leading striker in the Premier League. But his prolific run came shuddering to a halt just at the wrong time. After failing to convert an early chance in Santander, White was dispensed from the England set-up. His obvious disappointment seemed to impact upon his form for City. For the next nine games, he barely came close to scoring as the Blues slipped to fourteenth in the table. More and more critics were pointing the finger at City's style of play and White, too, believed it was time to speak out.

"I thought we were playing too much long-ball tactics and I went to see Sam Ellis about it. He listened to me, but didn't agree. Then, a few days later, Reidy called me into his office and told me to watch some videos. He said that when we were playing well, we were playing it long and Niall Quinn was at the heart of things. To be honest, he was right and I was won over. Quinny was incredible in the air, he could pass the ball with his head. Our only problem was that when we weren't playing well, it would just become aimless."

As City entered the final month of 1992, they were most certainly not playing well. A 2-1 defeat at Old Trafford brought Reid's problems into sharper focus. City needed some inspiration and the potential signing of Kare Ingebrigtsen from Rosenborg offered little solace to the faithful. Even Reid was beginning to ask whether it was a change in tactics which his club really needed.

"After the derby defeat, I sat down with the coaching staff and gave considerable thought to changing things around a bit," he said. "We've been accused in some quarters of taking the 'route one' approach too much, simply because we have an outstanding target man in Niall Quinn. But anyone who watches our training sessions at Platt Lane can see that we have much more to offer than that."

Keith Curle and Quinn reinforced their manager's message, making public pleas for patience from the supporters. But discontent was beginning to mount on the terraces and it surfaced at the club's annual general meeting. After the predictable declarations of support from the chairman's loyal coterie of followers, a lone voice dared to dispute the party line. Brian Williams, a small shareholder, seized the moment to challenge Swales's hegemony.

"You have been the chairman for fourteen years without a major success. You have not been a lucky chairman and you should give somebody else a chance," asserted Williams.

At the top table, Swales lifted his eyes and replied curtly: "I take your point, but I will not be taking your advice."

Outside the meeting, Swales spoke to the waiting media. His misjudgement of the prevailing mood was obvious. Times were changing, but City's chief was unmoved. He felt impregnable. "The only people who'll decide whether I stay in the job or not are the directors," he announced. "It certainly won't be the public."

His arrogance and weakening grip on reality only served to heighten the frustration among supporters. They were ignored, dismissed like naughty schoolchildren throwing a tantrum. Swales's kingdom was beginning to crumble but he could not even notice the cracks.

Yet this was no inexorable slide towards doom. There were still considerable grounds for optimism as City entered the New Year. While Lake's injury curse had deprived them of one glittering asset, another footballing gem had emerged. Garry Flitcroft, a Bolton-born midfielder with an impressive pedigree, was handed his debut early in the season. He was a product of the FA's National School of Excellence at Lilleshall and his polished and maturing style immediately caught the eye. Like a breath of fresh air, Flitcroft breezed into City's starting line-up and stayed there for most of the season. His vision and intelligence on the ball belied his 19 years of age and with striking blond hair and good looks to boot, City had found their new golden boy. Fitzroy Simpson, Reid's £500,000 purchase from Swindon in the previous season, struggled to match up to the precocious talents of Flitcroft. By the end of the campaign, City's home-grown star had made 28 League starts, forced his way into the England under 21 squad and been voted the club's Player of the Year.

While Flitcroft was the face of the future, a vestige from the past had also returned. Ray Ranson made 217 League and cup appearances for the Blues in the late 1970s and early 1980s. He was signed as a 14-year-old apprentice and emerged into the first-team with the likes of Dave Bennett, Gary Owen and Peter Barnes. A dependable defender, Ranson became City's regular right-back and played in John Bond's side in the 1981 Centenary FA Cup Final. Now, some 14 years after his debut for the club, he was required again to answer Peter Reid's mercy call.

Ranson, who had played for Birmingham and Newcastle since leaving City, was drafted in on a one-month loan at the start of 1993. With Andy Hill and Ian Brightwell both out, Reid desperately required some experienced defensive cover for his side. Ranson fitted the bill and he ended up spending the rest of the season at Maine Road, making 17 starts in an unexpected Indian summer. For the 32-year-old, it was a dream move and, perhaps inevitably, he was upbeat as he assessed the club's future prospects. "There is stability at the club now, the nucleus of a good side is here and the foundations are well set. So putting myself in the shoes of a Manchester City supporter, I'd be looking at the Nineties as an exciting period."

In reality the club was beginning its long and painful fall from grace. The stability which Ranson identified would very soon be shattered. After their ignominious exit from the FA Cup at the hands of Spurs, City's season merely limped laboriously towards a depressing conclusion. There was nothing to play for and little to hope for – except that United might self-destruct again on their way to the Championship. It didn't happen. Alex Ferguson's side claimed their first title in 26 years when their nearest rivals, Aston Villa, were beaten by Joe Royle's Oldham at Villa Park. While the Reds celebrated, the Blues retreated into the background to lick their wounds. City's last remaining crumb of comfort had been swallowed up by their despised neighbours. Hurt and resentful, the fans gathered for the final match of the season against Howard Kendall's Everton. Surely City could muster something to stir their supporters' flagging spirits, something to restore their faith in the future? But no: Reid's side were an utter shambles. Three-nil down after half an hour to an average Everton side, City were in danger of sinking without trace. Their young goalkeeper, Martyn Margetson, in for the injured Coton, was suffering most of all. His weak kicking was inviting wave upon wave of Everton attacks. Despite David White's goal just before half-time, the home crowd were beginning to despair.

Andy Dibble's introduction at the interval, in place of Margetson, did little to ease the torment. Within six minutes, Preki had made it 4-1 and City's loyal supporters had run out of patience. Familiar chants began to echo around the stadium. "Swales out," bawled pockets of supporters as they turned on the man whose early-season prediction of success now sounded so hollow. Eggs were pelted at the directors' box and abuse hurled at the chairman. He seemed bewildered but unperturbed by the protests.

A season which had begun so full of promise was descending into disarray. Curle's 73rd minute penalty restored some hope, but Peter Beagrie's second goal made it 5-2 moments later. Victory would have secured sixth place in the table, ahead of Liverpool, but defeat meant Reid's side had to settle for finishing ninth. It was hardly a disaster, but that was not the issue: it was the team who occupied top spot which really bothered the Blues. "It was a disaster for us," admits Chris Muir, "Peter Swales had staked so much on outdoing United and now they had beaten us to the Championship. He was crestfallen and I think we all knew it was extremely significant for the club."

Swales, the man who had so often gambled with the future of City, now had only one option – to bluff. He announced there would be £6 million for Peter Reid to spend during the summer. It was to be his "fighting fund" as City battled to match their neighbours and become Championship contenders. But Swales did not have the money, nor did he have any clear idea where to get it from. Though he knew the policy of "borrow and spend" had almost ruined the club in the early 1980s, he felt he had no choice but to follow that route again. The problem was, with City's overdraft reportedly topping £3 million, the bank was reluctant to bail Swales out again. "Peter always used to find money from somewhere, but this time his well seemed to have dried up. The supporters were crying out for big-name signings, but we just couldn't deliver," says Muir.

Reid had drawn up a shopping list of players he wished to sign and top of the pile was the Chelsea midfielder Andy Townsend. The Republic of Ireland international was intent on leaving London and had attracted interest from City, Aston Villa and Everton. Reid was prepared to pay whatever it took to secure his services. Swales was not. The City chairman baulked at the prospect of laying out more than £2 million on a player already aged 30. Aston Villa had no such qualms and agreed a fee of £2.3 million.

"We could have signed Townsend," countered Swales. "But we felt the fee was just too high. You have got to say to yourself: we are prepared to pay a good price but not over the odds."

It was the same story with the Blackpool winger Trevor Sinclair. Reid wanted him but once again Swales dragged his feet. After weeks of wrangling over a fee, Queens Park Rangers stepped in and signed the youngster in a £1 million transfer. Although Reid claimed he "would not lose any sleep over it," he was becoming increasingly alarmed at his chairman's attitude. It seemed as if Swales was purposely striving to obstruct any attempts to strengthen the squad. The City boss, who had been stalling over a new contract, began to wonder whether the ground was already being laid for a new manager. He decided to wait no longer and signed the deal on offer, a three-year extension to his contract. Swales was outwardly bullish: "The longer Peter Reid continues as manager, the more confident I am that he will win the title."

But the public facade could not hide the growing rift between manager and chairman. After a deal for Crystal Palace midfielder Geoff Thomas fell through at the last moment, Reid turned his attention once more to Paul Stewart. Swales was dumbfounded as the Liverpool midfielder had already turned down moves to City twice in the previous two summers. The chairman did not want to give him another opportunity to humiliate the club. Furthermore, he had grave doubts about the 28-year-old's attitude and his ability to help the Blues. When Liverpool demanded £2 million for their player, Swales was content to offer barely half that amount.

Reid was furious. He had seen transfer target after transfer target slip from City's grasp while supporters were beginning to question his ability to negotiate a deal. The only answer, it seemed, was to go public with his fears. He contacted the City reporter at the *Manchester Evening News*, Paul Hince, and asked if he would write a story on the current situation. Days later the *Pink* reported the Blues were in danger of losing their manager. Hince, a former City player, wrote that Reid was frustrated over the summer's transfer dealings and that his relationship with Swales had sunk to an all-time low following the failure to sign Stewart. Nobody was quoted, but Swales knew immediately where the story had come from. Hince and Reid were summoned to the chairman's office, where he confronted them both.

"He asked me outright whether the story had come from Reidy," remembers Hince. "I paused for a moment and could see the sweat pouring off Reidy, and then said 'No.' But Swales wasn't a fool and he turned to Reidy and said: 'If you ever pull a trick like that again, I will f*****g sack you straight away.' It was the first and only time I ever heard Swalesy swear and I think that indicates just how cross he was."

The City chief continued to maintain an uneasy truce with his manager in public. He rubbished the *Pink* story, asserting: "Any talk of the manager threatening to resign is ridiculous. I have no complaint about the way our business is being done. We are both working towards success for City."

In reality he pair were finding it almost impossible to work together. "Towards the end, they just couldn't have a reasonable conversation with each other. Every time Swales tried to broach a subject, he would just get a one-line reply. He just didn't know how to handle it," remembers Chris Muir.

Amid the acrimony, a pre-season tour to Holland seemed like a welcome respite. During the trip, Reid completed his only summer signing – an unknown midfielder from Ajax, Alphonse Groenendijk, who cost £500,000. Unfortunately, the tour would be remembered for different reasons. Just days before its conclusion, a number of English newspapers reported that City were set to be thrown out of their hotel because of rowdy and anti-social behaviour. Late night drinking and fighting were the principle allegations; not uncommon occurrences on a football tour, but this was exactly the sort of bad publicity which Reid needed to avoid in the current sensitive climate. According to David White, the City manager dealt with the fall-out admirably.

"It was all down to the players – of which I have to admit I was one. We had a friendly game the next day but, as a group, we decided to ignore the curfew and come in late. We had been stuck in this hotel for days on end and we just decided to let our hair down. It wasn't right, but these things happen in football clubs. The manager handled it very well. He gave us a serious dressing down and we knew exactly where we stood. When you talk about keeping discipline, I think Reidy should have come out of that incident well."

Instead, the reports which filtered back to Manchester merely raised concerns in the boardroom about Reid's style of management.

It seemed as if he and Ellis had lost control. The picture would get worse still on the final day of the tour. As Swales waited in Manchester for crisis talks with his manager, word arrived that the team's plane had been delayed – apparently because players and officials were getting drunk in the airport building. It was the final straw for City's high-minded chairman: he was livid. But, once again, White is quick to defend his former manager.

"It was nothing to do with the players getting drunk," he says. "The time of the flight was printed incorrectly on our itinerary. So, myself and a number of the other players, along with the likes of Tony Book, were just wandering around the terminal building. Reidy was on the plane, but there was just a misunderstanding. It wasn't a lack of discipline, yet there is no doubt a different image got back to the board."

As the City manager flew back to England, his fate was already sealed. His reign in charge was nearing its end, but the turmoil was only just beginning.

CHAPTER FOUR

Forward with **Franny**

A HUSH FELL OVER Manchester City's Platt Lane changing rooms. Peter Reid was ready to address his players. Looking drawn but still determined, the City manager rose slowly to his feet and stared squarely at his assembled squad. "I have just been given a vote of confidence by the board," he announced. "And from now on, John Maddock will be acting as the club's general manager."

Reid smiled and let out a nervous, derisory laugh. The room fell silent again – City's manager did not need to say any more. He knew now it was only a matter of when, rather than if, he would be sacked.

"There was a stunned silence," recalls David White, one of the players present. "But I think we had all seen the writing on the wall. The whole thing had been brewing up for some time and basically Reidy was just saying, 'It's all over lads.' He wasn't getting the backing which he had received previously and the chairman seemed to have lost faith in him. To be honest, I don't think Swales ever really wanted him as manager."

City's chairman was certainly showing little inclination to keep Reid on board. The pair had barely managed a civil conversation throughout a summer of broken promises and frustrated ambitions. Now, he had decided to introduce a third party into the equation. John Maddock was a bluff former journalist, a man well known in the insular world of north-west football. He began his career in the Manchester offices of the *Daily Express*, writing about local non-league soccer. Before long, he met Peter Swales, then the chairman of Altrincham Football Club. The two became close friends and confidants throughout the next 30 years as they steered separate paths towards the top of their trades. Up until 1988, Maddock was the northern sports editor of the *Sunday People*, where he used his privileged position with Swales to the paper's advantage.

"He told me stuff... how things were at the FA and Manchester City and it helped me because reporters used to come to me with stories and I could say it's not right because I know," says Maddock. "Basically, it meant the paper never made a fool of itself."

After leaving the *Sunday People*, Maddock broadened his interests and devoted more time to a sports promotions business, which he had run in conjunction with his journalistic career since 1971. His friendship with Swales, though, remained resolute with Maddock hosting events on match days at Maine Road and effectively acting as an unpaid consultant to the City chairman. "I brokered the deal which brought Howard Kendall to City and had also recommended Billy McNeill back in 1983," he says.

Now, with Swales stuck in one of the worst predicaments of his 20-year chairmanship, he turned to his old comrade. If anyone could sort out this mess, it was big John Maddock, Swales reasoned. "The board wasn't managing to have a dialogue with Reid and we thought Maddock would be the ideal man to handle the situation," explains former director Chris Muir. "He wasn't brought in to sack the manager, he was brought in as a buffer."

After an opening-day draw with Leeds and defeat at Everton, Swales decided it was time to act. Maddock was appointed general manager, with responsibility to liase between Reid and the board. For the first time during his tenure in charge, Swales claimed he was stepping out of the firing line. "It's a matter of trying something new," said City's chairman as he unveiled the new managerial team. "We have been highly successful as far as running a football club is concerned, but we probably haven't done as well as we should have done in terms of winning trophies.

"The summer has not gone particularly well so we are going to make a change. I'm going to step out of the day-to-day contact with Peter Reid. We've appointed John Maddock as general manager and he will work with Peter as I did in the past. Peter is a tough character, the same as myself, and I've had a few years working on that front and it's about time we tried something new. The only thing I will do now is tell the general manager what money is available and then let them get on with it."

Reid maintained the pretence in public, but privately he was seething. He had not been consulted on Maddock's appointment and felt the new hierarchy undermined his power base. As Maddock promised "fresh ideas" and "a fresh outlook," the City boss must have felt the noose tightening around his neck. But he was not prepared to go without a fight. As City's first-team squad prepared for a trip to Spurs – only the season's third match – Maddock took his place at the head of the team coach. It was a move steeped in symbolism as he endeavoured to assert his authority over every aspect of the club. For the players, it only served to heighten their frustration and bewilderment at the turn of events.

"It was just embarrassing," admits David White. "They were turning the club into a joke and there was nothing we could do about it. Maddock never spoke to the players and we didn't know anything about him. To be honest, most of us just thought it was a nonsense."

Their performances on the pitch, though, merely strengthened his case. An abject 1-0 defeat at White Hart Lane was characterised by a growing sense of disorder as players argued among themselves – and with the bench. It gave Maddock all the ammunition he needed to take on Reid and Sam Ellis. Yet he waited until the next game, at home against Blackburn, to pull the trigger.

"I quickly saw that things weren't right," says Maddock. "There was stuff going on in the background which wasn't right for a football club. They had a bad pre-season tour of Holland where there were accusations of heavy drinking. It was obvious that things needed sorting out. The football wasn't attractive, either, and people tend to forget that the club had only won four games since the beginning of February. Something had to give, something had to happen."

After another defeat, in the match against Blackburn, Maddock decided to go public. He barged into the post-match press conference, ahead of Reid, and unleashed an emotion-charged diatribe at the waiting media. His moment in the spotlight had arrived and he was ready to squeeze every last drop of melodrama out of it. Thumping the desk and with his eyes bulging out, Maddock declared: "The Manchester City fans deserve more than what they paid for tonight. People had better understand that there is a new regime at Maine Road. I am not a mouthpiece for Peter Swales. I am the supremo at Maine Road with a specific mandate from the board. "And that mandate is to sort out the problem which we have got at the moment. Make no mistake about it, I have the power to hire and fire and whatever has got to be done to put us back on line will be done. I am not a puppet or a messenger. I am the man in charge and I will take positive steps to put this club into shape."

It was the final straw for Reid, who had seen his authority undermined once too often. He challenged Maddock to explain himself but there was really no need to. By now, both knew there was only one possible outcome in their battle of wills. Less than 36 hours later, the City manager and his assistant were sacked on the "recommendation" of Maddock.

It was a humbling experience for Reid, who commented he was out of work for the first time since the age of 15. The man who had inspired City – both on and off the pitch – for the past three and a half seasons was leaving with his kingdom in ruins. After leading the Blues to the brink of Europe, his club had become beset by disharmony and disarray. Yet most of his players remain four square behind him – to this day.

Tony Coton is one. "Reidy is a man's man. He played hard and likes his social life and doesn't mind his players having a decent social life when it's right. Alcohol has been the ruin of me at times in my earlier days, but I can only remember one major incident at City that was drink-related. It was in Italy when two senior players got into an argument and it ended up as a fight. We saw the funny side of it later on and nobody could believe that I wasn't involved. There was no lack of discipline at the club and to use that as an excuse to sack Reidy was ridiculous. I genuinely thought we were on the right lines at that time and there was a great spirit in the camp. He'd got some decent players and I thought with one or two additions we wouldn't be far away. When he was sacked, we were just all stunned."

Niall Quinn decided to act. He publicly challenged the decision and questioned the authority of Maddock to make it. An eloquent and intelligent speaker, the Irishman made a compelling case and demanded a meeting with Swales. It seemed the players were on the brink of mutiny. "I don't have any problems with the players, it is at a higher level which is worrying me," said Quinn. "I shall be going to see Mr Swales and ask for a few assurances. There is a big problem there and there is no point in hiding it."

If the players were shocked, the press was vitriolic in its criticism of the sacking. Sports journalists on every newspaper turned on their former colleague, Maddock, and lambasted his decision. James Lawton, the chief sports writer at the *Daily Express*, was particularly acerbic.

"Manchester City were not content with sacking Peter Reid," he wrote. "They had to make a low-grade joke of it. They insulted the intelligence of their fans and their players. They sent out John Maddock, the general manager, whose only previous executive decision within football was to fill in his coupon, to explain how HE had decided to recommend to the board the dismissal of Reid and his assistant, Sam Ellis. I happen to know John Maddock as an amiable, intelligent man. But as a football man, I'm not at all sure he would qualify to run my local pub team."

Lawton's was a theme picked up by most of the press, with even the best man at Maddock's wedding, James Mossop, writing a damning assessment. It was an "unforgivable" act of treachery, according to Maddock, who to this day refuses to attend Football Writers' Association functions. "People were jealous and they just used the opportunity to settle a few scores," he says.

Yet, the image of Maddock as a hatchet man, acting on the orders of Swales, very soon became lodged in the collective consciousness. Whatever Maddock said and however much he blustered, the suspicion remained that City's chairman had merely used his friend as a cover to sack Reid.

There was certainly no doubt who the supporters blamed. They had seen this tactic before – sack the manager and buy some breathing space. It was the eleventh managerial change of Swales's reign. This time, though, the fans were not ready to be appeased. Reid's tactics had won him few admirers on the terraces but he still retained a strong groundswell of support. "We want Reidy back," sang the Kippax as the Blues took on Coventry in their next game, under the trusty stewardship of perennial caretaker boss Tony Book. Rather than solve the problem, Maddock had created a martyr: a symbol of injustice which would fuel the burgeoning discontent around Maine Road.

"Peter Reid still crucifies me," admits Maddock. "When he got an award at the Football Writers' function, he said I knew nothing about football. I thought that was sad, but there you go."

Chris Muir adds: "Looking back, we were probably wrong to sack Peter Reid. He has done a good job at Sunderland, but perhaps he and Sam Ellis just weren't the right partnership."

City turned their attention to finding Reid's successor. The speculation was intense, with many believing only a big-name boss would satisfy the increasingly unsettled supporters. On the morning of the match against Coventry, Maddock announced he was setting off in his car to meet the new man in charge. As he headed south, the guessing game was at full throttle. Gerry Francis, Terry Venables, Ron Atkinson, and even Rodney Marsh were mentioned but it was Leicester City's Brian Little who seemed favourite. The silver-haired, softly-spoken Geordie had spent his entire playing career at Aston Villa and was now proving his credentials as a shrewd operator in the managerial game. Successful stints with Darlington and Leicester had earmarked him as a future top-flight, high profile boss. But it was another Brian, with a distinctly lower profile, who was in Maddock's sights.

Brian Horton had served a long and eventful initiation on the shop floor of English football. The Hednesford-born midfielder quickly became accustomed to the realities of life in the working man's game after being rejected by Walsall at the age of 17. Undeterred, he battled his way back and carved out an honest, if less than illustrious, career with Port Vale, Brighton and Luton. His managerial life followed a similar route as he struggled to overcome the odds. After four seasons in charge of Hull, including a successful promotion challenge, Horton was sacked – only to be reinstated days later after a player revolt. He refused to return, though, and joined Oxford United as Mark Lawrenson's assistant. When Lawrenson resigned over Dean Saunders' transfer to Derby, Horton was left to steer the Maxwell-owned club through five turbulent seasons. Significantly, he had never suffered the ignominy of relegation.

But when Maddock unveiled his new manager after the game against Coventry, it soon became apparent that all Horton's experience would count for little. In an increasingly image-led game, City had opted for a man who seemed the epitome of substance over style. 'Brian Who?' screamed the back pages, while supporters reacted with a mixture of dismay and disbelief. He was the "professionals' professional," according to Maddock but the professionals at Maine Road were far from convinced.

"We just couldn't believe that Brian Horton had been given the job," says David White. "When we were told, there was uproar in the dressing room as everyone said, 'Who?' Some of the players literally hadn't heard of him. It took their breath away. Without knowing

Brian at all as a person or as a manager, my first reaction was that I'd had enough. I could see something good was being broken up and I couldn't take it."

The City board were equally suspicious of Maddock's choice at first. Freddie Pye, the club's vice-chairman, was asked to interview Horton prior to the appointment. He was reluctant, believing they needed a more experienced man to take control and defuse an inflammatory situation. Eventually, he agreed to a meeting and was almost instantly won over by Horton's infectious enthusiasm for the game. "He was very impressed and totally sold on the idea of bringing in Brian," recalls Maddock. "I knew him as a straight, honest, good manager – which he proved at City without any proper backing."

Horton and his assistant, David Moss, drove up to Manchester on the day of the Coventry game to be offered the job by chairman Swales. Both men knew it was an almighty gamble, but they could hardly have been prepared for what lay ahead. The first question at Horton's introductory press conference set the tone for the next few days. "A young Press Association reporter from London just stuck up his hand and asked, 'Who *are* you?'" recalls Paul Hince of the *Manchester Evening News*. "I have to say I found that grossly insulting because I'd known Brian for a long time and he was a fantastic professional wherever he went."

The harsh reality was that Horton was a nobody in the high-stakes world of Manchester football. His appointment did nothing to quell the escalating tension among supporters. The overwhelming majority chose to target their frustration at Swales. He became a hate figure, while Horton was considered merely an unfortunate stooge. Nevertheless, his refreshingly positive outlook and attacking brand of football was a welcome relief from the staid, more regimented regime of Peter Reid. Horton knew he desperately needed the fans on his side to have any chance of survival. A slim figure, whose cropped beard obscured his gaunt features, he was difficult to dislike. His wide blue eyes seemed desperate to escape from their sockets as he stared out, seeking some sense of reassurance. With his express-paced Midlands accent, Horton also had a habit of ending every pronouncement with a question – 'We played well, didn't we?' 'It's not good enough, is it?' and so on. But all the questions at the start of his Maine Road stay concerned his identity.

"The press were full of 'Brian Who?' and 'Horton Out' but the fans were brilliant," recalls Horton. "They never once shouted for me to go, even though certain quarters were trying to turn them against me. The Brian Who? business annoyed me because I'd played at City many times. People were saying, what's he done in the game? But that could apply to lots of managers who haven't played at a higher level, like Howard Wilkinson, Jim Smith and Ron Atkinson. The list is endless. I'd played at the highest level and I'd played at City many times, so I knew all about it. It was a big job and too good to turn down. We got six points out of six in the first two games, which was a wonderful start, but it was difficult to sustain with all the other outside pressures."

It was not just the supporters Horton needed to convince. The vibes seeping out of the dressing room were lukewarm. Keith Curle, the club's captain, could barely conceal his disapproval. "The decision has been taken over our heads and I suppose we'll just have to live with it," was his barbed assessment. But the new City boss was unbowed, declaring any unhappy players simply had to knock on his door. "I'm not in the business of keeping people here if they don't want to stay," he said.

David White had made up his mind. The sacking of Peter Reid and John Maddock's growing influence at the club had dismayed the Mancunian winger. He could not stomach another upheaval and resolved to get out as quickly as he could.

"I never gave Brian a chance, I have to admit," says White, who had joined the club on a YTS scheme in 1984. "The first thing he said to the players was that his door was open if anyone wanted to leave. I went to see him and put my cards on the table. I said that everything was going great before and now the club was going backwards. I felt we had gone two years back within the space of two months. I knew any new manager would say that it was a two or three-year job but that was just rubbish. I said I wasn't prepared to wait any longer and wanted to go."

It would be another four months before White got his wish – a move to Leeds United in exchange for David Rocastle. Originally, the deal had also included Steve Hodge and Noel Whelan moving to Maine Road, according to White, but City's indecision cost them dear.

"Brian Horton just ignored my transfer request for the first few months. So I went back to see him and told him I was deadly serious and that I didn't think my future was here. I knew Leeds United were interested in me and I never gave Brian Horton a chance to change my mind, which I regret now. Under the circumstances, I think he came in and did a good job. But I felt the wound was self-inflicted and a lot of the other players shared my disillusionment. They couldn't relate to Horton. I remember when I left, one of the other senior players rang me up and said, 'Where is your tunnel? Because we are all desperate to get out of here.' It just summed things up really."

The clamour for change was mounting among supporters as well. They were no longer prepared to tolerate their chairman's idiosyncrasies and losing habit. With United blazing a trail at the top of the Premiership, City desperately needed a hero to restore their pride and self-belief. On 5 September 1993, he emerged – a legend from a golden age still coveted at Maine Road.

It was the scoop of the year: "FRANNY LEE IN £8M BID FOR CITY!" was emblazoned across the back page of the *Daily Mirror*. As word began to spread around Manchester, City supporters rushed out to snap up a copy of the paper. It was the story they had been waiting for and they needed to see it in black and white. Alec Johnson, the *Mirror*'s long-serving football correspondent, was a personal friend of Francis Lee and had got the exclusive. Now, the traditional working-class paper of the North was ready to back City's working-class hero. The *Daily Mirror* would spearhead Lee's campaign to take over at the club.

Within hours of the final editions hitting the streets, Lee called a news conference to outline his plans. Sporting the same swagger which characterised his playing days, the former City player strode purposefully into the Stanneylands Hotel in Wilmslow, just yards away from his home. His blond locks glistening in the late summer sunshine and his portly physique encompassed snugly in a black pinstripe business suit, Lee was flanked by his son, Gary, and former playing colleague Mike Summerbee, both walking respectfully a couple of paces behind. It was the perfect image as City's saviour stepped confidently out of the shadows – pledging to deliver a bright new dawn for the club. The white knight had arrived right on cue.

"If it is the wish of the shareholders and supporters, I am available," declared Lee in a bullish statement of intent. "I'm prepared to personally make available substantially more funds than have ever been individually invested in this club and so will two of my colleagues. If this offer is not accepted, no-one can say that I did not try to help my old club."

Francis Lee was a born chancer, an ebullient character whose swashbuckling mentality could border upon arrogance. It was a trait which served him well as he forged his way to the top in the worlds of football and business. Born in 1944 in the back streets of Westhoughton, near Bolton, the young Lee never doubted his ability to succeed. As a youth, he attended Horwich Technology College as a traditional career path was mapped out in front of him. Like many of his contemporaries, Lee was earmarked as a potential draughtsman at the Horwich Locomotive Works. Sport was his escape route.

"There was nothing else to do, except for playing football and cricket," he recalls. "So I put my heart and soul into it. I've no time for people who go around moaning and have a chip on their shoulder. I always give everything one hundred per cent and don't worry about obstacles in the way."

By the age of 16, he was living out every boy's dream as he lined up for his home town club alongside their greatest-ever player, Nat Lofthouse. But if there was a semblance of nerves within the barrel-chested youngster, he did not show it. His debut was against Manchester City at Burnden Park in 1960 and, true to form, he bulldozed his way into the heart of the action, scoring past Bert Trautmann and setting up the winner for Lofthouse.

For five seasons, Lee was Bolton's leading scorer as his bustling style and instinctive striking talent combined to awesome effect. Yet, by 1967, he was ready to walk away from the game after a contract dispute with the club. Lee, who was on a week-to-week contract, wanted to leave to further his career but Wanderers were reluctant to let him go. He refused to play for three weeks and even trained on his own. The young striker was already displaying a volatile nature, both on and off the pitch. Joe Mercer and Malcolm Allison, meanwhile, were searching for the finishing touch to their Maine Road revolution. The 23-year-old Bolton striker fitted the bill and he was signed in a £60,000 deal early in the 1967-68 season. His wages nearly doubled to £60 a week, but the move had little or nothing to do with money. He had actually turned down an offer of £150 a week to stay at Burnden Park. "I just wanted to see how far I could get in the game," recalls Lee.

It was the defining moment in his life and completed a legendary trio of talents at the club. Colin Bell, Mike Summerbee and Francis Lee led the Blues to almost every honour in a glorious four-year spell. The Bell-Lee-Summerbee era would become the touchstone for all future City generations. For many, it was a cross they could not bear. While Bell provided the craft and Summerbee the skill, it was Lee who supplied the end product. He was the club's leading scorer season after season, as well as notching a record number of penalties in 1971-72, with a total of 15 in all League and Cup games, earning him the infamous nickname of Lee Won Pen. International honours duly followed as he collected 27 full England caps and played in the 1970 World Cup finals. Yet, four years later in 1974, City's new chairman Peter Swales decided to sell him. An offer of £120,000 from Derby County was accepted after a counter-bid from Manchester United was turned down. Swales, who was slowly dismantling the legacy of Mercer and Allison, used the funds for a deposit on Asa Hartford, who was signed from West Brom.

"You will regret the day you sold me. I promise you that," Lee warned Swales.

Later that season, the pugnacious striker returned to Maine Road and scored with a stunning 25-yard strike in front of the BBC's *Match of the Day* cameras. It was an extraordinary last-minute winner which left Swales cringing in the directors' box. Lee had made his point in typically emphatic style and Derby would go on to clinch the League Championship. His uncanny knack of success seemed in sharp contrast to the honest, yet uninspired, struggles of the City chairman. And Lee's golden touch was not restricted to the football field.

During his early days at Bolton, he spent his afternoons cleaning gravestones before buying a van to collect wastepaper around the streets of Westhoughton. It seemed a curious pastime, but would ultimately make him a multi-millionaire. Trade grew steadily as Lee somehow managed to combine the rigours of football and business. By the time he finished playing at Derby, his tissue paper industry, FH Lee, was employing 120 people and had a turnover of between

£7 million and £8 million. "I was worn out trying to play football and run the business so I felt it was the right time to retire," says Lee. "I was driving sixty thousand miles a year at Derby, it was life in the very fast lane."

He would later sell the business for £8.5 million and concentrate his energies on training racehorses. His interest had been aroused when he won £2,500 on a £13 accumulator bet and used the money to buy a horse for his Derby team-mate Rod Thomas. The Stanneylands Stud Farm soon became Lee's countryside retreat. Nestled in the narrow winding lanes of Wilmslow, the thatched house with its pebbled driveway was a warm and comfortable home. Behind it, the rolling fields of Cheshire provided Lee with the perfect environment to gallop his horses. Any questions about returning to football were fended off with a familiar reply: "I have too many other interests in my life. It would not be fair to place another onerous burden on my family."

The lure of returning to his former club, though, proved simply too great. Lee still craved more success and the challenge awaiting him would rank alongside any of the others he had encountered in the 49 years of his life. As he courted the press on that sunny September day in 1993, Lee could scarcely have conceived of the struggles which lay ahead. One of the bitterest and most protracted takeover battles in the history of English football would grip Maine Road for the next five months.

The battle-lines were drawn on the very first day when, after Lee's morning press conference, Swales retaliated with one of his own at the ground in the afternoon. City's commander-in-chief was not ready to relinquish control. In fact, he was furious that Lee had chosen to conduct his business through the media. Swales revealed, with some relish, that the club had already turned down a serious proposal to take over the club.

"I have to smile a little bit that people have come in with good strong offers and you didn't even uncover that one," said Swales. "It went through the proper channels and we considered it, but turned it down. Nobody ever bothered. Here we get a takeover bid that doesn't even start and it's in every paper. You can't really win sometimes at this stage. You think you wish the club would get as much publicity as Manchester United and now I'm thinking I wish we didn't get as much as we do."

There was no indication about the identity of the mystery investor. One newspaper suggested it was Lee's former team-mate at City, Rodney Marsh, a story which was quickly denied. In fact, there was another less-famous man lined up to take over the reins of power. His identity has never been revealed before. Steve Morrison was Chris Muir's next-door neighbour in Didsbury. He was also the managing director of Granada Television and renowned as a shrewd operator in the media world. A tough Glaswegian, Morrison was a graduate of the National Film School and joined Granada in 1974 to set up their northern documentary unit. The department was soon acclaimed as one of the best in the business, most notably producing *World In Action*. In 1987, Morrison was appointed Granada's director of programmes. He was also executive producer on the Oscar-winning film, *My Left Foot*.

By the early 1990s, he was brokering multi-million deals in the boardroom at Granada and would later become the chief executive of the Granada Media Group, a post he stills holds. As far as City were concerned, Morrison was the ideal man to steer the club into a new era. He could heal the rifts and restore the club's financial stability.

"Peter Swales, Stephen Boler and I talked it over and we all agreed that Steve would be the perfect man to take over as chairman," says Muir. "Swales contacted him and Steve said he was very interested and would give it all his consideration. But at the time, Granada were involved in some sort of merger with Yorkshire Television and Steve just could not become involved. I felt if he had come on the board as chairman, then we could have saved ourselves. "But it didn't happen and it was becoming obvious that we were going to lose. Peter's health was starting to go and he was simply not the same guy he'd been a year or so before."

The strain was beginning to tell on Swales as the campaign against him intensified. Supporters, under the banner of the "Forward With Franny" group, mounted organised demonstrations demanding his departure. Just days after declaring his intention to take over the club, Francis Lee joined the other key member of his consortium at City's home match against Queens Park Rangers. Colin Barlow was also a former player, a right-winger who played 179 League games for City in the late 1950s and early 1960s. A skilful operator with dashing good looks, Barlow went on to play for Oldham and Doncaster before pursuing a career in business. He had renewed his association with the Blues after meeting up with club director Ian Niven on a flight back from Marbella. Niven had persuaded him to invest some money into the club and Barlow was rewarded with four seats in the directors' box.

As he headed for those seats with his new comrade, Lee, ahead of the QPR match, the pair were mobbed by jubilant fans. In fact, Lee struggled to make it into the ground as thousands of well-wishers and supporters almost squeezed the life out of him. They cheered his every move and chanted his name – it was like turning back the clock to 1968. Peter Swales watched on, a few seats further back in the directors' box, as Lee took the acclaim of the fans. The indignity would get far worse for City's chairman over the coming months.

Perhaps naively, supporters thought Swales would concede his time was up and retire quietly into the background. But that was not his style. He was infuriated by Lee's "bullying" tactics and decided to stand his ground. He knew he might have to sell – but not to Lee, not at any price.

"I am disappointed at Francis and the way he's conducted himself," said Swales. "As for his backers, they are just opportunists. They have tried to incite mob rule but I won't give in to these people. I'll always consider offers, but I still don't think it's time to go. Make no mistake, I don't want to go.

"I know I have made mistakes as chairman. The handling of the Peter Reid dismissal, for instance, backfired on us badly and brought a lot of bad publicity. But when I became chairman twenty years ago, this club was in a mess financially. I have turned the situation around and that is something which I am very proud of. I don't expect a round of applause but the personal abuse I have been subjected to recently makes me wonder whether it has all been worthwhile."

Swales's intransigence only further inflamed the passions of supporters. An overwhelming majority wanted him to go, but he was not prepared to budge. The demonstrations, which had begun in a good-natured spirit at the QPR match, started to turn ugly. The ground began to resemble a war zone on match days as groups of fans staged angry, and sometimes violent, protests against Swales. When he still refused to accede to their demands, some elements of the campaign decided to raise the stakes even higher.

The City chairman was bombarded with death threats, his family was intimidated and terrorised, while one supporter broke into his invalid mother's bedroom at her nursing home. For Brenda, his loyal wife, it was a sickening experience. In an emotional interview at the family home in Bowdon, she admitted: "It was awful at the time here."

She has never spoken publicly about that trying time, until now. "From my point of view, I wouldn't let any of the grandchildren or my three daughters come round to the house. We had security men on the gate, it was really quite frightening. We also had a lot of death threats on the answer-phone. One day, when I walked to my daughter's, who lives around the corner, there were a couple of rather shady-looking characters and vans around. I was frightened, but Peter just made light of it."

By November, the situation was becoming intolerable for Brenda and her embattled husband. They returned home from a match against Sheffield Wednesday to find their house swarming with police and security guards. Mrs Swales has not returned to Maine Road since.

"I can remember that day so vividly. I came home and the house was surrounded with security men. I didn't know what was happening, so I went inside and looked out of the bedroom window. It was hard to believe, but there were police all around the back garden. Apparently, all the local pubs had received maps to our house, with a message asking people to come round and sort Peter out. It was terrible."

Swales nobly tried to shield his family from the worst excesses of the hate campaign. But the pressure was undeniably beginning to take its toll on his health. His face was drawn and his shoulders seemed ever more hunched as he endeavoured to battle on.

"The takeover killed him, I don't doubt that," asserts Chris Muir. "He had a major weakness – he would not admit that he wasn't well enough to carry on fighting. He should have just given up. I remember when it was all over, he looked terrible. His greatest love was Manchester City and it had been torn away from him.

"The problem was that a group of leeches, like the *Daily Mirror*, got involved in Francis Lee's campaign and it became very ugly. I felt Francis should have done more to distance himself from some of the things which went on. He should have called off the hard men and told them to behave. His hands are not dirty, but some of his camp followers do have a lot to answer for."

Lee remains steadfast, as ever, in his condemnation of the vicious campaign. He now knows exactly what Swales went through, having also suffered at the hands of the mob. During Lee's later years as chairman, a group of fans – which he believes were organised – issued threats against his family and his property. It was a chastening experience for the man who was once idolised on the terraces.

"There were a bunch of hot-heads making threatening phone calls and I know the same happened to Peter Swales," he says. "Of course I would never, and have never, condoned any activity like that. I never had any personal grudge against Swales. In fact, I occasionally used to sit with him on the train going down to London and we would chat about football. I never fell out with him and I never had an argument with him. At the end of the takeover season, I remember meeting up with him at one of Stephen Boler's functions at Mere Golf and Country Club. He congratulated me on helping to save the club from relegation and said we had made some good signings. He never looked better, really relaxed and well."

But as the takeover battle escalated towards the end of 1993, Swales seemed to become more and more determined to find an alternative to Lee. At the club's annual general meeting, the two men came head-to-head in public for the first time. While Swales sat impassively at the top table, Lee took his place at the back of the room. There was mutiny in the air but the atmosphere remained relatively calm until one shareholder stood up and praised the "wonderful chairmanship" of Swales. Suddenly, the meeting erupted into a chorus of boos. The top table seemed baffled, staring out blankly. Moments later, shareholders were asked to consider item four on the agenda: whether to re-elect Swales as a director of the company. On a show of hands, the City chairman lost 79-52. Cheers echoed around the room as the majority mistakenly believed they had ousted the chairman. But a vote based on the value of shareholdings quickly restored the balance of power. Nevertheless, as the meeting degenerated in front of his eyes, Swales must have realised his grip on power was beginning to slip away. He was reviled, it seemed, not only by supporters but by his own shareholders as well.

Within a matter of days, Swales stood down as chairman but retained his place on the board. It was seen as one last, desperate ploy to cling on to a semblance of power. He vowed to find a new chairman, but had already rejected a £2 million bid for his shares from the Lee consortium. The man whom Swales had lined up was Mike McDonald, a City-supporting businessman from Eccles. McDonald, a multi-millionaire, made his fortune in the scrap metal trade but had since diversified into engineering. He was a close friend of City's vice-chairman, Freddie Pye, and had offered to invest in the club before.

"Swales came to see me and said they were absolutely desperate for money," says McDonald. "He said he needed a couple of million pounds to get them out of trouble. I offered to lend them it, without any conditions, because I wanted to see the club sorted out. To be honest, at that time, they were having difficulty finding money to pay the wages."

Swales had now decided that McDonald was the obvious choice to succeed him. A deal was struck between the two men and McDonald believed he would soon be the new chairman. He even began negotiating transfer deals, agreeing to sell David White to Leeds United and inquiring about Nathan Blake from Cardiff and Bristol City's Wayne Allison. "That's the way I operate – I do move very quickly," continues McDonald. "But then what transpired shocked everyone."

Swales had called a board meeting at his house where he expected to rubber-stamp McDonald's appointment as chairman. But for the first time in 20 years, his colleagues were preparing to defy him. Three directors voted for the proposal (Peter Swales, Freddie Pye and Chris Muir), while four voted against (Tony Miles, Brian Turnbull, Gerald Doyle and Ian Niven). Swales was left reeling and it was the decision of the normally-loyal Niven to switch sides which was seen as critical.

Niven had Manchester City in his blood. Born a "stone's throw" away from Moss Side, he attended Ducie Avenue School and dreamed of playing for the Blues as a boy. Yet, after serving in India during the War, he returned to Manchester to work as a professional buyer for a wire manufacturing company. After falling out with a local publican, he decided to buy up the tenancy of the nearby Fletcher's Arms pub and go into direct competition. His establishment quickly became renowned as THE City pub in Manchester. Joe Mercer, Malcolm Allison and Mike Doyle were all regular visitors as Niven became a popular figure in the inner circle at Maine Road. In 1972, he joined the board and was instrumental in setting up the Junior Blues, a highly-successful young supporters' association, a few years later. He remained a trusted member of Swales's entourage throughout the turbulent 1980s and early 1990s. "I used to clean the toilets and pull the weeds out of the back of the Kippax," he recalls.

Now, Niven had decided it was time to stand up to his boss. He had been secretly speaking to Colin Barlow behind the scenes and had become convinced that Francis Lee was the only viable candidate to take over as chairman. The fanatical fan, who still proudly boasts about missing only five City games since 1947, was about to change the course of the club's history.

Chris Muir, who stayed loyal to Swales "until the bitter end," believes Niven was "flannelled" by Barlow and Lee. "Swales pleaded with Ian to stick by us, but it was too late," he says. "Barlow had already got to him. To be fair to Ian, he is obsessed with City and genuinely thought Francis Lee would be the saviour."

McDonald, meanwhile, was informed of the board's vote by a distraught Swales. But with Andrew Thomas and Julian Greibach both missing from the emergency meeting, Swales was confident he could still secure a majority in favour.

"I said that's no good to me," says McDonald. "Either way it was going to be a split board. The crowd didn't know me from Adam and there was a split board, so what chance did I have of turning the club around unless there was some united strength? "People have come to me since and said they made a mistake, but that's history now. What I don't understand is the character assassination which went on. I was getting stories from the papers saying I'd murdered people and done all sorts of things. I can put up with all that, but it intrigued me as to why."

With McDonald out of the equation, Swales had run out of options. His money had dried up, his empire was wrecked and his enemy was advancing. He had to sell and there was only one potential buyer: Francis Lee.

City's other major shareholder was Stephen Boler, a Middleton-born businessman who rarely visited Maine Road. A self-made millionaire, born in August 1943, he made his fortune in the tyre and exhaust business in the 1970s and profited from the DIY boom of the affluent 1980s. He owned the Kitchens Direct home improvements company and bought a £400,000 stake in City from departing director Simon Cussons in October 1984. His investment helped to prop up Swales, but Boler was more concerned with saving the black rhino on his South African nature reserve. He hardly ever intervened in the running of the club, preferring to back Swales's judgement. With both men owning a 30 per cent share of the club, their alliance was unbreachable. Greenalls, the brewing company, were the next largest stake holders, with 20 per cent.

Ashley Lewis, an accountant who handled Boler's business and personal affairs for almost two decades, says his boss was a hard but essentially good man. "He was a great motivator of people, that was one of his key strengths in business. Despite his tough exterior, he was a very fair person. He was never directly involved in the day to day running of City, but enjoyed a close relationship with Peter Swales. Basically, he was happy to take a back-seat role at the club."

By December 1993, Boler realised he could no longer afford to shore up Swales's position. A new Kippax stand had to be built to meet the requirements of the Taylor Report, which recommended that all Premiership and most First Division grounds must become all-seater by the start of the 1994-95 season. City had already spent the maximum £2.5 million grant from the Football Trust on their new Umbro Stand. They would have to find the money themselves to re-build the Kippax. Boler, who was acutely aware of Swales's financial plight, feared he would become saddled with the cost.

"Nobody had any idea where the money for the Kippax was going to come from," remembers Lee. "I think Stephen was just pleased that we were offering to take the responsibility away from him. To be honest, he also knew it was time for a change and always backed me."

Swales was beaten. His support on the board had ebbed away and now his major ally had also switched sides. The City chairman opened negotiations to sell his beloved Blues to Francis Lee and Colin Barlow. As Lee jetted off for his annual break in the Caribbean, he was confident a deal would be struck early in the New Year. However, as his accountants studied the club's books, it was clear something was not right.

"There was this big black hole in the accounts which nobody could explain," says Lee. "Suddenly, the deal was off for around a couple of weeks as we tried to sort out a compromise. Eventually, I got the nod from the accountants and I came back off holiday to complete the deal."

It was 4 February 1994, and the media were thronged at Manchester Airport for the arrival of City's saviour. For supporters, the wait was nearly over. For Peter Swales, it was the worst day of his life. He was just hours away from handing over control of his treasured club to the man who had plotted his downfall during a bitter five-month struggle. As Lee emerged, bronzed and buoyant, into the arrivals lounge, he confirmed his intention to take over as chairman before the end of the day. The final negotiations, though, would drag on all day and spill into the early hours of the next morning. After beginning at a solicitor's office in the city centre, the Lee consortium moved on to the Swan Hotel at Bucklow Hill, Cheshire, to complete the deal.

Arriving in his familiar white Jaguar car, Swales looked old and ashen-faced as he walked unsteadily into the hotel. At 12.24 am, he slipped quietly out of a back exit as Lee stepped triumphantly into the cold night air to announce his victory. Despite 30 hours without sleep, City's new chairman was jubilant. He had agreed a deal to buy 15 per cent of Swales's shares and a similar amount from Boler. As a sop, Swales was offered the title of Life President. He never accepted it and never returned to Maine Road.

Chris Muir, his closest ally, stuck by him until the end and even now says he "would be thrilled to bits to serve under him again." He adds, "I know all his failings, but behind it all, I think he was the right man for the job. He just made the mistake of staying on too long. At the end, he was not the man he'd once been. He was punch drunk. At one stage, he was untouchable. He was in a different class for wheeling and dealing. I always remember saying that if Swales and six starving people were sitting around the table and there was one piece of bread Swales would not say a word, but he would still end up eating the bread. He was that sort of person. But you cannot outsmart the rabble on the Kippax and it was them who defeated him." Muir left the board soon after Lee's appointment as chairman.

The supporters, who had campaigned so steadfastly for Lee, could now celebrate. As City entertained Ipswich just hours after

Lee's takeover, the scene was set for a huge party at Maine Road. Hundreds of blue and white balloons were released into the air as the new chairman strode purposefully into the directors' box. Dressed in a striking blue blazer and a striped blue and white shirt, he lifted his arms theatrically to the skies. City's favourite son had returned.

Earlier in the day, he had summoned Brian Horton to his house to spell out the harsh reality. The club's results had to improve or they would begin searching for a new manager. Horton had no complaints: he knew his side was in a shambles. Out of both cup competitions and third from bottom of the Premiership, City's squad was in need of drastic surgery. Defender Michel Vonk was partnering new signing Carl Griffiths up front as the Blues tried to compensate for the absence of Niall Quinn with a knee injury. Horton had been starved of cash during the divisive takeover battle and his only option was to wheel and deal. He had brought in Carl Shutt on loan from Birmingham to partner Griffiths. It was hardly an awe-inspiring forward line. Without a quick injection of cash, the Blues were clearly heading for relegation.

"With hindsight, if we had been hard-nosed businessmen, in it just to make a quick buck, we would have let the club go down before getting involved," says Lee. "It would have been much cheaper to buy the shares if City were in the Second Division. But I could not sit and watch as the club went down. We also had to start work on designing and building a new Kippax stand, otherwise we would have lost a large core of our support and that would have been disastrous."

In the event, Lee invested around £4 million of his personal wealth in the club. His fellow consortium members, Colin Barlow, John Dunkerley, David Holt and Gary Grant, each put in around £750,000. David Bernstein, meanwhile, who had joined Lee's takeover bid as a financial advisor, also provided around £200,000. In total, the investment was nearing £7.5 million. It was the largest amount ever invested in the club but it was still not nearly enough to overcome the problems which lay in store.

"The place was a complete mess," remembers Lee. "One of the first items at the first board meeting was to repair the boiler. We had a quote for around £15,000. I asked when it had broken down and Ian Niven replied it was in 1990! "It had just been patched up since then. Sometimes the referee and visiting teams had to wash in cold water. So I went down to look at this boiler and it looked like it had come off the African Queen! How it never blew up was a mystery. But that was not the half of it. There were people who had not been paid for three, six or eighteen months. In fact, some had been waiting for two years and had given up hope. It was like stepping into a disaster area."

Bernstein, who joined the board late in 1994 and became an increasingly influential figure in the new regime, believes the financial problems became almost insurmountable for Lee. Around every corner, there was another skeleton from the past waiting to leap out. A plan to turn City's social club into a new superstore was delayed two years because Swales had previously sold the building to Greenalls, the brewers, to repay his debts to them. City were paying to lease their own social club back from Greenalls. It was economic madness and there was nothing Lee could do about it.

"I think Francis underestimated the scale of the financial problems which he took over," admits Bernstein. "From the beginning, his hands were tied by a lack of available finance. It was a struggle from day one. You only have to look at the balance sheet to see that. Whatever was done at that time, and Francis did his best, it just wasn't enough."

Initially, Lee's arrival did make a difference. His mere presence at the game against Ipswich seemed to inspire the team as they fought back from 1-0 down to win 2-1 through goals from Garry Flitcroft and Carl Griffiths. But the revival was short-lived and two weeks later Horton's side were blown away 4-0 by Coventry City at Highfield Road. New players were essential to any hopes of survival. Paul Walsh was signed in a £700,000 deal from Portsmouth, while little-known German striker Uwe Rosler joined on trial from Dynamo Dresden. Born in Attenburg, East Germany, the 25-year-old forward had a modest scoring record throughout his early career. But on his debut for City, a reserve match against Burnley, he scored twice to stake his claim for a place in the first-team. His vigorous style and exuberant personality instantly charmed the crowd and even earned him comparisons to his chairman.

Horton had his strikeforce; now he needed a supply line. Another German, midfielder Steffan Karl, was brought in on a two-month loan from Borussia Dortmund. The Arsenal winger Anders

Limpar was seen as the ideal man to complete an attacking quartet but when he opted to join Everton instead, Horton switched his sights to Peter Beagrie, who was surplus to requirements at Goodison Park. The chirpy left-winger was signed for £1 million just minutes before the transfer deadline. Suddenly, it all clicked into place. As Easter arrived, the Blues faced three crucial games in the space of seven days. They won them all.

In the last eight matches, Rosler scored five goals, Walsh notched four, Beagrie got one and even Karl hit the decisive strike in City's 1-0 win over relegation rivals Southampton. Horton had saved the club from the drop and had almost certainly saved himself from the axe. By the final home match of the season, against Chelsea, the crowd were in party mood again, ready to celebrate their survival in the top flight and salute the Kippax's "Last Stand." The famous old stand would be demolished immediately after the game and fans arrived with chisels and hammers in hand, determined to acquire an everlasting piece of City's history.

Their new hero on the pitch was Rosler, who had become known affectionately as 'Der Bomber.' The 33,594 crowd sang his name almost incessantly and he was not about to disappoint his new adoring audience, scoring City's opener in a 2-2 draw. As soon as the season was finished, he was signed in a permanent £500,000 transfer and soon became a cult hero with supporters.

Meanwhile, the bulldozers moved in to tear down the Kippax, which had stood watching over City since 1923. Eleven years after its opening, the colossal bank of terracing helped accommodate the largest crowd assembled for an English football match outside Wembley: 84,569 for an FA Cup sixth round tie against Stoke. Now its time was over as football, and Manchester City, moved into a new era.

There was still one more dark secret lurking beneath the club's most famous stand. As the builders completed their demolition job, they discovered that the Kippax had been built on a mound of ashes. It was classed as contaminated waste and, as such, required particular attention. "Normally, it would have cost us £1 a ton to tip the waste," says Lee. "But because this was classed as contaminated, it cost us £28 a ton. It meant an extra £1 million went on the bill to get rid of the Kippax. Perhaps I should have known then that everything was not going to run to plan. In fact, it never does at that club."

CHAPTER FIVE

Fighting the **drop**

IT DID NOT get much better than this for Brian Horton. Relaxing in the sumptuous surrounds of Cheshire's Mottram Hall Hotel, he was enjoying a quiet drink with his old friend Ossie Ardiles. The following day, their two sides would come head-to-head in a Maine Road masterpiece. For now, though, Horton was taking it easy. His team had been picked, his tactics finalised and his mind was clear. The City manager was having the time of his life. After a career in the bargain basement of English football, he was mixing with the game's glitterati and managing one of the top clubs in the country. The industrious lad from Staffordshire had done well.

Horton and Ardiles made unlikely drinking partners. Their cultural backgrounds were as diverse as their playing styles. While City's manager had given yeoman service as an honest, wholehearted midfield general, his Tottenham counterpart was a World Cup winner in 1978 with Argentina. The artful South American moved to north London soon afterwards and lit up the English stage with his twinkling feet. Now he was back at White Hart Lane as manager after spells in charge of Newcastle and Swindon. In fact, it was during his time in Wiltshire that Ardiles crossed paths with Horton, then manager of Oxford. Despite their obvious differences, the pair hit it off immediately. They had an affinity: a vision of how the beautiful game should be played. Indeed, as they settled back in each other's company in the autumn of 1994, both must have been mentally preparing more or less the same team talk for their respective sides.

It certainly seemed that way as City and Spurs produced a vintage exhibition of football. It was a throwback to the classic confrontations of yesteryear as both sides flowed forward with enthusiasm and abandon. Tottenham had re-invented themselves following the £2 million purchase of Jurgen Klinsmann, fresh from his appearance in the 1994 World Cup, a tournament he had won with Germany four years earlier. The signing of one of the world's most charismatic players had stirred the imagination of English football supporters, but Ardiles' bold gamble of a five-pronged forward line featuring Klinsmann, Teddy Sheringham, Darren Anderton, Nicky Barmby and the Rumanian Illie Dumitrescu backfired spectacularly at Maine Road. The Blues romped imperiously to a thrilling 5-2 victory in a match beamed around the globe on television. Even the BBC's *Match of the Day* commentator John Motson struggled for superlatives to sum it all up. "It was the best match I have seen – in an entertainment and attacking context – in the English league for many years," was his exuberant assessment.

It was Brian Horton's finest hour as City manager. He had watched with pride as his expansive side demolished their world-renowned opponents. Paul Walsh scored twice against his former club, while Niall Quinn, Steve Lomas and Garry Flitcroft completed the rout. "Their side was full of good footballers but so was mine," says Horton. "We were magnificent that day and the game could have finished in an 8-7 scoreline to either side."

Two days later, Ardiles was sacked. Not for the first time, the elegant Argentinian was left to rue a result inflicted by one of Horton's sides. "It was ironic really because a couple of years earlier Ossie had got the sack at Newcastle after we'd beaten them by five goals when I was at Oxford," remembers Horton. "I rang Ossie after he'd lost his job after the City game. The strange thing is that Ossie would have loved that match at Maine Road because that's how he likes the game to be played."

While Ardiles was looking for new employment, Horton had never been more popular, as even the most sceptical of supporters warmed to his infectious personality and style of play. It was hardly surprising. The first seven home matches of the season yielded 21 goals as City produced some of their best football of the 1990s.

Niall Quinn was back after a long absence with a knee injury to link up with Uwe Rosler and Paul Walsh in attack. It meant Mike Sheron was surplus to requirements and he was sold to Norwich for £1 million. David Rocastle was also on his way out, to Chelsea, amid doubts over his long-term fitness. But City were not forsaking the skill factor – far from it. Peter Beagrie and Nicky Summerbee, bought from Swindon Town for £1.5 million in the close season, were assigned to the flanks. The pitch had been widened, reversing a decision made by Howard Kendall, and Beagrie and Summerbee were ready-made to exploit the extra yardage. A club steeped in the tradition of great wingers was clearly returning to its roots.

As the chairman surveyed his new kingdom ahead of his first full season in charge, he was predictably upbeat. "In view of the past record, if we could win a trophy and have a cracking run in the League it would be a successful season," said Francis Lee. "But providing we give a hundred per cent on the field and the lads play with great spirit and commitment and keep the fans entertained, then if we do just miss out I wouldn't be too disappointed."

That summer, Lee had been offered the chance to sign Klinsmann but the German striker opted for the glamour of north London instead. Horton, meanwhile, was shuffling his backroom staff, parting company with chief scout Bobby Saxton and youth coaches Terry Darracott and Jack Chapman. Responsibility for the scouting network went to Jimmy Frizzell, with former player Neil McNab taking over as a youth coach. The influence of the Brightwell family was also spreading with brothers Ian and David joined by their father Robbie, a former Olympic runner, who became the club's fitness coach.

Off the field, the Lee revolution was still in its infancy. City's chairman had pledged, during the long and painful takeover battle, to be more open with fans. He stayed true to his word and appointed a supporters' representative on to the board. Dave Wallace, the editor of City's most popular fanzine, *King of the Kippax*, was elected after a ballot among fans. It was lauded as a unique venture as the Blues "threw open their doors" to public scrutiny. In reality, Wallace's appointment was little more than cosmetic.

"It was started with all the best intentions, but basically it was just a sop," admits Wallace. "I think there was a difference of opinion about what the role should entail. They thought I should convey the board's views to the fans, while I thought it should be the other way around. "I did my best and I think we achieved one or two things, like setting up a fans' committee, but once I started to disagree with a few of their decisions, that was it basically. They ditched the fan on the board and after that the club went haywire!"

For the time being, however, Lee's grand plan remained on course. A new all-seater Kippax stand was starting to take shape. At a cost of £13 million, the impressive edifice was intended as a striking visual testament to the chairman's ambition for the club. But what really caught the eye was the spontaneous, uninhibited style of football displayed by Horton's team. While others had buckled under the strain of performing on such a big stage, Peter Beagrie and Paul Walsh were loving it.

"The fans adored Walshy and they still talk to me about him now," beams Horton. "I'd played with him at Luton and knew his character. I think that is sometimes the issue about handling a big club situation. I knew Beagrie could cope with it because he'd been there and done it with Everton and I knew Walshy was the same. Walshy was so bright as a player and had fantastic quality. You can't give people that. I decided to try to make my mark by being attack-minded. I'd always generally operated that way at Brighton and Luton during my playing days and the same applied when I was manager at Oxford."

City's extravagant flank play was being mirrored at Blackburn Rovers, who were on course for their first Championship since 1914. Horton recalls a conversation with the Rovers assistant manager, Ray Harford. "Ray thought I was too cavalier. They played with wingers but they operated in narrower positions whereas we played with our wingers out wide. Nicky Summerbee used to tuck in a little bit more than Peter Beagrie but they were so good to watch on their day."

The deadly duo were never better than on that sunny afternoon in late October when City's emphatic victory over Spurs earned acclaim across the nation. It completed a run of seven games with only one defeat as Horton's side edged into the top six. The fans were jubilant. This is what they had yearned for: an ambitious chairman presiding over a manager and team brimming with poise and panache. It was not only Horton's finest hour but arguably the high point in City's fortunes during the 1990s.

Almost inevitably, it would not last.

Francis Lee had an impeccable record against Manchester United as a player. In 16 appearances, he had been on the losing side only twice. But on Thursday, 10 November 1994, he watched helplessly as City slumped to the heaviest derby defeat in their history. United's Russian winger Andrei Kanchelskis ran amok, scoring a hat-trick as his side annihilated their neighbours 5-0. It was dubbed the demolition derby. Though no-one could yet know it, that result would mark the start of Horton's demise. Niall Quinn wore the captain's armband on that fateful Thursday night as Keith Curle recovered from injury. City's stand-in skipper was distraught; it was "his worst night in football."

"I'm a senior professional and I'm flattened. We're all shell-shocked. It was horrible to be out there and ripped apart and there's a feeling in my stomach I've never had before," said the Irishman.

The burden of expectations was again weighing heavily on Horton's shoulders. He knew results needed to improve, and improve quickly, just to keep his job. Although if he was feeling the strain, you would scarcely have known it. His wide blue eyes and attentive stare never dimmed, his demeanour remained as confident as ever. Yet as City travelled to Leicester ten days after the derby disaster, Horton's future hung in the balance; another heavy defeat and his days would be numbered. He needed his players to respond, and they did.

A Quinn goal secured three valuable points and earned his manager some breathing space. With victories over Ipswich and Wimbledon following in the next two weeks, it seemed Horton had emerged relatively unscathed from the Old Trafford wreckage. By the beginning of December, his side were back in sixth place.

Steve McMahon had departed to take over as Swindon Town's player-manager. The former Liverpool midfielder had been squeezed out of the first-team picture as Steve Lomas and Garry Flitcroft formed a youthful alliance in the centre. There was a new arrival to complement their maturing talents. Maurizio Gaudino, a former German international, was signed on loan from Eintracht Frankfurt and made his debut on Boxing Day at home to Blackburn. The long-haired midfielder had made a hasty exit from his homeland amid an investigation into a car theft ring. Just days before his arrival in Manchester, Gaudino had been arrested for questioning while recording an interview for German television. He was never charged.

Francis Lee, meanwhile, was preparing to leave for his annual midwinter break in Barbados. As the beach beckoned, City's chairman issued a public declaration of support for a manager whose future remained the subject of constant speculation in the tabloid press, with Ron Atkinson rumoured to be taking over. Horton was not Lee's man and despite the team's high standing in the table, there was a feeling it was a false position.

"People say a big club like City should have a big manager but that isn't always the case," maintained the chairman. "Brian has come up the hard way. One of the greatest managers in English football was Bill Shankly and he came from Carlisle, via Huddersfield, before he went to Liverpool to become a wonderful manager. I think it is a great way as a player and manager to start off and know what the bottom end of the market is like and know how tough it is to make ends meet. Brian has had a good grounding in that direction. As I told him, if he and David Moss are going to make it in the big time this is the place they're going to do it."

Five months later, Horton would be sacked after his team won just four of the remaining 25 League matches. His downfall began that December as City slumped to four defeats in quick succession at the hands of Arsenal, West Ham, Blackburn and Liverpool. Suddenly, the team which had been so prolific earlier in the season could not score and was missing the inspirational presence of goalkeeper Tony Coton, who was out injured. By New Year, the prognosis was looking bleak. The Blues were slipping further and further into the mire and only the promise of Wembley on the horizon could lift flagging morale.

For the first time in seven seasons, City had reached the quarter-finals of the Coca-Cola Cup, a rousing 2-0 victory at Newcastle in a fourth round replay having set them up for a tough but winnable trip to Crystal Palace in the last eight. Two more wins and the Twin Towers would be in sight. It seemed a feasible prospect, almost a fitting reward for City's great entertainers. But there was to be no consolation prize as Palace cantered into the semi-finals with a thumping 4-0 win.

"I think that result changed the course of my destiny at Maine Road. Everybody fancied us to get to Wembley and looking at the sides left in the competition that was probably the worst draw we could get," says Horton, who remembers vividly the course of events at Selhurst Park that were to conspire against his players.

"We were losing 1-0 when Steve Lomas got injured. He smacked a header against the crossbar and the goalkeeper whacked him and broke his nose. As he fell down he cracked a bone in his leg. The scoreline of 4-0 was ridiculous but we didn't deserve to lose that heavily. Palace scored a couple of goals that would have graced any game. It was unbelievable and I gambled at 1-0 down and put an extra forward on. But it just wasn't meant to be."

Their FA Cup ambitions were also extinguished a little more than a month later. Francis Lee was back from his Caribbean sojourn to witness another cruel twist in his club's season. Newcastle, managed by Lee's close friend Kevin Keegan, were a formidable outfit on their own territory. Yet City matched them in the opening exchanges until a controversial goal, originally flagged off-side, gifted their opponents the lead. Uwe Rosler equalised but Andy Dibble, in goal for the injured Tony Coton, was having a day to forget. His weak kicking and fragile confidence were ruthlessly exploited by the home side as they scored twice more to win 3-1.

All that remained for City was a desperate fight against relegation. By late March, they had slipped nearer to the edge after collecting only 13 points from a possible 48. With four clubs going down to accommodate a slimmed-down Premiership, the pressure was building on Horton.

It was Selhurst Park which once again provided the backdrop for another defining moment in Horton's tenure as City boss. With speculation over his future continuing unabated, he prepared his side for an inhospitable trip to take on Wimbledon. Just when he needed them most, his players were beginning to flounder. They served up an abject display, disintegrating in front of his eyes in a dismal 2-0 defeat. Horton was furious and did not appear for the after-match press conference. The waiting journalists assumed the worst; they surmised that the manager had been sacked and was already making a rapid retreat back to Manchester.

The truth was even more extraordinary. Horton had left the ground not daring to speak his mind. He was livid, not just at his players, but at his chairman as well. Lee had barged his way into the visiting dressing room after the game to castigate the team, an unforgivable breach of footballing protocol. Horton felt undermined, particularly as he had already lectured his squad on their inept performance.

"We were very poor that night and sometimes as a manager, and a player, you have to hold your hands up and admit it," recounts Horton. "I'd had a go at the players and it went all quiet. Franny then came in and thought nothing had been said, so he had a go. I told him I'd already spoken to the players and I think he realised his mistake."

Goalkeeper Tony Coton was one of those on the receiving end. To this day, he regrets not intervening on behalf of Horton. "After Francis Lee had gone out and shut the door I realised I should have told him to mind his own business and stuck up for the manager. I wondered if Brian was waiting for one of the lads to tell the chairman to get out but I missed my opportunity and I should have stood up and told him not to get involved."

Nevertheless, Lee maintains it was his right – as chairman – to speak to the players. And as a former player, he was more qualified than most to comment on playing matters. "I have been playing since I was two. I was a professional from the age of fifteen. I never gave less than one hundred per cent and I find it hard to watch other players giving less than everything. Everyone would say, 'You are such a good loser,' but I would be bleeding internally.

"I did used to go in the dressing room to say, 'All the best lads,' beforehand and always would say 'hard luck' at the end. The words used to stick in the back of my throat sometimes. What's wrong with that? I was the chairman. That performance against Wimbledon, though, was a disgrace. It was like watching the Red Lion play the Rose and Crown."

Horton remained resolute despite Lee's intervention. He was determined to do things his way, whatever the consequences. It seemed as if everyone was breathing down his neck: the media, the supporters and now even his boss. He maintained admirable restraint. If he was going to be sacked, it might as well be on his own terms.

"All the time I was there, I picked the side," asserts Horton. "Francis never interfered with team selection. I was my own man and I did what I wanted to do. I've always done that and if I got the sack, at least I could say I did it my way. Francis was such a good player and an international. It must have been hard for him. He'd been out of the game for a long time and to come back in and see how the salaries were now can't have been easy."

According to the tabloids, Horton's days were numbered and he was beginning to think they were right. By Easter, there was no doubt. City's manager realised he would be searching for new employment come the summer. Nothing had been said officially, but he could sense the prevailing mood. "It became apparent towards the end of the season that I might be going. You know in football, people generally know. I'd got the vibes I was going and the press were making a lot of it. A lot of names were being bandied about but I couldn't do anything about that. I just had to get on with it."

After their Coca-Cola Cup exit and the fiasco against Wimbledon, Horton must have wished he could forget Selhurst Park for another season. But the fixture computer had other ideas and City's next match pitted them against Crystal Palace again. Their luck was not about to change and, despite Rosler's solitary strike, the Blues lost 2-1. City's German striker was proving a rare ray of light in an increasingly gloomy season.

Ten days later, he confronted his fellow countryman Jurgen Klinsmann for the first time in English football. Rosler had missed the Spurs game earlier in the season and now came his chance to prove a point. In the clash of the Germans at White Hart Lane, City's leading man notched his twentieth goal of the season but it was Klinsmann, with his twenty-seventh, who emerged on the winning side. With six games left, Horton's men were just three points above the drop zone and had played more matches than most of their rivals. The manager's proud record of having never been relegated was under severe threat.

Forthcoming fixtures offered little hope of salvation. After the visit of League Cup winners Liverpool, the Blues had to travel to runaway leaders Blackburn. Even a point seemed an optimistic target from the two games. In the event, they managed to claim all six. Maurizio Gaudino's winner against Liverpool offered a lifeline, but it was victory at Ewood Park which saved the season. Twice City came from behind to clinch a pulsating 3-2 victory and effectively avoid relegation. Horton raced on to the pitch at the final whistle and celebrated extravagantly with his players. Against all the odds, he had rescued his side from the brink of disaster. Even now, he feels a warm glow of satisfaction as he thinks of that night.

"Sometimes in football management you have to try to prove people wrong and that is the way to answer them. The pressure I was under at City was nothing compared to being told as a seventeen-year-old at Walsall that I wasn't good enough to be a footballer. That's much harder than the press having a go at me and writing headlines like 'Brian Who?' when I was appointed. They knew who I was."

One unmistakable footballing figure had also arrived at Maine Road. John Burridge, a 43-year-old goalkeeper, was one of the game's most enduring characters, with a career spanning more than 20 years. He was hired as cover for Tony Coton and made a surprise return to front-line action against Newcastle in late April. Burridge was renowned for his eccentric habit of wearing goalkeeping gloves in bed and sleeping with a ball clutched to his chest. For the final three matches of the season, he was City's last line of defence as they looked to secure mid-table respectability.

Had they won their final match at home to Queens Park Rangers, Horton's side would have finished twelfth but a 3-2 defeat consigned them to seventeenth place, four points above the relegated clubs Ipswich, Palace, Leicester and Norwich. "I would have been reasonably happy with a mid-table position," says Horton. "I wasn't totally happy because we'd been sixth at one point. I had a go at our defender Alan Kernaghan after the game because Les Ferdinand had scored for them and I was annoyed because I wanted to win that game and finish on a high."

More than half the Premiership managers lost their jobs during the course of the season and within 48 hours of the final game, Horton was dismissed. His reign ended in a mire of confusion and contradiction.

Following the QPR game, he honoured a long-standing engagement at the League Managers' Association annual dinner. On the same night, City were holding their end-of-season get-together. The air was ripe with rumours about Horton's future. He had heard them all before, of course, but this time they were even more widespread. By the following morning, Horton's fears were realised. He picked up the morning newspaper to discover his fate. It was plastered over the back pages – City's manager had been sacked and they were already looking for a successor.

"It really hurt, I don't mind admitting that," he says. "As I was going down for breakfast with David Moss, it was ironic that Frank Clark asked whether it was true. I said, 'Well if it isn't it is now.' I rang the club and got hold of Francis Lee and he assured me he hadn't given the story out. But I went to see him as soon as I got back to Manchester and that was the end of it really."

A City director had let the news slip out after getting drunk at the club's dinner. It was a shoddy end to Horton's tenuous stint in charge. He had always seemed to be living on borrowed time but never expected such an undignified departure. Today Francis Lee claims he did not want to sack Horton, but says his hand was forced after the story was leaked to the press.

"At our annual dinner, somebody on the board said that Brian would be sacked the following morning but it was totally untrue. The next board meeting wasn't for another couple of weeks anyway. Brian rang me up at home when the story broke. I said I knew nothing about it and hadn't even seen the papers, but he was adamant. He wanted it sorted out once and for all. He demanded that I ask the board for a vote of confidence. Whether he wanted to get out because of the pressure, I don't know, but he certainly brought matters to a head.

"I was definitely of the opinion that we should not get rid of Brian because he had done well for us. I liked him. He was an honest lad and worked hard for the club. He had motivated the team when he first came in and they seemed to respond to him. In the second year, we just missed out on relegation, but could have finished in mid-table if we had won our final game of the season. It would have been worth around £250,000 to the club. But we lost and the players didn't seem to try.

"Anyway, I rang up all the directors and they were all in favour of sacking him. I asked them if they were quite sure about that. I think that last game had a big bearing on their decision. Everyone accuses me of being a dictator, but every single decision which the board made was unanimous when I was chairman. We talked things through and then came to an agreed verdict."

The players watched in frustration and Paul Walsh gave his gut reaction: "Since the day the chairman walked in there has been speculation about the manager's job and he has been badgered by the press and media from day one. I don't think it has come as a total shock because it has been rammed down everyone's throats for God knows how long."

It did not take long before Horton was back in work, accepting the managerial vacancy at Huddersfield after also speaking to Bolton and Derby. His 20 months in charge at Maine Road had at least turned him into a high-profile manager. 'Brian Who?' was now known throughout football. If his time in charge at Maine Road achieved little else, it at least earned him the notoriety which supporters and journalists seemed to demand. Looking back, his only regret is that he was not afforded more time as City's boss.

"I loved my time at City but I wish maybe I could have had one more year. I felt we were not far off and with a full side and a couple more players maybe we could have achieved something. I have no regrets about going there and would do the same again. I was in charge for twenty months which is the average length of time for a manager, so I can't complain."

Horton still lives in Manchester and his magnanimous attitude towards City has made him a regular on the supporters' club circuit. Yet the man who head-hunted Horton for the job still believes he bears the scars from his 20-month reign at Maine Road.

"City played attractive football under Brian and he brought in some very good players," affirms John Maddock. "It was only his relationship with Francis Lee that damaged the career of what could have been a very good manager. I don't think Brian ever recovered from it. He was never the same man. Don't get me wrong I think he is still a very good manager but at that time he was in his prime."

The club's hierarchy had acted. There was not much room to move around the boardroom table as the summer commenced. The number of directors had swelled to 14 following the appointment of Gary Grant and Brian Jervis. Their next task would to be find a suitable replacement for Horton.

CHAPTER SIX

A football **genius**

FRANCIS LEE might not have wanted to sack Brian Horton, but he knew exactly who he wanted to replace him. It was another Brian, a man whose name was legendary in Manchester football.

There was never any danger of Brian Kidd being met with the same derisory headlines which greeted Horton's arrival in the city. A working-class lad from the rundown Collyhurst district, Kidd scored on his nineteenth birthday in Manchester United's 1968 European Cup triumph. After a spell with Arsenal, he joined City in a £100,000 deal, scoring 21 League goals in his first season as Tony Book's side finished runners-up to Liverpool in 1977. His prowess in front of goal and whole-hearted approach quickly endeared him to the Maine Road crowd, who were content to excuse his Red roots.

After finishing his playing career, Kidd turned his hand to management, with little success, at Preston and Barrow but, after returning to Old Trafford to run their youth academy, he quickly established himself as one of the most astute coaches in the game. When Archie Knox left to join Glasgow Rangers, Kidd stepped up to become Alex Ferguson's number two during one of the most successful spells in the club's history. He was one of the lads, whose down-to-earth sense of humour endeared him to the players. By 1995, he was preparing United's multi-million pound squad for another Wembley appearance in the FA Cup Final. Yet, unbeknown to his Old Trafford colleagues, Kidd was already planning to take over as City's manager.

The offer to take charge had come in a secret meeting with the club's managing director, Colin Barlow, who had been to the same school as Kidd in Collyhurst. It was an area renowned for its football pedigree, with former United players Wilf McGuinness and Nobby Stiles hailing from the same side of Manchester.

Francis Lee, who still refuses to confirm whether Kidd was targeted, says, "We did shake hands with one man who had agreed to become our manager and he just had to ask his chairman. He was the sort of person who everyone would have thought would have made a good boss. But I knew there was a problem because he'd been ringing me for two weeks and then I didn't hear from him for four days. "When I finally got in touch with him and asked whether he had spoken to his chairman yet, he said he had not dared. I said, 'Well if you can't do that, then are you sure you're going to be a good manager?'"

Kidd had changed his mind at the last moment, leaving City's hierarchy with a big problem. They had a vacancy but no-one to fill it. Bolton's manager, Bruce Rioch, a former team-mate of Lee, was linked with the job but he was angling for a move to London and would eventually go to Arsenal. Ron Atkinson had long been named as a possible successor to Horton, but was now ensconced as the new boss at Coventry. The start of the season was nearing and, as City's search became more desperate, Lee even joked he might dig out an old track suit and take training himself.

His tongue-in-cheek remark merely fuelled the speculation in the press. There was even talk that one of the legends of German football, Franz Beckenbauer, might be appointed. But it was another World Cup winner, from closer to home, who was in City's sights.

Alan Ball was lazing on a beach in Spain's fashionable resort of Marbella when a call came in on his mobile phone. It was Francis Lee, offering him the "chance of a lifetime" to become City's manager. Despite 18 happy months on the south coast with Southampton, it was an offer Ball could not resist. After almost two months, the Blues had finally got their man, a big name who was renowned throughout football. But he was hardly the sort of accomplished manager the fans had hoped for. Dave Wallace, who was nearing the end of his term as "fan on the board," voiced his concerns in the press.

"We had spent all summer looking for a new manager and we had been promised all these great names, then they went and appointed Alan Ball!" recalls Wallace. "I, like many fans, could not believe it and I said so in the papers. Later on, I got a phone call off Franny and he was furious. He criticised me and said all the fans were delighted with Ball's appointment. All I can say is that he mustn't have spoken to any of the supporters I knew."

City's chairman remained confident in the ability of a man he had known since their schooldays together. Ball was from Farnworth and Lee from nearby Westhoughton, both suburbs of Bolton. They had played football in the same Bolton Boys under 14 team. "We even used to play in the same cricket league as well, Alan for Kearsley and myself for Westhoughton," says Lee. Both were destined to become international class footballers and, like Lee, Ball took his first steps to the top on the books of Bolton Wanderers.

He was considered too small to make the grade by the then Bolton manager Bill Ridding and went on to Blackpool where he was to collect the ultimate accolade as a player: a World Cup winners' medal with England in 1966. It was Ball's boundless energy in midfield which earned him a place in football folklore as he starred in that unforgettable 4-2 triumph over West Germany at Wembley. By the age of 21, Ball had been a part of English football's finest hour and was quickly establishing himself as one of the foremost players of his generation. A League Championship medal followed with Everton in 1970 before he was transferred to Arsenal for a record fee and then on to Southampton. A vibrant character, he won 72 caps for his country and had reached the pinnacle as a player.

Yet, as a manager he was a disaster area. With one of the worst records in football management, Ball was dubbed a serial loser. His striking red hair, squeaky voice and outdated flat cap made him an easy target; at times, he seemed almost a parody of himself. Ball's managerial fiascos had tainted his reputation, leaving him with an air of wounded pride.

He also possessed an uncanny knack of making a hasty retreat just before his clubs were relegated. In 1981, he exited Blackpool as they were heading towards the old Fourth Division for the first time in the club's history. He was hounded out by his own supporters at Stoke, who turned on him following a heavy defeat at Wigan. His escape act had not worked this time, after taking the club down in the previous season.

Ball's greatest achievement was taking Portsmouth into the First Division in the mid-1980s, although their stay in the top flight lasted only 12 months. In fact, some of his happiest times had come on the south coast as a player at Southampton under manager Lawrie McMenemy in the late 1970s and the pair were re-united when Ball went back to the Dell as manager in January 1994, soon after his former boss had joined the club's board. Ball kept the Saints up on a modest budget. Now he had been given his long-awaited opportunity to manage one of the biggest clubs in the land.

"Alan has done wonders at Southampton and I think he'll do wonders here. I was taken aback how quickly Southampton agreed to let him leave but you don't miss opportunities like that," said Francis Lee. "It's an important part of his managerial career and it'll be good for Manchester City."

Ball admitted he was stunned to get the call, "I'm absolutely amazed. It's all been a whirlwind and I'm a little shocked. I lived just up the road in Bolton until I was twenty-one years of age and I know what a big club Manchester City are and I'm excited about the prospect. I've got mixed feelings because it would have been my twentieth year, one way or another, at Southampton. My relationship with Francis goes back an awful long way and he has sold Manchester City to me."

To many, it seemed like another example of the old pal's act. The critics claimed Lee needed somebody quickly so he turned to one of his mates, a man whose managerial record scarcely warranted the chance to run a big club. It is a charge which Lee fiercely denies to his day. "We weren't close friends, that is a total myth," he says. "Right from being kids, we used to play against each other at football and cricket and we hated each other's guts. Alright, we played in the same England team together but that did not come into the reckoning when we appointed Alan. He was just the best option available."

As Ball settled into his job, it was clear this was not going to be an ordinary manager-chairman relationship. Lee admitted he had given his new appointee a list of the players' names and "his opinion on each of them." The City chairman was evidently not intending to restrict his attention to non-footballing matters.

Nevertheless, Lee's influence was having an effect off the pitch. The club was enjoying a boom in its commercial and merchandising activities as football's popularity continued to soar. Ball knew a winning team on the pitch was paramount to keep the money rolling in. As he commented rather curiously: "It's very important we keep up with the leading pack. These teams are heading to the moon and if we don't get on that spaceship then we'll be left behind."

The players were introduced to their new manager before a training session at Manchester University's playing fields. As they looked out over the wide expanse of football pitches, their eyes were drawn to an approaching figure emerging out of the distance. Ball marched confidently across the neatly manicured turf towards his assembled squad. He knew exactly what he was going to say, having rehearsed it over and over again in his head. The sight of almost 50 professionals ranked en masse might have daunted many newcomers – but not Ball.

"Let me tell you about me and what I'm about," he piped, breaking the silence. "I'm a winner. They all go on about winning this and winning that but I'm a World Cup winner. None of you can out-drink me and none of you have been to better parties than me. I've done it all. Let me tell you, I'm only after success and that's all I'll strive for here and that's what we'll get."

City's players were stunned. They had expected a rousing introduction but this seemed bizarre. A speech which Ball had intended as an inspiring rallying cry to his new squad had simply managed to alienate some of his most important players. The City manager had been warned that there was unrest in the camp. If he hoped his address would suppress the fractious elements in his squad, he was wrong. Tony Coton was one of the players present: "It was hardly the kind of things to say to a team packed with vast experience and seasoned internationals."

For Coton, there was a more personal affront to come. As one of the most senior players and a member of the England squad, the highly-regarded goalkeeper decided to introduce himself to the new man in charge. "I wanted to tell him about an injury I'd picked up at the end of the previous season and explain that I'd have to miss the first couple of days of training," says Coton.

He knocked on Ball's door and asked to have a quick word. "Yes, come in Andy," came the reply, as the new boss mixed up Coton with City's other senior goalkeeper, Andy Dibble. It was an embarrassing and crass insult to a player with five years' experience at Maine Road.

"I couldn't believe it," says Coton. "To be honest, I couldn't believe that Alan Ball was the manager in the first place. If you'd said to me that Brian Horton had got the sack and named me a hundred managers who were in with a chance of taking over, Alan

Ball would not have been in my hundred. My view is that Francis Lee just wanted someone he could manipulate and everybody saw through that."

Ball's challenge was clearly to appease City's discontented senior players. Niall Quinn had almost moved to Sporting Lisbon for £1.5 million over the close season but the deal had broken down. Terry Phelan had been placed on the transfer-list after failing to agree terms for a new contract. The others – Keith Curle, Paul Walsh and Uwe Rosler – viewed Ball with a considerable degree of scepticism. He was in bullish mood as he spoke out on the eve of the new season.

"What I've said to the players is that I have to earn their respect and they've got to earn mine. But, so far, the senior players who are supposed to be at loggerheads with the club have impressed me with their attitude."

Francis Lee had another player on his mind as he sat patiently in Manchester Airport's departure lounge, awaiting his flight to Geneva. It was supposed to be a secret trip as the City chairman homed in on his top summer transfer target. But when four other football chairmen joined him on the flight, Lee began to wonder whether his cloak and dagger operation had been uncovered.

"They were all going to the European draws in Geneva," remembers Lee. "They wondered why I was on the plane when we weren't even in Europe. I said I was going on a skiing holiday. We actually signed the player that afternoon in the hotel."

The new signing had caught Lee's eye during a spot of late-night television viewing. The City chairman sat bolt upright as a 5ft 6ins player began to dominate his screen. Within minutes, Lee was smitten and determined to bring the little maestro to Maine Road.

The player in question was Georgi Kinkladze, a wonderfully-gifted 22-year-old who had already graced the international arena with his native Georgia. Born in Tbilisi, the young Gio lived through the ravages of civil war, surviving as some of his closest friends fell victim to the bitter conflict. In the early 1990s, there had been bloody scenes in the streets of his birthplace as rival factions fought for control following the country's independence from Russia. His only refuge was the game he loved – football. Kinkladze had a mesmerising natural ability and was ready to abandon his homeland to make his fortune in the West.

"I watched him for around three months and I thought he was a marvellous talent," says Lee. "I sent our chief scout, Jimmy Frizzell, to watch him play for Georgia against Wales. Jimmy came back and said, 'If you've got an orchestra, this guy will conduct it because he is exceptional.'"

Lee did not need convincing. He contacted Kinkladze's club, Dynamo Tbilisi, and arranged a £2 million deal. City's signing was unveiled on the same day as Alan Ball arrived to take over as manager. There was one slight problem – Kinkladze could not speak a word of English.

"My wife, Gill, and I felt so sorry for him," says Lee. "He was living in an hotel on his own so we would go round to look after him. He was one of the nicest lads you could wish to meet, he did not smoke or drink much, and was very conscientious."

Kinkladze was not the only arrival as Ball embarked on a late summer spree in the transfer market. The former German national goalkeeper, 34-year-old Eike Immel from VfB Stuttgart, was signed to cover for the injured Coton and Andy Dibble. Ball also swooped for one of his former players, Kit Symons of Portsmouth, who arrived in a swap deal, with Fitzroy Simpson and Carl Griffiths going in the opposite direction. The transfer also involved City handing over a cash adjustment of £800,000. Maurizio Gaudino, meanwhile, returned to Germany but his fellow countryman Uwe Rosler signed a four-year contract to ward off any potential buyers.

Behind the scenes, there was more change. Ex-Manchester United player Alex Stepney was appointed goalkeeping coach and there was a familiar face back in the treatment room as Roy Bailey returned from his three-year exile. Controversially sacked by Peter Reid, Bailey took over from Eamonn Salmon, who went back into private practice. But it was the man chosen as Ball's assistant who was seen as most significant. Asa Hartford was steeped in City tradition after eight years as a player during two spells in the 1970s and 1980s. His original move to Maine Road in 1974 only materialised after a transfer to Leeds United fell through due to the young Scot's hole-in-the-heart condition. It was a problem which never seemed to hamper his progress at City as he made more than 300 appearances. Capped 50 times by Scotland, Hartford had most recently been coaching at Blackburn. A quiet and loyal lieutenant, he was seen as the perfect foil for the more emotional Ball. Sam

Ellis he was not – and as the season went on, it seemed City needed a stronger figure to rein in Ball's extravagant tendencies.

As the campaign kicked off, chairman Lee had no doubt that his managerial pairing would prove an unbeatable double act. And, as ever, he was not afraid to articulate his optimistic predictions. Writing in the match programme for City's opening home match against Spurs, he was fulsome in his praise for Ball and Hartford: "They will put this club back on the map. I don't think it will be too long before we regain our place at the forefront of English football. We've got a manager who knows the game inside out and has won the highest honours. He may not have been here long but already he has earned the respect of the players because they appreciate he knows what he is talking about. I'm surprised he's not been given the chance at a really big club before. I wanted him as manager even before I became City's chairman!

"When the takeover campaign was at its height, I telephoned Alan, who was then at Exeter, and asked him if he would become the manager once I became chairman. That's how much faith I had in him and I was delighted when he said yes. But the other situation dragged on and Alan took the Southampton job."

Now that Ball was in charge, it was evident his job would be far from straightforward. His chairman was already warning of the need to cut costs and demanding that players justify their earnings. "We have to set about trimming the senior squad. It's still too big and unwieldy and the wage bill is horrendous. We want quality, not quantity, and Alan is already taking the necessary steps to sort things out. Invariably, the manager, and sometimes the chairman, carries the can when things go wrong on the pitch.

"I want our players to stand up and be counted and accept some responsibility for the struggles of the last couple of seasons. Some of them are picking up fabulous wages and I want them to start earning them. Money should NOT be their motivation. Their chests should swell with pride every time they pull on a City shirt. Alan Ball says this is the manager's job he has been waiting for and that he is willing to 'die' for the club. If the players go out with the same determination we'll be on our way."

As the fans digested Lee's programme notes, their side stuttered to a 1-1 draw against Spurs. City would not collect another point for the next two months as the club endured the worst start to a season in their history. Ball's side scored just three goals in their first 11 League games and managed to concede 21. The bright new dawn was turning into a disaster. Ball stumbled into the transfer market in a desperate effort to arrest his team's alarming slide. Scottish striker Gerry Creaney from Portsmouth was bought in a £1.5 million deal which saw crowd favourite Paul Walsh move to Fratton Park in part-exchange.

"I don't think playing in the Premiership is going to be a problem for me," declared Creaney as he confidently assessed his future with his new club. His optimism was short-lived as his woeful lack of fitness became obvious in the higher division. By the end of the season, the 13 and a half stone forward had started only six games. His transfer was a complete flop.

City's other leading strikers were also beginning to toil, with Uwe Rosler managing only three League goals before Christmas. The once-lethal German striker had lost his touch and had fallen out with the manager. Their personality clash came to a head late in October as City faced successive trips to Anfield in the space of three days. Already red-hot relegation favourites, the Blues were torn apart. After losing 4-0 in the League Cup, Ball's side had to face even further humiliation in their next visit. They were trounced 6-0 and Rosler, disgusted with the performance and the plight of his club, tore off his boots and hurled them into the crowd of visiting fans at the end of the game.

As the players and fans felt the embarrassment of defeat, Ball wandered into the post-match press conference and unashamedly declared: "I enjoyed that." He went on to explain he "enjoyed" watching a Liverpool side in all its pomp put on such a wonderful exhibition of attacking football, even if it was at his side's expense. It was an incredibly ill-judged remark. As the hordes of City fans headed back down the East Lancs Road and the M62 to Manchester, they could scarcely believe what they were hearing on their car radios. Throughout the match, they had mocked their manager, singing sarcastically, "Alan Ball is a football genius." But it was not funny any more. Their club was falling apart at the seams and Ball seemed clueless how to fix it.

For Michael Brown, it was all a rather unsettling introduction into the professional game. The Hartlepool-born youngster had broken into the first-team three games into the season and was sent off on his debut after coming on as a second-half substitute. A tough-tackling, all-action midfielder, Brown had been signed as a 14-year-old after one of Peter Reid's youth scouts, George Smith, spotted him in Hartlepool. He played in the 6-0 reverse at Anfield and could already detect an uneasy atmosphere in the dressing room.

"Bally was great with me but I think that was because I was young and he could mould me," says Brown. "But I don't think he was as good at dealing with the older, more experienced lads. Quite a few of them fell out with him and by Christmas they could sense that the club was trying to off-load its top earners. Francis Lee never gave any team talks or anything like that, but you just got the feeling that he was calling the shots behind the scenes."

But Ball was the dominant force in the dressing room. Brown, one of the younger members of the squad, would sit wide-eyed as his manager launched into animated tirades after matches: "Bally would do a lot of shouting and was extremely passionate about the game. In the dressing room, he would go berserk sometimes. I've never known another manager like it. The problem is that it works for some players, while others need a consoling arm around their shoulder."

The suspicion that Lee was interfering in team affairs began to spread throughout football. As Ball and his players suffered so badly, it must have been extremely difficult for Lee to keep his counsel. Yet he maintains, that while he offered advice, he did not interfere. "Bally used to ask my opinion on things and I would tell him, then he would go off and do something totally different. I think he just used to do what his missus told him! I couldn't interfere anyway or he would have got the League Managers' Association on to me."

Between the two Liverpool games, City opened their redeveloped training ground complex at Platt Lane. It was a far cry from their previous decrepit headquarters as the club forged a partnership with the city council to build modern facilities and an upstairs restaurant. It was to be shared by City and the community, with the club using it during the day, leaving it free for the public in the evenings. Throwing open their doors to supporters was nothing new at a club renowned for its accessibility and friendliness. But, with the team in such deep distress on the field, and a hungry media feeding off any juicy gossip to fill column inches, it did not take long for rumours to spread.

Ball's future was already being questioned as the season entered its fourth month and City had still not managed to win. Lee, though, was not prepared to turn his back so soon on his first managerial appointment as chairman. "Alan is my choice and he is tip top in my opinion," he said in an interview with the *Mail on Sunday*. "There is no doubt in my mind that he will get it right but he has to be given a chance. I have known Alan a long time and before he took the job here I warned him that there was an attitude problem with some of the players.

"It has been a long, hard eighteen months for me as chairman. At times it has felt like climbing Mount Everest with people tugging at the rucksack. But I know Alan will get it right. He is my appointment and I will stay loyal to him all the way. Even if we were to be relegated this season he will remain manager of Manchester City so long as I am chairman."

Then, after a wait of nearly seven months, City won a League game. Nicky Summerbee's goal earned them a precious 1-0 victory over Bolton Wanderers on the day before Bonfire Night. As one wag put it, people were lighting fires all over England to celebrate City's victory. The change of mood was stunning. By the beginning of December, City had climbed off the bottom of the table after winning four out of five League games.

Georgi Kinkladze scored his first goal for the club in the 1-0 home win over Aston Villa. It was a result which secured the November Manager of the Month award for Alan Ball after a remarkable turnaround in fortunes. Kinkladze was at the heart of it all. The Georgian was dazzling; his breath-taking skill and sharp acceleration left the fans drooling. With Rosler badly out-of-sorts, it was Kinkladze who quickly became a terrace hero, an icon for fans who needed something to grasp on to. Manchester United might be topping the League but City fans could claim to possess the most exciting player in the land.

If the rest of England had any doubts, they were convinced later on in the season when Kinky scored a wondrous solo goal against Southampton, dribbling past four hapless defenders before chipping the ball over the goalkeeper. The images were beamed around the globe – it was something very special. Ball compared it to Diego Maradona's second goal against England in the 1986 World Cup. For Lee, it only reaffirmed what he already knew.

"Gio is probably one of the best players ever to be seen at Manchester City," he says. "We just needed another two players on the same wavelength as him. If the team were passing the ball to one another, he was okay. But once you started to play the long ball, he was gone. The problem was that none of the managers could decide which was his best position." Lee has his own ideas, but there is little doubt it was not easy trying to accommodate Kinkladze into a team pattern. He was a free spirit on the field and any attempt to rein in his attacking tendencies seemed doomed to fail.

"It was difficult for me when I first came over to England," admits Kinkladze. "The culture was so different from Georgia and I could not speak any English. It was the fans who made the difference. They made me feel so welcome and I began to think of Manchester as my home. My mother used to visit me from time to time and I made friends in the team, like Nicky Summerbee. But that first season was difficult. City were struggling and sometimes I felt all alone."

Ball must have known exactly how he felt as City's revival stalled as suddenly as it had begun. The high hopes of November nosedived during December. Ball's side went another four League games without a win and, as they stumbled back down the table, the manager plunged into the transfer market again to sign a player he had long admired. Martin "Buster" Phillips was a spindly, blond-haired winger from Exeter City. Ball had forecast, during his time in charge at St James Park, that Phillips would become "Britain's first £10 million player." It was an unfortunate dose of hyperbole which did little to aid the youngster's development. Now, with Phillips aged 19, City were able to tempt Exeter with a more modest offer of £350,000. Ball remained convinced that his signing was destined for the top.

"In my opinion, we have signed the most exciting young player in English soccer," he declared. "We had to move now because the stands were full of scouts watching him every week. But Martin has been signed for tomorrow, not for today." Unfortunately, tomorrow would never come. Phillips was sold on to Portsmouth three years later for £75,000 after only a handful of first-team appearances. His new manager at Fratton Park was a familiar one: Alan Ball.

The flame-haired one was concentrating on re-aligning his City squad as 1995 drew to a close. Terry Phelan was sold to Chelsea for £750,000 while central defender Michel Vonk was transfer-listed. Arriving through Maine Road's revolving door were two foreign players. Ronnie Ekelund, who had played for Ball at Southampton, was signed on a two-month loan from Barcelona, while the troublesome left-back slot was to be filled by a former German international Michael Frontzeck signed in a £300,000 deal. City needed a boost, but the signings once again proved disastrous. Ekelund returned to Spain after a month and Frontzeck was quite simply hopeless. In 11 League appearances, he was substituted on seven occasions and sent off once. Any international qualities he once possessed had long since deserted him. One of City's most promising home-grown players, meanwhile, was facing a painful exile on the sidelines. Richard Edghill, who had established himself as a key player over the past two seasons, suffered a devastating cruciate ligament injury in a League game at Leeds.

Another of City's mainstays was also contemplating his future. Tony Coton had decided it was time to act; he was going to confront his manager and ask about his chances of a recall to the first team. The 34-year-old had spent almost six years at Maine Road, twice winning the club's coveted Player of the Year prize. Yet by early in the New Year, he still had not made a single appearance in Ball's side as Eike Immel maintained an ever-present record. Coton was fit again after a persistent leg injury and was raring to get back into the action. The word was that he could be set for a recall.

It was a frosty Friday morning in early January and there was a tingle of excitement around the training centre at Platt Lane. The third round of the FA Cup beckoned and City were due to play at Leicester City on the following day. Coton was making his way to the manager's office. He thought there might be some good news coming his way.

"I remember asking the reserve team coach, Les Chapman, whether Bally might have mentioned about me being back in the team," recalls Coton. "Les said he hadn't heard anything and if you can get the manager's nose out of the *Racing Post* on a Friday morning, you've done well."

Undeterred, City's goalkeeper arrived at Ball's office. The manager was relaxing in his chair, with his legs stretched out and his feet perched on the table in front of him. Wearing a track suit, his familiar flat cap and a pair of flip-flops, Ball looked an unlikely figure of authority. Nevertheless, Coton set out his case: he had played more than ten reserve games and was desperate to get back into the team. Ball's prompt reply left Coton frozen to the spot in disbelief.

"He said I'd been a great servant to the club and everyone recognised that, but he was going to let me go and would keep the fee low. It really took me back because it was the last thing I was expecting. He said there might be a deal on because he fancied the Sunderland left-back, Martin Scott."

Coton promptly replied he did not want to join Sunderland and emerged from Ball's office in a daze. He could hardly believe the club were contemplating selling one of their most experienced players at a time of such crisis. Furthermore, he did not want to go. "As I walked out I felt like a schoolboy who'd been punished for something he hadn't done."

Coton was later named as a substitute for the match at Leicester but his Maine Road career was over. He would never play for the Blues again. The proposed move to Sunderland fell through as the Wearsiders could not match Coton's wages and the £400,000 fee. But the word was out that City were prepared to sell one of the most experienced goalkeepers in the country. Alex Ferguson, a long-time admirer, stepped in. He was desperate for a reliable understudy to Peter Schmeichel as Manchester United chased a League and Cup double. Coton was offered a contract and he accepted, even though he knew the move would infuriate City fans, who had taken him to their hearts. For them, a move across town to the sworn enemy amounted to an act of heresy.

"I agreed to go to United until the summer and I saw it as a chance to get an insight into one of the most famous and successful clubs in the world," says Coton. "I knew I'd get slaughtered by the supporters but as the days went by they'd find out the truth. I knew I was only staying at Old Trafford for a few months. I could have stayed at City but I knew for a fact that I would not get into the team. I didn't even train with them half the time."

With Coton a fixture on their substitute's bench, United completed the Double for the second time in three years. But City's former keeper did not want to remain a replacement. He still craved first-team football and the experience at Old Trafford had whetted his appetite. Over the summer, he received an offer from his former boss, Peter Reid, to rekindle the move to Sunderland. He accepted but after only a few months, Coton broke his leg and was forced to retire.

"I enjoyed my career at City but it's still hard to get the bitter taste out of my mouth at the way it ended. I also had six seasons at my other clubs Birmingham and Watford and I'm sometimes asked back to functions but I'd have reservations about going to back to City even though some of my best friends support the club. Francis Lee still goes along to matches and I haven't got any time for him or Alan Ball. Ball came up to shake my hand once when I was on the coaching staff at Sunderland and they were playing Portsmouth. I found that a bit strange because that was the only dealing I'd had with him apart from the day he said I could go." Coton was later to return to Old Trafford as goalkeeping coach.

It was at United's ground that City were to experience another critical moment in their turbulent season. After overcoming Leicester and Coventry in two replayed ties, the Blues drew their deadly rivals in the FA Cup fifth round. It was a golden opportunity to resurrect their season. Ball's side set about the task with relish and deservedly took the lead through Uwe Rosler in the first half. The German raced on to Kinkladze's slide-rule pass and chipped the ball over Schmeichel to send the visiting fans into raptures. Their joy would be cut short as United equalised in the most galling circumstances. With half-time only seconds away, referee Alan Wilkie awarded a penalty for an innocuous Michael Frontzeck challenge on Eric Cantona. The Frenchman duly converted the spotkick and punctured City's belief. A Lee Sharpe winner in the second half completed their misery. Ball's men, who had fought so gallantly, felt cheated and demoralised.

Michael Brown was part of the team that day and believes the result changed the course of the season. "I never thought we would lose the game after Uwe scored. But then, after the penalty, we couldn't recover. The players were distraught at half-time. Who knows what would have happened if we had won that game? Things like that can change the whole season and I think that decision had a massive impact on us."

With their money-spinning run in the cup now over, cash was getting tight again. Ball had signed Nigel Clough in a £1.5 million deal from Liverpool as he looked to add experience and goals to his midfield. But, according to former director John Dunkerley, Ball was ordered to recoup funds as well. Dunkerley admits the battle against relegation was conducted against a backdrop of financial worries. "Alan Ball had to get rid of a lot of players because there was so much debt at the club," says Dunkerley. "They were trying desperately to cut the bills down."

Although the club was rarely specific about the extent of debt, it was estimated they were more than £10 million in the red. When an offer of £3.5 million from Blackburn Rovers was received for Garry Flitcroft, it seemed as if it was too good to turn down. But Lee is adamant it was "Ball's decision" to sell Flitcroft and he came to the board with the proposal. Money, he claims, had little to do with it.

"Everyone criticises me for the sale of Flitcroft, but it was Ball who made the decision," says Lee. "I happen to think it was the right decision as well. Bear in mind, Garry has only scored a handful of goals in the last five years. He is a lovely lad but you need your midfielders to score. "We had Nicky Summerbee on the right and he has not scored ten goals in the last five years, along with Steve Lomas who is not exactly prolific. It wouldn't matter if you had Jimmy Greaves and Alan Shearer up front, with that midfield you would not score enough goals."

Yet for many, Flitcroft's departure – just days ahead of the transfer deadline – was akin to raising the white flag in their relegation battle. Fans were dismayed as City off-loaded one of their best homegrown players at a time of such desperate need. For Flitcroft, it was a massive wrench to leave the club he had joined as a schoolboy. "I got a call off Alan Ball and, as soon as I came off the phone, I knew my time was up at City," says Flitcroft. "I didn't want to leave. The club was so close to my heart and all I could do was just hope they would stay up without me."

As Flitcroft left, another Georgian arrived. Mikhail Kavelashvili was signed in a £1 million deal from Russian club Alania Vladikavkaz and was hailed as "better than Kinkladze." Within a few minutes of his debut, it seemed that the Georgian striker might live up to his billing. He scored from close range against Manchester United at Maine Road, but by half-time Eric Cantona's penalty and a goal from Andy Cole had put the visitors 2-1 ahead. The scene was set for another of City's strikers to prove a point. Uwe Rosler climbed off the substitute's bench to equalise and then dramatically pointed at the name on the back of his shirt in a gesture clearly directed at

Ball. Their simmering feud had boiled over in the most public arena of all – the Manchester derby. But it all counted for nothing as Ryan Giggs settled the game in United's favour with a stunning 30-yard strike.

Afterwards, Rosler made no secret of his contempt for Ball. "I'm happy with my performances in the second half of the season and I couldn't understand why the manager dropped me," he declared. "But at the end of the day, I'm playing not for Alan Ball, but for a fabulous football club and my team-mates."

Typically, Ball was not prepared to take Rosler's criticism on the chin. He hit back, claiming, "The most important thing is that players shouldn't be bothered about themselves at this moment in time. All they should be worrying about is the club and their own personal thing should not be talked about."

There was still plenty to worry about as the Blues entered the final few weeks of the season. Successive defeats by United and Wimbledon had plunged City back into seventeenth place, on the brink of the relegation zone. Rosler was recalled to the starting line-up for the visit of Sheffield Wednesday as the tension began to mount. With relegation rivals Coventry and Southampton both having a game in hand, victory was essential for City. Rosler's goal ensured the three points but at the final whistle there was little relief as results from elsewhere filtered in. Coventry's 1-0 victory over Queens Park Rangers condemned the Londoners to the drop but offered hope to Ron Atkinson's side. Yet, it was the result at the Dell which really rocked City. Southampton had defeated Champions-elect Manchester United 3-1, with Alex Ferguson infamously ordering his team to change kits at half-time. The Old Trafford manager claimed his players were struggling to see each other in their new grey away strip.

It was another two weeks before City could play their next match, a daunting trip to high-flying Aston Villa. Michael Brown was back in the side at left wing-back after Ball had finally given up hope on Frontzeck. The gamble paid off as Brown's excellent cross from the wing was converted by Steve Lomas to secure an unlikely 1-0 win. The players were jubilant, but not for long.

Brown explains, "Everyone had written us off and nobody expected us to even manage a draw at Villa Park. To be honest, the players felt if we could get anything out of the game, then we would be alright as the other teams were away as well. When we came into the dressing room at the end, the atmosphere was just brilliant – it was as if we had stayed up. But then somebody said both Coventry and Southampton had won as well. We were just shattered. All the elation just evaporated within seconds."

With City now third from bottom, their destiny was out of their hands as the final day of the season arrived. Bolton Wanderers and QPR were already down, and it was between City, Southampton, Coventry and Sheffield Wednesday for the third spot. Wednesday had been dragged into trouble after a terrible recent run. City's opponents were Liverpool at a packed and pensive Maine Road. With tension seeping down from the stands, the home side froze as their uninterested-looking visitors cruised into a 2-0 lead. It seemed that Ball, who had played the game with such passion, was going to witness his players being relegated without much of a fight. Rosler's penalty restored some hope and when Kit Symons equalised, the crowd began to believe again.

Before the match, Ball had insisted his side would ignore any signals from the crowd regarding the progress of their rivals. But with still more than ten minutes left, word had somehow reached the players that a draw would keep them up. The whispers were wrong; City still needed to win. Yet Steve Lomas kept the ball near the corner flag to waste time in one of the most enduring images of the decade for City fans. Amid the confusion, Niall Quinn, who had been substituted, was watching events unfold in the dressing room. He raced on to the touchline and urged his colleagues to continue attacking. It was a farcical episode on a day of such enormous importance. Despite a late bombardment on the Liverpool goal, City could not find the winner. They were relegated on goal difference, while Manchester United claimed their third League title in four years with victory at Middlesbrough.

Afterwards, an emotional Ball emerged grim-faced from the dressing room, leaving behind his tearful players. He had no excuses, except to say his side's pitiful start to the season had cost them dearly. "This is the worst day of my career and it's a blot on everyone's life but occasionally in life setbacks prove to be a blessing in disguise and sometimes you have to take a step backwards before you can start moving forwards again. You have to be man enough to say we weren't good enough at the end of the day but I'd rather say we weren't good enough for the first dozen games and we've paid dearly for that. In the last twenty-five games, we've picked up something like thirty-six points which is a very good haul."

Niall Quinn, who had kept his composure throughout the afternoon, voiced the view from the players. "City are a huge club and don't deserve to be in this position and we've got to carry the can for that. We can only apologise to the fans who've travelled the length and breadth of the country and given us not just their money and their support but part of their lives as well. I only hope we're all given the opportunity to take club back up where it belongs." It was Quinn's last game for the club. He was sold to Sunderland that summer.

For Ball, it was also the beginning of the end. His mission to turn City into one of the Premiership's top sides had ended in miserable failure. He was Lee's man, but today the former chairman admits he was not the right man for the job. "With hindsight, I thought he was a good coach but maybe not a great man-manager," says Lee. "The problem was that he said the wrong things in the newspapers. He would tell the players off and then criticise them in public. But you cannot do that; it turns them against you and you still need them to play for you. There was a certain amount of unrest within the club and ultimately he had lost the faith of the senior players."

But Lee had also criticised the players near the start of the season. He seemed to have encouraged Ball's antagonistic attitude, warning him about the troublesome elements within the squad. When his manager responded in typically vehement fashion, Lee should not have been surprised.

Three days before City were relegated, there was a shock in store. The man once regarded as Mr Manchester City passed away. Peter Swales died of a heart attack at the age of 64. He had never been back to Maine Road since losing his battle for control with Lee two years earlier. Swales had been offered the opportunity to return to football as a director at Blackpool, but he turned it down. Nothing could replace City. Yet the man who cared so deeply about the Blues never spoke publicly about the club after he left; it was probably just too painful.

A minute's silence was impeccably observed by the 31,436 Maine Road supporters ahead of the final game of the season against

Liverpool. Many believed it was the pressure of the campaign against Swales which had contributed to his rapid decline. But his widow, Brenda, bears no bitterness, her memory and respect for her husband give her the strength to carry on, allied to her strong religious beliefs as a member of the Baptist Church. She still lives in the same house in south Manchester which she shared with Peter during their marriage. They were together for 41 years, a defiantly old-fashioned couple who treasured their time together out of the public eye. The man who held a vice-like grip on power and possessed a notoriously ruthless streak was also a devoted husband and a dedicated family man. He rifled through 12 managers during his time as chairman, but there was only ever woman in his life – Brenda. She has not re-married and remains loyal to her husband.

"Peter was an extremely good listener and had a special gift of being able to understand people," she says. "I remember when I was young, he used to listen very carefully to older people and what they had to say. He wanted to learn from them. Peter did a lot of things to help other people. He would sort out their problems but he wouldn't say anything to anyone about it. After I'd been widowed for some time, somebody said to me, 'I can't understand why you've not got another man.' I said that I didn't want another man, because I've had the best.

"I know City took over his life but that was fine with me because I was happy whatever he was doing. I didn't know anything about the running of the club because when he came home, he never talked about it. He was only concerned with our three daughters and me. I know he always wanted to win, but it's not like running a business. He'd been successful in his own record shop business but football isn't quite the same. You get the terrific highs and lows and I was there all the way."

A month before Swales's death, his grandson Daniel was born. Needless to say, Daniel's favourite colour is blue. It could have something to do with the heavy influence of the colour around the Swales family home. Brenda has learned to cope with the loss of her husband and still proudly displays photographs and mementoes from his involvement in the game. "It's so strange but no-one has told Daniel to be blue. I like blue and love to wear clothes that colour," saya Brenda. "Daniel wanted a skipping rope for his fourth birthday but it had to be blue."

Yet Swales always attempted to shield his family from the stress of life at Maine Road. Even at the height of the takeover campaign, he refused to take his problems home with him. "He never said anything wrong about anybody, even to me. He never complained about anybody and he always found the good things in people. Sometimes, being a woman, you'd say, 'Go on tell me something' and he'd just look at me and never did. It's very unusual in this day and age. I suppose at times I was a bit upset about what was going on at City and perhaps I would have said something, even though I was supposed to be the religious one. Yet he showed more of that quality than me."

Former colleague and friend Ian Niven believes Swales made life harder for himself because of his reluctance to share any problems, preferring to bottle them up. It has also taken time for Brenda to bring herself to discuss the final months of her husband's controversial reign at Manchester City. She now realises that the enormous strain of the battle for control took its toll. By the end, the pressure was showing.

"I think possibly I can talk about it more now than I could when he had just died really. He'd worked hard all his life and he'd probably decided that it was time for somebody else to have a go. I look at these football managers and you can see the stress they go through. Peter didn't look so good at the time of the Francis Lee takeover. You don't realise it when you are with them all the time. It took me ages to bring myself to look at old video tapes of him on television. But when I've looked back, I thought he did look a bit rough compared to other photographs of him. His health was always fine and he had regular check ups. In 1994, I didn't realise how much the takeover had taken out of him because he never showed it. Once he'd finished at City, it was lovely for me because I saw more of him. He was home more often. Not that we did much more because we weren't ones for gadding around and socialising. We were just together and that was nice for me. I'm sure he missed City but he never said so.

"He looked so well just before he suffered his heart attack. We'd just had a photograph taken with one of our baby boys and he looked great on it, which is why his death was such a shock. Peter came into the TV room at home and felt pains. I rang for an ambulance and we took him into hospital. The next day he had another funny turn and he was taken into intensive care. He didn't die for another ten days. For those days I thought he was getting a little bit better each day. The day before he died he looked really well and we thought we'd cracked it. He rang up and said he was ready to come home.

"He was in Wythenshawe Hospital. Normally you can't park anywhere near the hospital and you have to walk miles but I got right near the front entrance. I thought everything's going well and he won't have far to walk. Each day he had walked a bit more so I thought I'd be all right here and parked the car.

"As I got in through that hospital door, I felt very strange. I got into the corridor where his room was and there was a receptionist and I asked, 'Is everything all right? I've come for Peter.' She told me just to wait in this room and I knew instantly what had happened. As I got to the hospital he must have died. I just sort of knew then. It was a most strange feeling and it was as if he had passed his strength on to me. I know it sounds odd but he did."

That resolve now enables Brenda Swales to face up to key questions concerning one of the fiercest and dirtiest battles ever fought for control of a football club.

Does she have any regrets about what happened regarding the takeover campaign, led by Francis Lee?

"No! I didn't know what was going on apart from what was in the newspapers. One of my daughters would say have you heard such a thing on the radio and I would tell her not to listen. To be quite honest I never listened. I might have seen the newspapers but that wasn't the way to cope with it really."

Did Peter Swales suffer a heart attack at the time of the takeover of the club?

"I can't remember now. Time is most peculiar. He had a funny turn when my daughter got married and then he was all right. He had tests on his heart. I felt he was just tired because he was working so hard."

Do you think the turmoil at City contributed towards his death?

"I don't know. You can't say really."

The writing on the wall. Fans mass outside Maine Road to campaign against Peter Swales.

Before the bubble burst. Hundreds of balloons are released as supporters celebrate Francis Lee's first day as chairman in 1994.

So much to do. *Chairman Francis Lee in pensive mood during that first game.*

Two victims of the Maine Road merry-go-round.

Frank Clark *shouts instructions from the sidelines.*

Steve Coppell *on the day he resigned as manager.*

Brian Who? *Brian Horton surrounded by his management team from left to right Tony Book (seated), Horton, Dave Moss, Eamonn Salmon.*

A football genius?
Alan Ball in trademark flat cap after taking City training.

Who pulls the strings? *Peter Reid and Sam Ellis after becoming the new managerial team at Maine Road.*

"I enjoyed that!" *Uwe Rosler competes with Liverpool defender Mark Wright during City's 6-0 defeat at Anfield that led to Alan Ball's ill-chosen remark.*

Back where we belong! *City's players mob Shaun Goater after the equaliser at Blackburn in 2000. Left to right: Jeff Whitley, Shaun Goater (obscured), Mark Kennedy, Kevin Horlock.*

A football genius

Sweet taste of success. *Joe Royle with his Nationwide Manager of the Month Award in May 2000.*

Power behind the throne.
Chairman David Bernstein ahead of City's play-off semi-final at Wigan in 1999.

Are you bitter about the things that went on?

"Peter was never was bitter and never gave anyone else cause to feel bitter. When he died somebody gave me a leaflet and it said about being bitter and angry but I didn't feel that at all because I thought I've had so many happy times and wonderful memories and you have to think of those."

Like all other City fans, Brenda Swales prefers to dwell on the happier times, even if they were few and far between. "Fortunately I can block out all the bad times and think of the good times because I think that is important. My special memories are going to Wembley and I can remember clearly the goal that got us promotion at Bradford City in 1989. "It was nice because the two of us would just come back here and be together. All Peter wanted to do was to be in his house. He didn't like parties or anything like that. He wasn't one for change and was just very content with me and the family really."

Even without her football-mad husband, Brenda still watches the game he loved. "I've watched City on the television and they've invited me to go along to a match but somehow I couldn't really go. I haven't been to Maine Road since that day I left after the Sheffield Wednesday game in 1993. But I'm still a City fan and it's the first result I look for every Saturday."

She has, in fact, seen City on a couple of occasions in recent years when they were playing at Bloomfield Road. She was in the directors' box as a guest of the Blackpool and former City director Chris Muir, an old family friend. "I sit a little way back and watch the wives of the chairmen and managers and I know what they're going through. It's very stressful but very enjoyable. I used to think about City quite a lot when Peter was in charge. They were his life and I was in it wasn't I? He used to say, 'You get more worked up than me,' because I did. It's an emotional game.

"I wondered how I'd feel watching City play again. But the strip has changed and the colour is not quite the same. Everything has changed and it was an odd feeling because I didn't feel anything. I thought this isn't my team any more in that respect, not the team I knew."

CHAPTER SEVEN

Thirty-five **names**

ALAN BALL SURVIVED three games into the new season. His side were tipped as favourites for promotion but patience had worn pretty thin at Maine Road. A summer of soul-searching had hardened the hearts of City's loyal followers. Francis Lee warned his manager on the eve of the campaign that "serious questions" would be asked if the club did not start making "obvious progress." The pressure was on and Ball knew a false start would cost him dearly.

"The first twelve months at City have been very tough for me and I've been hurt," he commented at the club's pre-season photo call. "I've been hurting all summer but that's gone now and I've got to look forward and be positive and believe we can have a good season."

It was not to be. Despite a victory over Ipswich in their first game, defeats at Bolton and Stoke rocked City back on to their heels again. As his side trailed 2-1 at Stoke's Victoria Ground, Ball found himself under attack from all sides. He had endured an equally unsuccessful stint in charge of the Potteries club in the late 1980s and their fans had not forgotten. The "Ball Out" chorus echoed around the ageing stadium. In the previous season, supporters had coined an Alan Ball anthem to the theme of Oasis' *Wonderwall* song. It was an affectionate, if slightly sardonic, ode to their manager: *"I said City, you're gonna be the one that saves me, because after all we've got Alan Ball."* Now, though, Ball had no chance of saving himself.

As he emerged from the dressing room at Stoke, Ball was a man on a mission. He knew his time was up, but he was not ready to go quietly. The manager pushed his way into the post-match press conference and launched an astonishing verbal attack on one man.

"The problems at this club are not due to the players or the management," he raged. "The problems at this club are down to that man." Ball pointed his finger in the direction of Paul Hince, the City reporter for the *Manchester Evening News*. "You would have thought your local paper would give you a little bit of backing but unfortunately Paul Hince has decided there will be a witch hunt and so be it. At least I'm finding out who my enemies are."

Hince was shocked. The previous night's edition of the *Manchester Evening News* had run a back-page story claiming "FANS WANT BALL OUT," after the newspaper's Deansgate offices were overwhelmed with phone calls and letters from disgruntled supporters. Yet to blame the club's plight on a newspaper and its reporter seemed risible.

"It was ludicrous," says Hince. "Remember, I never played one game for the club during that period. The editor did, in fact, write a one-paragraph editorial accepting the blame for City's demise, saying that we would insist on printing the results!

"I did not have a bad relationship with Bally, but I don't think he trusted me and the chairman didn't help matters. In all the time Alan Ball was at Maine Road, I only put my name to two critical articles. Once was before the Aston Villa match when there was a meeting of the plc board and a director rang me up and said they were going to ask questions of his stewardship and why they were struggling against relegation. Bally objected strongly to that story and I know he marched into the board meeting waving a copy of the paper, saying how could he manage when this sort of thing was going on.

"The second critical article was after they'd lost to Bolton and Bally refused to speak to the press and said you'd better ask my wife. That went in the paper in the column reserved for the manager's comments and over the next forty-eight hours we were flooded out with fans saying it was time he went. So by the Friday night we had to reflect the fans' opinion.

"His attack on me after the Stoke game surprised me more than anything else. I couldn't believe after what had happened to the club over the past twelve months that he could point the finger at someone and say it was because of the negative press they got from the paper. For one thing it wasn't true and what the hell has that got to do with it anyway?"

Ball's reign ended 48 hours after the Stoke game. A brief formal statement was read out by club secretary Bernard Halford at a news conference: "A meeting was held last night at which Mr Alan Ball tendered his resignation as manager of Manchester City Football

Club, which was accepted. The chairman and board would like to place on record their appreciation for his endeavours and efforts while in his period of office and wish him well for the future."

Another unfortunate chapter in Ball's hapless managerial career was over. Officially, he had jumped ship but the truth was that the board had forced him out. Ball had lost the trust of his players and had used up all the good will from fans. After Niall Quinn had departed to Sunderland over the summer, Keith Curle followed suit and joined Wolves. The team was breaking up and Ball had seemed unable to find any suitable replacements.

"The club was just in chaos," remembers Michael Brown. "Everything was changing and it was obvious the fans had had enough of Alan Ball even before the season started. You can sense when something is not right behind the scenes and it was pretty obvious to the players that the club was in a mess."

Alan Ball's last act as manager turned out to be one of his most significant. Paul Dickov was signed in a £1 million deal from Arsenal and made his debut as a substitute on that fateful day at Stoke. The diminutive Scottish striker would later change the course of City's history but he could do little to save Ball. The manager, who had been ridiculed for his high-pitched voice and unusual dress sense, left feeling embittered and angry at his treatment.

"The society in this country at this moment is shocking," he raged. "To be abused doesn't really bother me. Unfortunately, in this day and age in this country, we've got phone-ins and fantasy leagues and they all want to be managers. There are no heroes any more. The manager is there for fodder. He is not a person any more to be looked up to. He is there to be ridiculed and laughed at and unfortunately that's a poor part of our game."

He refused to apportion any blame to his chairman, stating emphatically that Lee "did not interfere." He received advice, but ultimately the final say belonged to him. Their friendship, it seemed, had stayed intact, although the pair rarely speak nowadays. Ball went on to manage Portsmouth, one of the sides which indirectly sent City down to the Second Division, but his return to Fratton Park would also end with the sack. Lee's loyalty to his former England colleague remained until the bitter end at Maine Road. As the board demanded Ball's sacking, once again Lee dissented. He did not want to get rid of Ball, unless there was a definite replacement waiting in the wings.

"Everyone on the board was saying, 'We have got to sack Alan Ball' but I wasn't so sure," reveals Lee. "I distinctly remember saying, 'Who are we going to get in his place?'"

The reply was George Graham. The former Arsenal manager was back in circulation after serving out a suspension for receiving illegal payments during his time at Highbury. Graham was still renowned as one of the game's top managers after steering the Gunners to two Championship triumphs in three seasons at the turn of the decade. A tall and suave Scot, he had also savoured cup success on the European and domestic stage. He seemed the ideal candidate to fill the vacancy at Maine Road and all the noises coming from him suggested he wanted the job.

"What has happened up in Manchester is a bit sad really because I'm quite friendly with Alan Ball and he was one of my team-mates while I was at Highbury as a player," sympathised Graham. "I'm interested in any big ambitious job. I have been interested in a few jobs recently but I didn't think they were ambitious enough but Manchester City definitely come into the category of a big club. They are one of the biggest clubs in the game. It's a big job and I would be interested."

An appointment appeared imminent after Graham was interviewed and offered the job. But Lee soon realised that things were not going to plan. "I knew George was a tricky bugger," he says. "I couldn't get hold of him on the phone so I started to think there was something funny going on. In the event, it transpired that George had already been offered the job by the new regime at Leeds. He was using City to put pressure on Leeds to make a quicker decision."

Graham was duly appointed as the manager at Elland Road, leaving City still hunting for a replacement for Ball. Graham's public snub had not made the search any easier. Lee, keen to defend his territory, stated Graham might "live to regret" his decision to join Leeds.

While the guessing game continued, Asa Hartford was placed in temporary charge of the club. The reliable right-hand man was suddenly thrust into the glare of the spotlight. He had been a manager before but had no desire to repeat the experience.

"People have asked me if I have applied and I certainly haven't," he said. "I'm happy working for the club in the capacity I'm in at the moment and I'd like to remain in that role if and when a new guy comes in. I've got no desire to be the manager. I'm happier working with the players on the coaching side of the game. It's a more difficult job being a manager now than it was six or seven years ago. I've been an assistant manager for about four or five years and I enjoy that role."

But the players did not want to take 'no' for an answer. They held a team meeting and agreed that Hartford was the right man to take over. Lee says, "Kit Symons came to see me and said the players wanted Asa to be manager. I said I had no problems with that and they should show their backing for Asa on the pitch. Unfortunately, they went out and lost embarrassingly."

With such intense focus on the club, winning matches was becoming increasingly difficult. Every move was being scrutinised by a fascinated media but the drama had only just begun. It was quickly becoming the biggest farce in football.

Hartford replaced goalkeeper Eike Immel with Andy Dibble and moved into the transfer market to sign the versatile Eddie McGoldrick on loan from Arsenal. In early September, City returned to the Potteries to win 2-0 at Port Vale with goals from Uwe Rosler and Paul Dickov. On the same night, Manchester United were in the slightly more glamorous surrounds of Turin, preparing to face Juventus in the Champions League. Twenty years earlier, it was City who travelled to Italy for a UEFA Cup tie against the famous Turin side. Now, though, as the Red half of the city was aiming to conquer Europe, the Blues were struggling just to survive in the Nationwide League.

Their next match was at Crystal Palace, a fixture given extra spice because of the two men in charge at Selhurst Park. Both the Palace boss, Dave Bassett, and the club's technical director, Steve Coppell, had been linked with the City job. Bassett's case was strengthened as his young side ran out 3-1 winners. Afterwards, he took centre stage in the cramped press room at the back of the main stand and attempted to deflect questions about City.

"If Cindy Crawford asked me to take her out I'd have a problem, but I know she ain't so why should I talk about turning something down that I haven't been offered?" asked Bassett. "Do you want to write tonight that I've turned down Newcastle, Man United, Man City, Everton, Liverpool and Rochdale, because it's not the case. So I can't stop speculation. You lads all start it. You get your rumours from somewhere... by the way, I've just put a bid in for Franco Baresi."

He was kidding no-one. As he sloped off, presumably for more talks with City's hierarchy, Bassett expected to take over at Maine Road before the week was out. He had been offered the job before – back in 1987 when Mel Machin eventually took over – but had opted to join Watford instead. This time, the former non-league player had decided the time was right. A proven man-manager, achieving six promotions with Wimbledon and Sheffield United, Bassett's credentials suggested he might succeed where so many others had failed.

Three days after the Palace defeat, City suffered further humiliation at Third Division Lincoln. It was the first round of the League Cup and Hartford's side succumbed to one of the most humbling defeats in City's history. Despite taking an early lead through Uwe Rosler, the Blues slumped to a demoralising 4-1 loss. The newspapers branded the performance "a disgrace" and splashed photographs of shame-faced players over their back pages. Michael Brown remembers that night well.

"Asa was nominally in charge after Bally was sacked but I think Franny was still calling the shots," he says. "Franny called me round to his house and asked me why I wasn't playing well any more. He then said he would play me at Lincoln and if I did well then I would stay in the team. In the event, I was played on the left wing, which was laughable, and we lost 4-1."

Less than 48 hours later there was to be another bombshell, this time delivered by Dave Bassett. After initially accepting the offer to become City's manager, he had changed his mind. Francis Lee was flabbergasted. He had met with Bassett the night before and a deal had been struck.

"When he was leaving after shaking hands to become our new manager he said, 'I am a Southern League player who became a manager. I have never played the game at your level or perhaps know it at your level.' I looked at Colin Barlow and we both said to each other, 'What an odd thing to say.' The following morning, Dave rang me at 6.30 am, woke me up and said he could not accept the job. To be honest, I never got a satisfactory reason why he had changed his mind so quickly."

Bassett's about-turn had further tainted the job. Suddenly, it was being dubbed as the position which nobody wanted. Bassett made a valiant attempt to offer an excuse, but it could not deflect the damage inflicted on City's image. "Francis Lee bent over backwards and pulled out all the stops to convince me that Manchester City was the right job but I had to make a decision which I thought was right for Dave Bassett," he said. "The pull of working with the players at Palace swung it that way. I want job satisfaction. The contract Francis was offering was infinitely better than the contract I'm on at Crystal Palace so it's not down to money. He was making several million pounds available for players and he did his best to convince me to go to Manchester City. Other than kidnapping me he did everything possible."

With Bassett out of the equation, City turned their attention back to his colleague at Selhurst Park, Steve Coppell. Former manager Howard Kendall was also considered but his current club, Sheffield United, refused permission to make an approach. Coppell was still a relatively young man who appeared enthusiastic about returning to the day-to-day duties of a club manager. He did not have to travel far from his home in south east London for his job interview. It took place in Finchley at the home of businessman David Bernstein, who had joined the Maine Road board just under two years earlier.

"I interviewed Steve in the front room at my house," says Bernstein. "I almost felt like putting up a plaque to say this is where we interviewed the manager who will turn around City's fortunes. Obviously, it didn't quite turn out that way."

Bernstein had become an increasingly influential figure at Maine Road since becoming a director late in 1994. He had initially been enlisted as a financial advisor for Francis Lee's takeover bid. "It was suggested to me through a contact in Manchester that I should meet up with Mike Summerbee to talk about the Francis Lee takeover bid. Mike introduced me to Francis at Mottram Hall. We had never met before but hit it off immediately. I offered my help, although it was very late in the day."

Born in St Helens in 1943, Bernstein was the only City supporter in his school. He qualified as a chartered accountant before moving into the world of business. By the early 1990s, he was the joint managing director of the Pentland Leisurewear Group and a non-executive director of sports clothing company Blacks Leisure. Despite moving down to London in the early 1970s, he had not lost his affinity with Maine Road. His wife, Gillian, and four sons were quickly converted to the Blue faith as Bernstein managed to maintain a long-distance love affair with his chosen team. When he was offered a chance to join the board, it was an opportunity he could not turn down.

"I felt very privileged and was delighted to accept, as I suppose every supporter would be. I invested a certain amount of money with the consortium and once Francis took over, I became an insider and we talked together quite a lot. When I came on the board, I got involved more quickly than I expected. When you come into a situation like this, it is totally awe-inspiring. I had a lot of experience in boardrooms, but I thought I would be very much on the periphery here.

"But I got drawn in very quickly. I was particularly involved in financial and structural issues. Both areas are a strength of mine and I helped Francis a great deal in that respect. As time went on, though, I became his first port of call on a number of issues. It was mainly financial matters at first, but after a while it was everything.

"Francis dealt with things, but he would phone me almost daily. People used to joke that if you had a problem, 'Phone David.' That wasn't the case at the beginning, but it developed over the three-year period. We had a very regular dialogue during 1996, which was a particularly traumatic time for the club. I had a degree of influence, but Francis was in charge, there's no question about that."

Bernstein, who owned around one per cent of the club, became Lee's most trusted lieutenant. And the London-based businessman, who was now also the chairman of fashion chain French Connection, had decided that Coppell was the answer to their managerial woes.

As City's latest boss emerged from the grey Mercedes which had drawn up outside Maine Road, there was a brief burst of applause from the waiting fans. Coppell, a trim figure looking smart in a dark stylish suit and tie, walked briskly up the steps and into the ground. The Liverpudlian knew his way – he had been there many times before, as a player with Manchester United and as a manager with Crystal Palace.

Aged 41, he was articulate and – for football – a deep thinker. Back in the 1970s, he had combined his studies at Liverpool University with a part-time career at Tranmere Rovers. His incisive play on the wing earned him a move to Manchester United and he went on to win 42 caps for England. At £30,000, Coppell was described by United boss Tommy Docherty as "the best signing I ever made."

As an up and coming manager, Coppell had guided Crystal Palace to the 1990 FA Cup Final against his old club. He was an intelligent tactician who had broadened his knowledge by studying coaching methods abroad. Now, after three years away from the pressures of management, he was stepping into arguably the hottest seat in football. Yet he seemed totally at ease as he faced the glare of the media on his first day in charge in early October.

"It's nice to be back in Manchester. I still consider myself a Northerner so it's good to be not quite home but not far from home," were his opening words. "This is a magnificent opportunity and that is the way I look upon it. I want to do well here. I'm determined to do my best and get this club back in the Premiership. It's a great chance for me and I just hope I can repay the faith that Francis Lee and his board and the Manchester public are now placing in me. "I'm excited about the potential but that means nothing now. It's all about the team and getting the players in the right frame of mind and giving them an environment in which they can produce their best on a week to week basis."

It was an impressive debut as he skilfully handled the questions from the floor, including the vexed question of how a man with such deep Red roots could be accepted by their arch rivals. "It's a long time since I was a player. I'm just a faded image on Denis Waterman's *Matches of the Seventies* television series. It's not about the past, it's about the present and the future."

For his number two, Coppell turned to former England colleague Phil Neal, who was manager of Cardiff City at the time. Neal had become one of the most decorated players of his generation during a glittering career with Liverpool. He was Bob Paisley's first major signing in 1974 and after winning eight League Championship medals at Anfield, embarked on a career in management as player-boss at Bolton Wanderers. He later went on to manage Coventry and was assistant to Graham Taylor during England's ill-fated bid to qualify for the 1994 World Cup. Channel Four's infamous television documentary chronicling the campaign, which portrayed Neal as the manager's parrot, copying his touchline instructions, did little to enhance his reputation.

But he was excited to be invited to join the Coppell team: "It's great to be back. When Stevie gave me the opportunity there was only one way forward and that was to come back to the North West. It's the Mecca of football and I'm privileged now to be with what is undoubtedly one of the top six clubs in the country and I'm looking forward to a big challenge."

Neal could scarcely have imagined how great the challenge would be. But at least City had managed to temporarily halt their managerial search. The relief was almost audible as Coppell took charge of his first home match against Norwich City on 19 October. The match-day programme printed a full list of all the people who had been linked with the manager's job in one way or another. It offered a graphic illustration of how the club's plight had begun to dominate the back pages. There were 35 different names: Francis Lee, Asa Hartford, George Graham, Bruce Rioch, Dave Bassett, Howard Kendall, Kenny Dalglish, Alan Curbishley, Tony Woodcock, Howard Wilkinson, Terry Venables, Lennie Lawrence, Lou Macari, Ray Wilkins, Bryan Hamilton, Tommy Docherty, Ron Atkinson, Martin O'Neill, Brian Kidd, Steve Bruce, Frank Clark, Stuart Pearce, Danny Wilson, Jack Charlton, Johan Cruyff, Steve McMahon, Willie Donachie, Neil Warnock, Sammy McIlroy, Jim Jefferies, Denis Smith, Chris Waddle, Sam Allardyce, Brian Flynn and Steve Coppell.

In the event, only Coppell, Graham and Howard Wilkinson, who had left Leeds, were actually interviewed for the job, although the club did speak to a number of foreign managers as they cast the net far and wide.

Coppell, meanwhile, was having to get used to commuting as he switched between Manchester and London, where his family was based. After away matches at QPR and Reading, it was back to Maine Road for the visit of Norwich and then Wolves before he was back south for games against Southend and Swindon. His record was mixed, picking up two victories, one draw and three defeats in his six matches in charge. Within minutes of the final whistle at the County Ground, Coppell was rushing off – with familiar travel bag in hand – to catch a train.

There was no game the following weekend because of international commitments but rumours were beginning to spread about the manager's health. It was being suggested he was going to take an enforced break to recover from illness. When City called a hastily-arranged press conference on the morning of 8 November, it was clear the rumours had some substance, but few could have imagined what was to happen.

Coppell, looking pale and gaunt, twitched nervously as he sat down next to his chairman to face the assembled media once again. It was same room in which he had been unveiled as City's boss some 32 days earlier. This time Coppell looked very different from the confident and eloquent figure who had assumed control. Glancing up just briefly, he barely paused as he read out a pre-prepared statement word for word.

"If you don't mind I'd just like to read the statement and then go and not answer questions," he said in a strained voice. "For the last eighteen months I have wanted to manage a football club so when I was given the job as manager of Manchester City I was proud, excited and delighted. I was also determined to be a success and return the club to its rightful place in the Premiership. I'm not ashamed to admit that I have suffered for some time from the huge pressure I have imposed on myself and since my appointment this has completely overwhelmed me to such an extent that I cannot function in the job the way I would like to.

"As this situation is affecting my well being, I have asked Francis Lee to relieve me of my obligation to manage the club on medical advice. I am therefore resigning solely for personal reasons. I am extremely embarrassed by this situation and I would like to apologise first and foremost to Francis Lee and his board who have done everything in their power to help me.

"Francis has been particularly understanding and I'd like to thank him for that. I'd also like to thank and wish good luck to the players and staff. Their attitude and approach has been superb over the last six games and will hold them in good stead over the coming months. "Finally I would just like to say sorry to the supporters of Manchester City who have, to a person, made me feel very welcome. This is obviously not the way I intended events to happen. This is the hardest thing I have ever had to do and I can only say that the decision I have made is an honest one made in the best interests of the club as well as myself. Thank you very much."

With that, Coppell was gone. He darted out of the room, through into the Blue Room which led to the directors' box and scurried across the pitch to his car. He seemed in a daze, even shrugging aside a request from a senior club official who wanted a brief word. The spotlight was suddenly shifted back on to Francis Lee, who was left to try to explain Coppell's baffling actions.

"Phil Neal will be the manager for the foreseeable future," he blurted out, before re-iterating the reasons for Coppell's resignation. It was "stress", he maintained, but the rumour mill was already beginning to churn again. For the next few days, the dressing room was rife with outlandish suggestions; at one newspaper, reporters were encouraged to ring up health clinics in New York and ask to speak to Mr Coppell. It was also suggested that the former United man had merely fallen out with his chairman, a charge which Lee fiercely denies.

"The real reason why Steve resigned has never come out and I am not about to betray his confidence," says Lee. "Suffice to say, it was personal and private. He came to see me the week before he left and was in a very distressed state. He said he was very poorly, he had problems in his personal life and was becoming a nervous wreck.

"Rather than tough it out, he decided to give in to it. I have got letters from him thanking me for the way I looked after him. He said he was going to Manhattan when he resigned to get away from it all. I even offered to get my son, Gary, to drive him up to Scotland so he could relax up there for a while. Steve was so upset, but it was nothing to do with football or the football club. There is no doubt about that."

For Bernstein, who had been instrumental in Coppell's appointment, it was particularly galling. Just as it seemed the club had turned the corner, they had hit another brick wall. "I was absolutely shocked," remembers Bernstein. "Francis rang me at home and I remember it was a lovely Sunday evening. He said, 'We've got a problem, Steve wants to resign.' I told Francis to delay him and I set up a meeting with Steve, but he was intent on leaving for the reasons he gave in his press conference. I asked if he had any problems with the board, and he said no. I felt humiliated, like the rest of the fans did. I would pray that City would not appear in the papers, but we were there all the time, and it was always the most appalling news."

It was left up to Neal to inform the players of the latest twist in City's season. The former Bolton manager had no inkling why Coppell had left so abruptly. He knew, nevertheless, it was a great opportunity for him to stake a claim for the top job. "I have been in the managerial game ten years so I know exactly what the stresses are," he said. "I faced it when I had that short reign at Coventry. I was six and a half years at Bolton and I was allowed to manage and I've left assets that they're probably building their new stadium with now at Bolton. I've got a reasonable track record and I just hope we can turn it around and make the Sky Blues sing again."

Eddie McGoldrick's first instinct when he heard of Coppell's resignation was to get in touch with a man he regarded as a friend, as well as a boss. The pair had been together for five years at Crystal Palace in the late 1980s and early 1990s. He was Coppell's only signing during his brief time in charge, apart from a loan move for Crystal Palace's Simon Rodger. Now McGoldrick, who cost £300,000 from Arsenal, wanted to know why his former boss had walked out without any real explanation. The Republic of Ireland international left a message on Coppell's mobile phone but it was never returned.

"Steve was a down to earth chap who took everything in his stride," says McGoldrick. "He was a great tactician who put a lot of work into the opposition and how to combat them and there was no sign at all really of what was to unfold over the next thirty-two days. The only possible thing I could link to it is that we had four away games down south in his first six games in charge and he didn't actually get a chance to stay in Manchester. "There were a lot of stories flying about and certain rumours, but I think they were all unfounded. I do believe he had a few personal problems off the pitch in terms of his marriage situation and I don't think travelling up and down the motorway really helped."

Coppell himself refuses to elaborate on his reason for leaving, beyond saying it was "personal and private."

Phil Neal's first match in charge ended with a group of supporters attempting to storm the front entrance at Maine Road in a furious protest. It was not against their caretaker manager but against a regime which had consistently failed to deliver on its promises. The club had become a laughing stock and was now hovering dangerously above the relegation zone after a 3-2 home defeat by Oxford United. Andy Dibble was jeered by frustrated fans after his errors led to two of the goals. For Neal, it was a crash course in life at Manchester City. He vowed to carry on, even as supporters turned their attacks on to their chairman for the first time. Lee could no longer rely on the undivided loyalty of his subjects; many of them now blamed him personally for the club's plight.

Neal, City's fourth manager of the season, lasted longer in the hot-seat than any of his predecessors. Yet, after seven weeks, the club was still haunted by the spectre of relegation as Neal's side slumped nearer to the foot of the table. It was obvious he was not going to last. The once-proud club had become the butt of endless wisecracks as people joked that City were running their own manager of the month competition. There was also the one about the contestant on *Mastermind*, whose specialist subject was Manchester City managers, season 1996-97. Not surprisingly, Neal found it difficult to laugh as his future hung in the balance.

"I'm very honest with people and I want people to be honest with me. I've made that point to the chairman and everybody else. If he has decided to sack me then let me know. If I'm not involved in the future of this great club then would Mr Boler, or whoever is influential in whatever policy is going to be laid down, please have the goodness to tell me. I'm not here to be a whipping boy. It's unfair on me and Manchester City. I won't walk away. I'm here to help Manchester City and the fans deserve the club to be great again. I'm staying here because somebody needs to stay and direct the traffic."

The caretaker boss was not even invited to the club's annual general meeting, held in the top suite of the new Kippax stand. Any attempts from the floor to discuss his future were blocked as the standard reply came from the top table: "An annual meeting is not the time to discuss any employee's future."

The main topic of discussion instead centred on a new share issue which would raise almost £12 million for the club. Major shareholder Stephen Boler was ploughing in £5 million through new shares, while John Wardle and David Makin, joint owners of the Heywood-based sportswear company JD Sports, were matching his investment. With Francis Lee also putting in around £1.5 million, it was the largest total amount ever injected into the club.

The deal, which helped defuse mounting criticism from disgruntled shareholders, had materialised as a result of two chance meetings. Lee had met Boler at a dinner party at a friend's house in Wilmslow. It was good timing as Boler had some spare capital following the floatation of his home improvements company, the Limelight Group.

David Bernstein, meanwhile, had spent the past 12 months searching for potential investors. The club had been linked with a number of takeover deals earlier in the season, including a supposed bid from a group of Saudi Arabian businessmen. Bernstein was determined not to leave any stone unturned. "Myself and Francis spoke to so many potential investors at that time," he recalls. "Almost all of them turned out to be time-wasters. There is so much hot air in football. The problem was that we were 'in play' at that time. We were seen as having great potential because we were under-performing and our low value attracted a lot of people."

Bernstein was introduced to David Makin through business connections. Both were in the leisurewear industry and were avid City supporters who could talk for hours about the plight of their beloved club. Makin, tall and fresh-faced with short dark hair, was a season ticket holder, who blended into the crowd in the Kippax. Nobody could have imagined the man who hid his face under a City baseball cap was about to plough millions of pounds into the club. His partner John Wardle was more striking in appearance with his silver hair and personable manner giving him the air of a successful businessman. Their double act had earned them great wealth in the sports retail market and now there was another vital decision to be made. Makin desperately wanted to invest in his favourite club but sought the backing of his friend, Wardle, who did not share the same level of devotion to the Blues.

"I persuaded David and he managed to get John Wardle on board as well," says Bernstein. "Funding was so tight and we desperately needed to sort something out. John and David were the perfect sort of partners because they not only made a significant investment but were strong supporters of the club as well."

As City continued to fester in the doldrums of the First Division, it was clear the new cash was desperately needed. Under Neal, the club had slumped to fourth from bottom of the table – losing their fifth away match in succession at Barnsley on 28 December. It was a miserable 2-0 reverse, but the club's fans continued to proclaim their Blue faith from the terraces. "I'd rather be in Barnsley than Barbados" was the refrain from the visiting end, a reference to their chairman who had retreated to his West Indian hideaway for his annual break.

The contrast could hardly have been greater. It was a bitterly cold day in South Yorkshire, but underneath his bobble hat it was still possible to detect a wry smile from Phil Neal. He was even seen to conduct the fans as they mocked their absent chairman. Neal knew his time was up and resigned by "mutual consent" a few days later. As he cleared his desk at the club's Platt Lane training ground, his successor was sitting in a BMW in the far corner of the car park waiting for him to leave. It was another tragi-comic scene in City's slapstick season.

Frank Clark had spent his first Christmas in years at home, with his feet up, in the comfort of his favourite armchair. He had resigned his post at Nottingham Forest days earlier and spent the festive season with his family before stepping back into the crucible of football management. Clark boasted a fine record as a player and a manager during a long career. A native of the North East, he had played for Newcastle in their 4-3 defeat to Manchester City in May 1968, a famous victory which clinched the League Championship for Joe Mercer's side. Clark had played at left-back with the strict instruction to mark Francis Lee. Now the pair were to work together to try to recapture the glory days.

Clark had become a European Cup winner at Forest in 1979 and, after more than a decade managing at Leyton Orient, was summoned back to the City Ground to succeed Brian Clough on his retirement. An avuncular figure with a shy personality, Clark steered Forest to a finishing position of third in the Premiership in 1995 behind Blackburn and Manchester United, a feat which earned him the Manager of the Year award from his fellow managers. The following season, he guided the East Midlands side towards the quarter finals of the UEFA Cup before their fortunes slumped and Clark walked away from the politics engulfing the club.

Clark met Francis Lee and David Bernstein at the Edwardian Hotel near to Heathrow Airport. Lee was about to jet off on holiday to the West Indies and was hoping to finally conclude City's frustrating four-month search for a new manager. The Maine Road chairman and his right-hand man were quickly convinced that Clark could restore some order and stability to their troubled club. "He was the most senior manager available," remembers Lee, while Bernstein admits he was "very pleased" to get Clark on board. Yet, the meeting in London was to become a major source of contention between the three men. The cause was Tony Book.

After 30 years of loyal service at Maine Road, Book's time was up. 'Skip', as he was affectionately known, had captained City during their golden era. Though he did not join the club until he was 31, he was to lift almost every trophy in the game during the late 1960s and early 1970s – the League Championship, the FA Cup, the League Cup and the European Cup Winners' Cup. After retiring in 1973, he joined City's coaching staff, first as assistant to Johnny Hart and then to Ron Saunders. When the latter was sacked, Book stepped into his shoes and led the club to more success in the 1976 League Cup Final and then claiming runners-up spot in Division One in 1976-77. After leaving the hot-seat in 1980, Book coached the club's youngsters and later the first-team. A remarkably fit and popular figure around Maine Road, he was almost like one of the fixtures and fittings.

Yet, there would be no place for Book in the new set-up. Somebody had decided that he was no longer needed. Lee fiercely denies the decision had anything to do with him.

"One of Frank Clark's pre-conditions on taking the job was that Tony Book must go," says the former chairman. "I was going on holiday so I made it clear to David Bernstein that, because of Tony's long association with the club, we must do it in the proper way. I said that I wanted David and Bernard Halford to explain it all to Tony. But it never happened. David was my right-hand man and this is where he first let me down.

"Bookie says that Frank Clark told him that it was me who wanted him out of the club. Nothing could be further from the truth. When I came back off my holiday, I sorted out a financial package, I made him an honorary president of the club and arranged his testimonial which raised a substantial amount of funds. As soon as he had collected all his money, he slagged me off in the paper.

"But there is no doubt: Frank Clark said to me and David Bernstein in the Edwardian Hotel that he wanted to get rid of Tony Book and he cannot deny that."

But Clark DOES deny it. He is adamant he did not want to dispense with Book's services and believes it was the wrong decision to let him go.

"I didn't sack Tony Book and Tony knows I had absolutely nothing to do with that," maintains Clark. "I don't know who did it, or why it was done, but the decision was made before I got to the club. It was a disastrous decision, by whoever made it, because when I got there the kit situation was in an absolute shambles and no-one had a clue how to do it. Tony's main job at that time was to be in charge of the kit."

It seemed there was already tension in the relationship between chairman and manager. Clark was determined to maintain his autonomy and keep Lee at arm's length. His 'strictly-business' approach even extended to social occasions. The City boss would decline dinner invitations at the Lee household, preferring to keep his counsel on football matters. In fact, he seldom spoke to his chairman about team affairs.

"The only time Frank ever spoke to me about football was when he wanted to buy a player," adds Lee. "Mind you, it didn't stop him coming around to our house and keeping us awake playing his guitar until all hours, pretending to be Carl bloody Perkins!"

It was also rumoured that Clark was not even his chairman's choice. It was suggested that Lee favoured Howard Wilkinson and that Clark had been foisted upon him by Stephen Boler. But early in the New Year, the South African-based businessman issued a statement to set the record straight.

"Let me make one thing clear. Frank Clark was Francis Lee's choice right from day one. It was Francis who approached Mr Clark to offer him the position. Mr Clark was the manager Francis wanted and I was happy to support that choice because, like him, I believe we have finally got a man who will put our club back on track. "As far as I am concerned, Francis will remain as chairman in every sense of the word for as long as he wants to be. I have no intention of joining the board either now or in the foreseeable future. I have made a substantial investment in the club and it would be naïve if I didn't offer my advice from time to time."

Five million pounds is a lot of money and no matter how much he supported Lee, Boler was anxious. He was keen to come face to face with the man who would be spending his millions. Lee set up a meeting and still clearly remembers Boler's words of warning that day.

"Stephen had just put in that extra five million pounds and I introduced him to Frank Clark," recalls Lee. "When Frank had left the room, he said 'Don't let that bugger waste our money.'"

A fit-looking 53, Frank Clark had the air of a man confident in his ability to handle the fierce pressure at Maine Road. He strode on to the pitch to salute the fans on his first game in charge. It was an uncharacteristically grandiose gesture from a man renowned for his unassuming nature. His lugubrious expression was exaggerated by a trim moustache and sober dress sense. "I felt like I should have been wearing a fedora," he joked afterwards, in a reference to some of City's brasher managers of the past. Yet, Clark had no doubts that his more measured style could satisfy the huge demands of the Maine Road supporters.

"A club that can get 30,000 fans when they are fourth from bottom of the First Division and can take 6,000 to Barnsley doesn't sound like a job from hell to me," he remarked.

"We'll be bringing players in who will get us out of the First Division but will also be able to perform in the Premiership. I've signed a three and a half year contract and hope to see that out. Obviously, stability is something that has been lacking here."

Clark appointed Alan Hill, a trusted deputy from his Forest days, as assistant manager and the one-time Liverpool defender Richard Money became first team coach along with Asa Hartford. "We worked well together as a team," says Clark. "Alan Hill had the role of a roving commissioner at the club. He didn't coach the team but he was an integral part of the management set up and would be involved in team selection and how we would play. He was assistant manager but he was also chief scout and involved in the youth scheme. He was also very good on the PR side. He did a terrific job going along to supporters' clubs and making sure the players got there. That is a big part of Manchester City. When I first got there that side of things was in a bit of a shambles and players were going out to meetings on Thursdays and Fridays before match days which wasn't right. Richard did most of the coaching with the senior squad and they were both very good at their jobs."

Heavy snow fell in Manchester as Clark arrived at his new club. His first game at Birmingham was postponed as the cold weather began to disrupt the winter fixture programme. But Clark was determined to warm the spirits at Maine Road and summoned his players for a get-together in the top tier suite of the Kippax. The squad watched in disbelief as their new boss produced a guitar and proceeded to sing to them.

"The lads just couldn't believe it," remembers Michael Brown. "We were all falling about laughing. But he did restore a happier atmosphere around the club for a while. The problem was that nothing really changed and very soon things were getting out of control again."

But Clark's appointment undeniably galvanised the club as they pushed clear of relegation trouble. After nine League games without a defeat, optimists were even contemplating a late charge for the play-offs. In early February, Clark's rejuvenated side strode to an invigorating 4-1 triumph on a Sunday afternoon in Oxford. Georgi Kinkladze scored twice to cap a superb solo performance alongside Uwe Rosler in attack. Making his debut in midfield, Kevin Horlock looked a class act. A £1.5 million capture from Swindon, the Northern Ireland international was Clark's first signing in a prolific spending spree. Unfortunately, he would also prove to be one of the few successful purchases.

Paul Beesley was signed for £500,000 from Leeds United, but was sold on to Port Vale for £50,000 the following season. Northern Ireland goalkeeper Tommy Wright was recruited in a £400,000 deal from Nottingham Forest, but found his progress beset by injuries. Ged Brannan, meanwhile, was bought in a £750,000 deal from Tranmere Rovers to bolster City's midfield. The 25-year-old never seemed to settle and was later off-loaded to Scottish side Motherwell for £378,000.

Nevertheless, there was one signing in the last week of the season which would prove fundamental to the club's future. It hardly elicited a mention in the newspapers and the player in question would not trouble the first-team for another 18 months. Nicky Weaver, an 18-year-old goalkeeper from Mansfield Town, had only made one senior appearance when he learned of City's interest. The Sheffield-born youngster had been spotted by goalkeeping coach Alex Stepney in a youth game. Just one glimpse was enough to convince Stepney that he had stumbled across a major talent. Clark acted on his coach's advice and agreed a £200,000 deal with

Mansfield. Weaver arrived with his father, Alan, at Maine Road to complete the signing.

"I remember his dad was very enthusiastic about Nicky and it's great to see a father backing his son like that," says Francis Lee. "I said to him he reminded me of my father when I first joined Bolton."

As well as new players, there were also changes behind the scenes. Colin Barlow, the man who masterminded Lee's takeover, stepped down as managing director but remained on the board. Taking his place was Mike Turner, who assumed the role of chief executive. A lifelong City supporter, he joined from Liverpool Football Club, where he had helped to expand commercial operations from an annual turnover of £1 million to £6 million in five years. He knew the sports retailing sector as well after 13 years with boot manufacturers Puma. Now, he was charged with maximising the commercial potential of City's abiding support. Turner, a small balding man, was a chirpy character whose friendly approach lightened the mood around Maine Road. He was a drinking pal of former general manager John Maddock but had been recommended by the new JD Sports contingent at Maine Road.

In February 1997, Francis Lee reached his third anniversary as chairman at Maine Road. It was time to reflect on a difficult period in the club's history and hope for better times ahead. With money available from the share issue and a change in manager, Lee had reason to believe the future was looking brighter.

"It's been a terrible 1996, but seven is my lucky number so I look forward to 1997," declared Lee. "It's been a stormy three years and it's been very difficult with relegation, which was hard to accept. Playing in this League has been a culture shock after everybody was tipping us as favourites to come straight back. The last three years hasn't been as expected. A myriad of problems needed to be sorted out but we're on our way now."

Asked where he envisaged the club in another three years, he replied: "Obviously in the Premiership, playing at the new stadium and bombing along being one of the big clubs in Europe."

For the moment, City had to be content with finishing fourteenth in the First Division after a run of draws cooled any hopes of a belated surge into the play-offs. For a change, City's fans enjoyed the rare luxury of a meaningless final game against Reading. Nevertheless, the 27,260 supporters who gathered at Maine Road had a definite agenda in mind. It was the "Keep Kinkladze" campaign as fans filled the ground with banners, urging their Georgian hero to stay. Speculation was rife that he was preparing to move on rather than face another season in the First Division. At the final whistle, Frank Clark ushered Kinkladze to the centre circle to receive the crowd's acclaim. It seemed like a poignant farewell to City's most popular player. A month later, though, he signed a new three-year contract and pledged his future to the Blues. It seemed the supporters' impassioned pleas had worked.

Meanwhile, a refreshed Steve Coppell ended the season as a play-off winner at Wembley and looking forward to a return to the Premiership. By a strange twist of fate, he had resumed management duties at Crystal Palace three months after his exit from Maine Road. He took over from Dave Bassett, who completed the managerial triangle by filling the void at Nottingham Forest left by Clark.

CHAPTER EIGHT

Laser **surgery**

THE FAMOUS Sky Blues were no more. Manchester City were toning themselves down as they prepared for another season in the Nationwide League. The club unveiled a darker-coloured strip produced by the Italian sportswear manufacturers Kappa. From now on, City would be known as the Laser Blues. Tradition was discarded as the shirt became an instant best-seller.

Frank Clark was still looking for someone to wear the number nine jersey in his team. He had his sights fixed on a former soldier, 22-year-old Lee Bradbury from Portsmouth. Two years earlier, the strapping centre forward had cost Pompey a mere £500 when he signed from Isle of Wight club Cowes. He had bought himself out of the army to pursue his career in football and it was proving a shrewd decision as he began to flourish at Fratton Park. The 6ft 2ins marksman hit 15 League goals in his first full season for the south coast club. It was enough to convince Clark, and his backroom staff, to make him City's record signing.

Birmingham City were also showing an interest in Bradbury, but dropped out of the bidding at £2.5 million. Yet City ended up paying out £3.25 million to get their man. It was way over the odds and Clark's desperation to recruit a striker was to cost them dear. The deal was brokered by one-time City forward Paul Walsh who was now acting as Bradbury's agent. He later admitted that the move had come far too soon for his client, who was still adapting to the rigours of professional football. It did not take long for Francis Lee to come to the same conclusion.

"I was on holiday in Portugal when we signed Bradbury and I had never seen him play," recalls Lee. "I remember asking Frank Clark time and again whether he has sure this was the player he wanted. Frank assured me that he was, so we went ahead with the deal.

"But I can tell you this, we would definitely, definitely, definitely, DEFINITELY not have signed him if I had seen him play. As soon as I had seen him three or four times, I knew we had made a terrible mistake. When you have been a striker and have played with – and against – some of the best players in the world, you can tell. After half a dozen games, I felt like jumping off the Kippax."

Lee must have had an uneasy feeling as he recalled Stephen Boler's words: *"Don't let that bugger waste my money."*

Clark's summer spending also included the £1.35 million purchase of defender Tony Vaughan from Ipswich Town. The fee was set by a Football League tribunal and proved to be wildly excessive for the former City ball boy. Vaughan, a year younger than Bradbury, was also unproven at the highest level and struggled to settle into his new surrounds. A more modest £500,000, meanwhile, was invested in the versatile Dutchman Gerard Wiekens.

All three of Clark's newcomers were on parade in the opening day fixture at home to Portsmouth. The visitors grabbed a late equaliser to clinch a 2-2 draw and deflate the carnival atmosphere among the 30,474 crowd. Clark's side had failed to match the great expectations of their success-starved supporters, a trait which was to be repeated far too frequently over the coming weeks. The Blues did not manage a single League win in August and crashed out of the League Cup to Second Division Blackpool, with Bradbury missing the decisive spotkick in a penalty shoot-out. It was clear City's early-season optimism was going to be tested to the limit.

By the end of the first month, Clark had already used almost 20 different players. His campaign strategy was under review as he sought a way to turn around City's fortunes.

"When I arrived at the club, I decided fairly drastic measures were needed because we were third from bottom of the table," explains Clark. "I put Georgi Kinkladze up front as a floating player, knowing he'd pick the ball up in dangerous areas and do enough to win us games. It worked short-term because it stabilised things and got us well away from the relegation zone. But I was worried we wouldn't score enough goals with that system to get us into the promotion picture, which had to be the target for a club like City. So we bought Bradbury and I was intending to play him, Uwe Rosler and Georgi Kinkladze all in the team. I felt the three of them could score enough goals between them to get us up there, but it didn't work out for whatever reason. We kept changing it and ended up going round in circles. We finished up getting confused ourselves."

If the manager did not know his mind, what chance did the team have? The results were certainly confusing. After a glorious 6-0 triumph over Swindon Town at Maine Road, it seemed as if the season would take off. But Clark's side picked up only one point in their next four League games. Suddenly, the relegation fears of the previous season were back to haunt them. As the supporters lost confidence in their new-look side, Maine Road became an inhospitable venue to play football – unless you happened to be on the visiting team. Clark admits many of his players simply could not handle the pressure.

"When you come and play for Manchester City you've got to be able to handle that big stage, especially when things aren't going well. It's a double-edged sword. It's wonderful to get 30,000 people in there when you are really struggling at the bottom of the First Division. The support was fantastic but when the expectations go up and they're not fulfilled then obviously, like every other crowd, fans tend to turn against the players and you've got to be able to deal with that. We had a few who couldn't handle it when things weren't going very well."

After finally discovering his scoring touch, with two goals in two games, Bradbury's season was set to go from bad to worse. The young striker cracked his vertebrae playing for the England under-21 side and was sidelined for four months. With Uwe Rosler also out, Clark was left with few striking options. He gambled on a succession of back-up forwards from his squad – Chris Greenacre, Ray Kelly, Barry Conlon and even Gerry Creaney – but none could fill the void.

After successive home defeats to fellow strugglers Port Vale and Huddersfield, Clark felt compelled to act. He swapped Nicky Summerbee for Craig Russell, a hard-working but uninspiring striker from Sunderland. Inexplicably, Clark proceeded to play the 23-year-old at left wing-back, a position alien to him. As Russell later observed, "Even Alan Shearer would struggle if you played him at left-back." City's manager seemed to be losing the plot. He was under fire for his transfers, team selection and tactics, while supporters also began to question his powers of motivation. Everyone agreed: Clark was a nice guy, but his dour, phlegmatic demeanour hardly inspired confidence.

The manager was not the only one suffering. City's captain was enduring the lowest ebb of his career. Kit Symons had looked an accomplished central defender alongside Keith Curle in his first season with the club. But by the autumn of 1997, with the team toiling near the bottom of the table, he was picked out for blame. To even be playing Stockport County in a League match would have been unthinkable a few years earlier. Now, with City trailing 3-0 after half an hour at Edgeley Park, the visiting supporters turned on their skipper.

"It's probably the lowest I've been in football," admits Symons, who was relieved of the captaincy 24 hours later and never recovered. At the end of the season, he joined Fulham on a free transfer and enjoyed promotion in his first season at Craven Cottage.

"Once City went down to the First Division my form suffered terribly," he continues. "They were my worst two years in football, my confidence was shot to bits. I ended up almost non-existent and everything that could go wrong, went wrong. Some sections of the crowd started having a go at me. You don't feel like going out socially and you have to watch where you are going so you don't get into trouble."

The match at Edgeley Park also marked a watershed in Eddie McGoldrick's career. It was his last appearance in a blue shirt and, at the end of the season, he retired with a back injury. Symons was later to regain the captain's armband after the appointment of Joe Royle, but the job was jinxed with Kevin Horlock, Gerard Wiekens, Ian Brightwell and Jamie Pollock all trying their luck without much success.

There seemed to be no end to City's troubles. By Christmas, Clark had used 30 players in his quest for a winning formula but the club was still anchored near the foot of the table. Inevitably, Lee faced recriminations from supporters as their post-match demonstrations were rekindled after a 12-month absence. Yet, this time, there were also murmurs of a rebellion in the boardroom as the club's power brokers shifted uneasily.

The annual general meeting was a predictably rough ride for Lee as he faced a barrage of complaints about his running of the club. Only days before, City had been forced to settle out of court after all-time great Colin Bell had taken them to an industrial tribunal claiming unfair dismissal from his coaching job. Shareholders demanded to know how one of the club's legends could have been treated in such a way. Lee would later admit the club was wrong to sack Bell, stating, "We should have found another role for Colin. It was handled badly." How often that could now be said?

Lee's role was coming under increasing scrutiny as the year neared its end. The chairman was having to fend off endless takeover talk as speculation centred around the 26 per cent stake of Stephen Boler. He insisted it was not for sale, but privately spoke bitterly about his £5 million investment being "squandered" by Clark. The next biggest shareholding was held by John Wardle and David Makin with 19 per cent. By December, they were ready to make their move. Dennis Tueart was appointed to the board as their representative. The former City player had left an indelible mark on an outstanding career with his instinctive overhead kick in the 1976 League Cup Final. The audacious stroke of genius was enough to clinch a 2-1 victory over Newcastle United. It also assured him a place in City folklore.

Despite an affinity with his native North East, Tueart had settled in Manchester after retiring from playing football. He set up a corporate hospitality business, but maintained strong links with the game. Now, at the age of 49, he was joining a new streamlined board. Isle of Man tax exile David Holt, former managing director Colin Barlow and John Dunkerley, all allies of Lee, stepped down. As part of the re-shuffle, a new deputy chairman was also appointed. David Bernstein's influence had been steadily spreading behind the scenes for the past two seasons. He was now officially installed as Lee's number two, yet still little attention was paid to his promotion.

It was Tueart who grabbed the headlines as he spoke about "rattling a few cages" around the club. He added: "I understand a lot of business ethics and how business is run. I also know what ticks inside a footballer's brain and perhaps I can add a little bit to that. I have certain views and opinions and John Wardle and David Makin felt I had something to contribute. I will keep in close contact with Frank Clark and make sure we are on hand to help him if he wants." Clark, weary of the internal politics at Maine Road, famously told Tueart that the best way he could help was "to keep his mouth shut."

The changes in personnel were not restricted to the boardroom. City's Georgian dynasty continued to grow with defenders Murtaz Shelia and Kakhaber Tskhadadze joining Georgi Kinkladze. Lee had also agreed a deal to bring in Georgian striker Shota Arveladze but Clark, who had never seen him play, vetoed the move. Another of their compatriots, Mikhail Kavelashvili, had been farmed out on loan to Grasshoppers of Zurich. Kinkladze was also looking for a way out; he had had enough. Just before Christmas, he intimated privately that he wanted to leave.

Another player planning his exit was Uwe Rosler. The German striker had rejected a new contract and had already agreed to return to his homeland. Rosler, whose City deal was due to run out at the end of the season, had signed a pre-contract agreement with Bundesliga side Kaiserslautern. He hoped to keep the arrangement secret but his chairman soon found out.

"Uwe rented his apartment off my son, Gary, and he told him that he was leaving in May and would not be renewing his tenancy," reveals Lee. "It turned out he had already signed an agreement with Kaiserslautern. I told Frank Clark he should never play him again. I don't care who you are, if you have already signed for another club, you cannot concentrate on the business on the pitch."

With his leading player wanting out and his front-line striker already signed up for another club, Clark was facing an onerous task to turn things around. By the middle of February, his side had won only one of their five League games since the turn of the year. With Bury the next visitors to Maine Road, Clark knew anything less than a victory could be fatal to his job security. His demoralised side duly lost to their small-town neighbours with barely any resistance. One disgusted supporter forced his way on to the pitch and ripped up his season ticket, to cheers of support from all around the ground. Afterwards, police on horseback tried to contain an angry mob outside Maine Road's front entrance. But the most surprising protest of all was yet to come.

Presenter Jimmy Wagg was introducing the next caller on BBC *GMR*'s post-match phone-in. "And we're now joined on the line by one of the major shareholders at the club, David Makin," announced Wagg, with a hint of incredulity in his voice. It was scarcely believable that one of the club's owners had made an unsolicited telephone call to the radio station.

Makin was a Kippax regular who liked to blend into the background, despite the wealth which had enabled him to buy a chunk of his favourite club. He was shy of the spotlight but had now decided to use a public platform to launch an amazing attack on Francis Lee. His emotional outburst dealt a devastating blow to the regime.

"The reason I am not at the ground is that about six months ago, maybe four or five months ago, I saw my backside with the chairman. I think there is a massive chemistry problem within the club. I really do. He overrides everybody. He tries to be dominant. I am in business and I know if you haven't got a happy workplace then there are problems. I don't think City is a happy workplace and, frankly, I think there is a problem. So everybody is looking at Frank. Yes, I'll be honest, so am I. His tactics have left a hell of a lot to be desired but, by the same rule, I think it's upstairs and I think Francis should do us all a favour and live up to what he said [a reference to Lee's statement that he would get out within three years if City hadn't won anything].

"I get down like the best of the City fans and I've had enough. I will be doing my best in the next few weeks to remove the chairman because he is staying there and I don't know whether he is bloody minded or stubborn. He is being proud. If I was him I think I would put a moustache and a cap on and hide. I know there are people ready behind the scenes ready to take over. I am not going into any details.

"It can happen – that's for certain – and I think it should. I have seen enough and I know the fans are hurt. I still go in the Kippax. I have been near to tears with the best of them. The first thing I would do when Francis has gone is to find the guy who has probably been barred for throwing his season ticket away on the pitch and put him in the directors' box. It sums up how the fans feel.

"I own about ten per cent of the shares, or my missus does, because I was sick of it, I just wanted to get out. I was just gutted. I know for a fact that there are people waiting to take over Manchester City. I am privileged to know that information. I just want to go on record as saying – because the guy won't listen himself and maybe this is a way of pushing things along – that I believe the chairman, if he has any pride, should be walking away.

"There is no doubt that with the fan base they've got a chance of getting back to the top. But it is eroding, there is no doubt about it. My kids are in a

primary school where there are not that many City fans. Now when I was at primary school, it was 50-50."

LEE WAS OUTRAGED. He knew he had made enemies during time as chairman, but this was unforgivable. "I thought it was disgusting what he did. The share price of JD Sports had just gone down by fifty per cent but I did not go on the radio and call him about the state of his business."

Makin's tirade certainly did the trick. The board's façade of unity was destroyed. They were split down the middle and now everyone knew it. The following day, chief executive Mike Turner issued a statement from the board as they struggled to regain their authority. It read: "We understand the fans' frustrations and the manager is fully aware that the team's performance has to improve to reflect the high expectations of our fans." It was a thinly-veiled warning to Clark. The only problem was that nobody told him about it. The City boss was informed of its existence by the *Manchester Evening News.*

"I'd be grateful if someone would show me that statement. I didn't know it was being made and I've not seen it. From what I've heard it doesn't say anything new. I assume it was the powers that be trying to pour a bit of oil on troubled waters but it would have been nice if someone had mentioned it. I think I know in the short term the results have got to improve," said an aggrieved Clark, who was to confront his chairman over the matter.

With their next match less than 48 hours away, the City manager hurriedly set up a deal to bring in 37-year-old Peter Beardsley on a month's loan from Bolton Wanderers. It meant the former England international would achieve a unique record of playing for both Manchester clubs and the two Merseyside clubs. He would also have three managers in the space of two days: Colin Todd, Frank Clark... and Joe Royle.

Beardsley, unaware of the maelstrom he had stepped into, trained with his new team-mates on Tuesday morning in readiness for his debut against Ipswich Town the following night. Frank Clark was also looking ahead as he set off to watch Sunderland play Reading at the Stadium of Light. He wanted to run the rule over Reading, who were due to play his side in seven days' time. Joe Royle was also on his way to the North East but not for business. He was out of work and planning a few drinks with his old friend Peter Reid after the match.

Royle never made it to the game. While preparing to set off, he received a call to come and take over as manager of Manchester City. Clark was also contacted and informed the chairman wanted to speak to him. He offered to turn back, but was told the meeting could wait until the next day. By the time he returned from Sunderland, Clark was beginning to suspect his fate had been decided. By the following morning, there was no doubt. As he headed towards the Platt Lane training ground, the top story on BBC *GMR* confirmed his worst fears. He had been sacked and Joe Royle was waiting in the wings. Like Horton, Clark had found out about his dismissal through the media. He turned his car around and set off to Francis Lee's house.

"He sped into our driveway and furiously demanded to know what was going on," says Lee. "I tried to calm him down and told him it was nothing to do with me. John Wardle and David Makin had instigated it, but of course they left me to tell Frank the bad news. "

Wardle and Makin had taken control. Their representative on the board, Tueart, had contacted Royle late on Tuesday afternoon to set up a meeting. By the end of the evening, they had agreed a deal and Royle was ready to take over. The boardroom coup was complete: Maine Road had new rulers.

"It was the first contact I had with the club, which is the honest truth," says Royle. "I was being linked with City all the time but I never put myself forward and I rang Frank Clark later to tell him that. Francis Lee officially appointed me, but he didn't offer me the job. In fact, I know he wanted Frank to stay on. To be honest, the whole board were not keen to see Frank go, but they were forced into a corner by the team's results."

The power base had shifted and it could hardly have been more openly demonstrated. Lee was left on the sidelines as his manager was sacked and a new man was brought in. "I felt that even though Frank was having a bad time, he might have been able to save us from relegation," says Lee. But his views suddenly counted for nothing as a different top order at the club was established. Its driving force was Makin, whose radio outburst lit the blue touch paper. Yet he slipped back into the shadows as quickly as he had appeared. His business partner John Wardle was left to act as the front man, standing quietly by as the new manager was unveiled.

"John and David are very low-profile people," says David Bernstein. "For a number of reasons, they did not want to get particularly involved in the running of the club. They never pushed themselves forward." But nobody could question their overall authority. For the first time in years, even Bernstein was on the outside. He had not been on the interviewing panel for Joe Royle, but maintains he was fully consulted as Wardle and Makin homed in on their target.

"I had felt for a long time that he might be the right man for the club, although I didn't know him personally. I mentioned it on a number of occasions. I felt he was very positive and almost a natural manager for this club. We had to deal with the Frank Clark situation. What had to be done, had to be done. Of course, we made the decision to sack Frank with great regret. He is a very decent man, there is no question about that."

Clark left feeling embittered by his treatment. He claimed to have been the victim of a poisonous smear campaign, fuelled by a malicious element in the club. As he cleared out his desk at the training ground, he spoke about a "vendetta against the club," notoriously labelling his enemies as "the fifth column." To this day, Clark remains unaware of the identity of the mysterious forces who were undermining his efforts but is convinced they were there.

"You always get leaks in a football club because it is that kind of industry. You get leaks in government and politics and that's what makes the world go round. But a lot of the stuff that was leaked was detrimental to the club. It looked as though it was leaked deliberately to cause trouble or embarrassment to the football club. That was the kind of thing I meant by the fifth column. There just seemed to be a faction somewhere, not either in the club or on the fringes, but with a little bit of influence who were looking to do the club down. I never took it personally. It was the club that was suffering and that is what really disappointed me. I couldn't get to grips with it and I couldn't isolate the sources of these stories and it was very difficult."

Clark had arrived as one of the most highly-rated managers in the game. He left with his reputation in tatters. "My biggest regret about Manchester City is that it seems to have been the kiss of death as far as my managerial career is concerned. Once I was sacked it's not their responsibility to get me another job, but I've never really been in with a shout anywhere else. It seems as though I've just been totally wiped off the list of prospective managers for any other club in the country because of what happened at City. It's disappointing, but it's something I've come to live with." For one man, at least, Manchester City has ruined his life.

With Clark went his assistant Alan Hill and first-team coach Richard Money, later to join the academies at Leeds and Coventry respectively, and fitness coach Peter Edwards. The trio had almost been sacked weeks earlier. City's board had decided that Clark's backroom team were part of the problem and drew up plans to dispense with their services. Once again the story was leaked to the *Manchester Evening News* by a former director and shareholder. Clark demanded an explanation from Lee, who quickly dropped the plan. But Lee remains convinced that Clark was ill-served by his coach, Money.

"I think Frank's problem was that his coach had a big say in who to sign and, apart from Kevin Horlock and Nicky Weaver, they were all bad buys," says Lee. "I mean how can you swap Nicky Summerbee for Craig Russell? It's just beyond belief. Some of the players who came in were on big money and others were only on average money, so I think that created a bit of tension in the dressing room. I always remember telling Frank at Christmas that he did not have to play players just because he had paid a lot of money for them. But ultimately I think he just signed too many poor players. When the supporters began to realise that, they started to boo the team and the atmosphere within Maine Road deteriorated rapidly."

Joe Royle was not worried about the scare stories as he settled back into the rigours of management. This was the kind of job he had been waiting for during his 11-month sabbatical from the game. He had turned down 14 job offers since his departure from Everton, including the chance to take over as Northern Ireland manager. None appealed to him like the challenge of returning to his former club. He knew it was a formidable challenge. City were staring at the threat of relegation into English football's third tier for the first time in their 104-year history. Clark's 54-man squad was demoralised, while the club was riddled with division and dissent. But as Royle faced the press just minutes after his predecessor had slunk out of the club, he could hardly have been more positive.

"No-one has a bad word about the club. Anyone who speaks about the club smiles and says it's a great place. Anyone who has played here has nothing but affection for the place and you never get a job of this size when things are going well. I'm here to do what I have done before and that is firefighting to start with. We have fifteen games left and we need to get one more point than the bottom three clubs."

Almost nine years earlier, Royle had turned down the City job after a last-minute change of heart. The Blues went on to appoint Howard Kendall and became trapped in a downward slide which eventually led to relegation and upheaval. While City struggled, Royle continued to prosper. The Merseysider guided Oldham into the top flight for the first time in 68 years as well as steering them to two FA Cup semi-finals and the final of the League Cup. In 1994, he decided to end his fairytale story at Oldham and took over from Mike Walker as Everton manager. A year later, he had led the Goodison Park club to victory in the FA Cup Final.

It was a proud moment for a man already steeped in the club's heritage. As a 16-year-old, he had become their youngest debutant when he forced his way into Harry Catterick's team in 1966. Four years later, Royle was a championship winner as his burly physique and eye for goal became a potent weapon in Everton's armoury. In 1974, he joined Manchester City and scored 31 goals in 119 appearances, collecting a League Cup winners' medal along the way. After spells with Bristol City and Norwich, he retired through injury in 1982 and shortly afterwards took up the managerial reins at Oldham. Big Joe was dubbed Jovial Joe as he became renowned for his sharp wit and wicked sense of humour. After scoring four goals on his debut for Bristol City, Royle emerged from the dressing room to tell the waiting reporters: "I hope you're not expecting me to do that every week!"

His Scouse wit was in evidence again as he met his players for the first time at Maine Road. The shell-shocked squad were still absorbing the news of Clark's sacking. To deflect any tension, Royle launched into a joke-laden speech which, at times, bore little relevance to football.

"He was just like one of your mates when he arrived," says Michael Brown. "He was having a laugh and joke with everyone. I remember his first team talk was really funny – it was all about nights out and girls – nothing much to do with football." It was a far cry from Alan Ball's first meeting with the same players when the subject matter never strayed far from his World Cup medal. Royle's refreshing approach filtered back to the boardroom. At last, the directors believed they had found a man with the charisma and communication skills to lift their club out of the doldrums.

"His personality shone through immediately," says David Bernstein. "He has the confidence and ability to communicate. When he comes into a room, he lifts it. I have seen it so many times. It must have the same sort of effect on the players. He's great company as well and has a fantastic sense of humour. He was exactly what the club needed – a lift and a new sense of stability. He represented so much of what we wanted to achieve."

Within 24 hours of his appointment, Royle had renewed the managerial partnership which had worked so well at Oldham and Everton. At 46, Willie Donachie was two years younger than his colleague and had been coaching at Sheffield United in the months following his departure from Everton. A shrewd Scot, he was steeped in the traditions of City after spending 12 years with the club in the 1960s and 1970s. He was a model professional whose cultured displays at left-back earned him 35 caps for Scotland and a League Cup winners' medal with City in 1976; his cross had led to the winning goal. Since retiring from playing, he had become regarded as one of the best coaches in the game. Now Donachie, a fitness fanatic with a distinctive and deliberate Scottish accent, was coming back to his adopted home.

"City means an awful lot to me and I just consider myself a fan," he said on his return. "It hurts me to see them struggling near the foot of the First Division and it is frightening to even consider them going down. When I played here in the 1970s we were getting bigger crowds than Manchester United and beat them more or less every time we played them. But I don't want to dwell on the past. I'm here to help City now and our priority has to be staying up this season."

Their survival mission did not start well, with City losing 2-1 to a strong Ipswich side at Maine Road after conceding two late goals. The following morning, Royle was due to address his first board meeting and he knew exactly what was top of his agenda. He stepped confidently into the boardroom, took off his jacket and announced:

"We have to sell Kinkladze." They were effectively his first words as Manchester City manager.

"I told the board we had to sell him," says Royle. "I had my own ideas about Gio before I came to the club and I'm happy to admit that. I knew he had to go."

If Royle was expecting any voices of dissent from around the table, there was no need to fear. Most of the directors just nodded in grim recognition that Kinkladze's time was up. "I think most of us had come to the same conclusion anyway," recalls Bernstein. "There was a strong feeling that something was very wrong. Although Gio was a great talent, it was not working for us."

The fans, however, would not be so easy to convince. They adored Kinkladze and many considered it lunacy to even contemplate selling him. Amid the torment of the past three seasons, he had been the shining light in City's side.

"I knew he had fantastic skill," admits Royle. "In fact, after George Best he is the most naturally talented player who has appeared on these shores. The problem was that when the side won, he was fantastic, but when they lost, the other ten weren't good enough. You cannot have one player who's not putting in as much effort as the rest. At the end of the day, you have to ask yourself why the club went down twice if he was such a good player.

"But I want to stress there was never any vendetta. Gio is a nice boy. I wasn't making a big statement to the crowd or anything like that. The fact was that the team was not playing well with him in it. In all honesty, I wish he was arriving here as an eighteen-year-old next week. Don't forget, he'd been over to Argentina before he came to England and they questioned his attitude. It all came too easy when he arrived in England. He became a legend before he became a player. The fans idolised him and I don't blame them for that. They were crying out for a hero."

Kinkladze would make only sporadic appearances in the closing stages of the season. After playing in Royle's first two games in charge, the midfielder picked up an ankle injury which kept him out for almost a month. He returned to first-team action for City's trip to relegation rivals Port Vale on 14 March. It would prove the breaking point in his relationship with Royle.

The manager had decided to shuffle his pack after a disappointing home defeat to Oxford United. Ged Brannan was drafted back into midfield, Neil Heaney was given only his third start of the season on the left-wing and Kinkladze was ordered to play on the right. The Georgian was incensed. He did not consider himself a right-winger and had run out of patience with the club and with Royle. "I wanted to leave. I had made my mind up," says Kinkladze. "It was nothing personal with Joe Royle. He just arrived at the wrong time for me."

But it did get distinctly personal after City surrendered to Port Vale in a woeful 2-1 defeat. Kinkladze was anonymous, barely breaking into a sweat. Royle, the man who had so successfully forged a "dogs of war" spirit at Everton, was furious. In the dressing room afterwards, he confronted City's star player and the pair's uneasy truce was torn apart. "Gio had a nightmare and the manager went ballistic at him," recalls Michael Brown, who had come on as a substitute at Vale Park. "They had a real bust-up and Gio didn't play again until the last two games of the season."

Royle adds, "I told Gio that we needed our big players at such an important time. The problem was not just that he played badly at Port Vale, but he didn't even try. He just sulked because I'd put him on the right-hand side. I wouldn't say we had an altercation. I never got more than two words out of Gio all the time I was manager."

The fall-out in the dressing room was nothing compared to the seismic shift in the boardroom. The match at Port Vale also officially marked the end of Francis Lee's travails as chairman and two days later, the man who brought Kinkladze to Maine Road announced his resignation. In fact, Lee had already stepped down before the game at Vale Park. He had known the end was near for some time as the team laboured on the pitch and his power in the boardroom ebbed away. His grand plan to revive the glory days had failed.

"I knew long before that I was going to have to fall on my sword. Unless the team started performing on the pitch, it was going to be my problem. Nobody else was going to take any of the flak. There were all these things going on behind the scenes. And I was left high and dry on my own. If there was any trouble, there was nobody around, except me, to fend it off. Everyone else was in the trenches with the hatches battened down. I was General bloody Custer! David Bernstein was my right-hand man, and he is doing a good job as chairman now, but he knows where he let me down. But that's life. None of this back-stabbing matters if the team is winning."

Lee felt betrayed by his friend, but for Bernstein the partnership had to be sacrificed for the sake of the club. Lee's problem was that the team had only won 53 times in the 181 League games during his chairmanship. It was not nearly good enough. The supporters who had heralded his arrival watched as their team plunged into the recesses of the Nationwide League. They had lost faith in their white knight and urged him to ride off into the sunset. The mass support for Lee had turned into disillusionment and, ultimately, something more sinister.

"I had told the previous board meeting that I thought my time was up. There was a lot of unrest and it was affecting my family's health. There had been threats to burn down my factory in Bolton and, whatever you may think, you have to take it seriously. We had to double our security at the factory and at home, just in case.

"I decided to have an easy-going life instead. I suppose it would have been much easier not getting involved in the first place, but it was such a unique challenge and that is why I stuck at it so long. But eventually I thought, 'You're not going to win this one, Francis. There are too many horrible pigs around the club.'"

Francis Lee had been a winner all his life – on the football field, in the boardroom and on the racetrack. Defeat was a new experience and he had been humiliated in public. There was private heartache as well, with the death of his mother a few days before he stepped down as chairman. In the end, it had all become too much.

Looking back, Lee still remains proud of his record as chairman. He knows he will forever be judged on the results, yet believes they tell only half the story. He still enthuses about the hidden revolution which took place off the pitch. The culture of the club was changed, he claims, as a new marketing and merchandising strategy was implemented. Lee believes it is the success of that policy that has ensured the abiding loyalty of City's support.

"The big story of the 1990s is how City have gone from crowds of 23,000 in the Premier League to sell-outs every week now. I believe that is due largely to the way we changed the marketing of the club. When the attendance was around 23,000, we used to give away around three or four thousand tickets to local schools and the Junior Blues. In fact, the Junior Blues had fallen flat when I arrived. The first thing I did was to make it compulsory for players to go to meetings. I used to go myself as well and send my son, Gary, along. It started to expand quite rapidly which helps build up the fan base. In 1993, the membership was around two and a half thousand but when I left it was around double that amount. When you think about those children growing up and getting married, you are talking about tens of thousands of people becoming lifelong City fans.

"Platt Lane was a dump when I took over. The place was falling apart and the club did not even have a gym. I set about rebuilding Platt Lane, with help from the city council. Nowadays about 150,000 people use the building as part of our community scheme. If just ten per cent of those retain an affinity to the club, then it is enormous. We also built the dome (an indoor training centre).

"But perhaps the most important development is the eleven Manchester City coaching schools around Manchester. Around six hundred to seven hundred kids go through that scheme every week, which works out at around 30,000 children, between the ages of seven and fifteen, every year. It was launched in 1996 and I reckon more than 120,000 kids have been through the schools since then. It doesn't cost City a penny either. All the money comes from the lottery and sponsorship."

With the proliferation of supporters' clubs and internet sites as well, Lee believes City's fans now have stronger links to their football club than ever before. He even tried to forge a closer bond with the support, personally replying to hundreds of letters – by telephone. "I used to get between one hundred and one hundred and fifty letters every week and I would ring them up and try to explain our side of things. I used to spend every Sunday morning doing that, because I thought it was important."

Chief executive Mike Turner had worked side by side with Lee to develop the club's commercial and corporate activities. The pair, alongside commercial manager Geoff Durbin, managed to increase the number of corporate supporters from 520 to 2400 in nine months. Turner was also instrumental in turning the social club into a new City superstore and club administration offices.

"It was an unpopular decision at the time with a lot of fans, but it had to be done," says Turner. "We were making around £60,000 a year in franchise payments from the souvenir shop, but the superstore had a turnover of £2 million in its first year."

Turner collaborated with Lee to tie up a kit deal with Kappa. The laser blue shirts, which were struggling so badly on the pitch, became the best-selling replica strip in the club's history. "They even out-sold Rangers and Celtic shirts in Glasgow for a couple of weeks," says Lee. "We used the Gallagher brothers from Oasis to help promote them and the lads were very good."

But not even Oasis could save Lee. As he handed in his resignation to the board, his friend and colleague Turner offered to go as well. He was informed of Lee's impending departure over the telephone by the heir to the throne, Bernstein.

"As soon as I had congratulated David on becoming chairman, the first thing that sprung into my mind was that I should go as well," says Turner. "I had worked so closely with Francis and if he wasn't seen to be doing the right things for the club, surely that meant I wasn't either? I do have certain principles and I didn't like the way things were going at City. I didn't like the way Francis Lee was forced out. "I offered my resignation, but David Bernstein said that wasn't on the agenda. I think I still had a job to do for them, in terms of weeding people out and doing the unpopular things."

Turner would survive for another eight months before finally resigning. He has gone on to work as commercial manager at Wembley Stadium and remains unflinchingly loyal to his former boss at Maine Road. "It's only now that you think, 'By God, Francis was unlucky,'" says Turner. "You can say he chose the wrong managers but the board were also responsible for making those decisions. If Frank Clark had been a success, it could have all gone right for Francis."

To this day, Lee also remains adamant that he did not fail as chairman. "People can think what they like. I know I did not fail. A lot of people who were associated with the club know I did not fail. It was the players who failed. Unfortunately, it doesn't matter what happens off the pitch, the fans are only interested in results. They mask everything else. "The whole atmosphere of the club rests with the players that go out on the pitch. If they are motivated, they will run through brick walls for you. That is one of the great things which Joe Royle and Willie Donachie have done now. They have made average players believe in themselves. Unfortunately, I felt that was always lacking when I was in charge."

As Lee stepped down, citing the pressure on his family life, one of his former allies from the takeover bid, John Dunkerley, suffered a heart attack. While a director, he had divided his time between his home in Spain and Manchester, where his own pet project was the redevelopment of the Platt Lane Complex. Looking back, Dunkerley believes there were too many favours handed out during Lee's tenure in charge. "It was an old pal's act from what I could see," he says. "It wasn't a business. When the fire alarm went off, the staff would all come out and I didn't know we had that many people working for us. I thought to myself, 'What do they all bloody do?'"

The man in charge of all those employees was now David Bernstein. After almost four years in the background, Lee's number two was ready to step forward. But his entrance was very different from his predecessor's. Few could forget Lee's first day in charge as he saluted the fans from the front of directors' box. But there was to be no fanfare this time. Looking poised and determined, Bernstein assumed his new role with a quiet dignity. There were no theatrical gestures, just a few firm handshakes and sober assurances.

"I will be more low profile than this club is used to," he announced, in what some saw as a dig at the previous two chairmen. "At the end of the day, my job will be to hire and fire managers. I don't want to become known as a firer. Nothing would give me greater pleasure than to see Joe Royle leading us into the new millennium and beyond as manager."

Stability and unity were Bernstein's watchwords as he slipped almost effortlessly into the seat of power. He said there would be no more wild promises and instead the club would become "more professional and stable at all levels without the constant hype that plagues us." After trying unsuccessfully to shore up Lee's regime, he was now going it alone. Yet, with a personal stake of around one per cent in the club, he needed the backing of City's major shareholders. John Wardle joined the board, at Bernstein's request, in a public show of support.

"I would not have taken the position of chairman if I had not had the unanimous support of the board and major shareholders," says Bernstein. "I said if they wanted me to do it, I had to have everyone's support and there had to be money available. I said I'm not a miracle worker. John and David were the main providers of what was needed financially. "I think that having a small stake has helped me in a number of ways. I have always been independent, a professional manager if you like, and not governed by a huge financial investment. Of course, the cautious side of me had reservations about taking over as chairman, but that was completely overwhelmed by the feeling that this was a once in a lifetime opportunity. These things do not come around twice."

Despite the changes on high, there was no respite on the pitch. Royle brought in four new players, but it was clear the fight against relegation would not get any easier. Ian Bishop was signed on a free transfer from West Ham, almost nine years after he had left. Royle also snapped up one of his stalwarts from Boundary Park, Richard Jobson, on a free from Leeds. The most expensive purchase, Jamie Pollock, from Bolton, was bought with £1 million supplied by Wardle and Makin. But perhaps the most significant arrival came with only minutes to spare before the transfer deadline. Bermudan striker Shaun Goater was recruited from Bristol City for £400,000 in what was to prove one of the shrewdest buys Royle ever made. The manager sought a character reference for his new signing from Alex Ferguson, who had brought Goater into English football after the gangly striker impressed in a friendly match against Manchester United in the Caribbean.

Goater was far from impressive on his debut as City took on Bradford at Valley Parade. Clean through on goal more than once, he seemed to have left his radar behind in Bristol as he sliced the ball hopelessly wide. With Goater way off beam, the Blues lost 2-1 and Royle was left to continue his search for a winning formula. A total of 38 players had worn the club's colours that season, more than in any other year since the Second World War. There was no stability or continuity, a factor which Willie Donachie now believes was critical in their demise.

"I think part of why we were relegated was because we were too fair to players," maintains Donachie. "Instead of giving everybody a chance we should have been more ruthless and said this is the squad we're going with and ignored the rest. If anything that is the big mistake we made. When we first came there were far too many players whose hearts weren't really in the club. I don't blame them. If you're one of fifty-four pros and you aren't in the team then you're not going to be happy. In the reserves there used to be ten old pros who were very cynical and didn't want to try, basically."

Donachie had also sensed a change in attitude among the supporters. "There were a lot of people feeling sorry for themselves and that saddened me. They were taking the mickey out of themselves and laughing at themselves. All the pride had gone out of the fans even though they were turning up in large numbers. It is one of the top six clubs in the country but the club had become a laughing stock."

City were in deep trouble near the bottom of the table. Despite Royle's wheeling and dealing, his team had won only once in eight games. Their final home match of the season against relegation rivals QPR was critical. A win would have kept them out of the relegation zone ahead of their last game at Stoke. With the pressure on, Royle made an about-turn and drafted Georgi Kinkladze back into his side. The fans had been clamouring for his recall and Royle knew his side were sadly lacking inspiration. Even Francis Lee wrote a letter to David Bernstein, informing him that Kinkladze was keen to play. The player had opened his heart to his mentor after a lengthy spell on the sidelines. With the game barely 40 seconds old, the Georgian underlined his immense ability by scoring a stunning free kick.

"I brought him back for the QPR game because I felt he might just lift the crowd in that hothouse atmosphere and that was what we needed," remembers Royle. "I wasn't being stubborn not playing him. To be honest, a lot of the time he was supposedly injured, although we had our doubts. When he scored in the first minute against QPR, it looked like a marvellous gamble but 20 minutes later when he hadn't touched the ball again, all the doubts returned."

The visitors fought back. Mike Sheron equalised after capitalising on Martyn Margetson's mistake, but the goalkeeper's embarrassment was soon overshadowed by an outrageous own goal. Jamie Pollock, running back into the penalty area, looped a header into his net to hand Rangers a 2-1 lead. The goal effectively saved the Londoners from relegation and Pollock was later voted the most popular man in the world on an internet poll hijacked by QPR fans. Despite Bradbury's second-half equaliser, City could not find a winner. The point was not enough and their destiny was now out of their own hands. They needed to win their final fixture at Stoke and hope either Port Vale or Portsmouth could only draw.

There were plenty of things thrown on that last day of the season. Rival fans hurled bricks and bottles at each other as they waged a running battle on the waste ground outside the Britannia Stadium. And Georgi Kinkladze tossed his boots into the crowd. For the lucky fan who caught them it was a souvenir of the saddest day in the club's 104-year-old history. It was Kinky's final gesture as he waved a tearful goodbye after three years at the club. City had reached an all-time low and one of the most talented players in Europe had been a part of one of the most rapid declines in the history of English football. The club had dropped down two divisions in the space of three seasons and were now consigned to football's third tier. Joe Royle's firefighting job had failed but, through the ashes and rubble, he would build more solid, stable foundations and the club would be re-born. Now, though, was a time for anger in the sweltering heat at Stoke, on that awful Sunday afternoon in the first weekend in May.

The madness outside had been widely predicted after City fans were allowed to buy tickets direct from the Stoke ground. There were hundreds more without a place inside who sat and watched the drama unfold from the steep, grassy bank overlooking one corner of the pitch. When Shaun Goater scored after half-an-hour, scuffles broke out around the ground as the tension became too much for both sets of fans. With Stoke also needing victory to survive, it seemed the Manchester club had taken a vital step towards safety. Yet, as results from elsewhere began to filter in, it was clear both sides were doomed. Port Vale were soon in command at Huddersfield and went on to chalk up a 4-0 victory. Portsmouth, meanwhile, now managed by Alan Ball, clinched an unexpected 3-1 success at Bradford.

A handsome 5-2 victory at Stoke, their best away result of the season, merely increased the anguish of City's players and fans. New club doctor Warren Groarke, unaware of the permutations, asked innocently why the players seemed so sad after winning so comfortably. He was soon put right. City were down, paying the price for 11 home defeats, the worst home record in the country apart from Doncaster, who ended the season by losing their Football League status.

Within a few feet of a distraught dressing room, Joe Royle was, for once, almost lost for words. "I think we've been improving as a team but it doesn't matter now because we're down. The players are inconsolable and they know they've let the fans down. But I've told them this is a start and we must go on from here."

A few miles down the road, David Bernstein issued a public apology at a pre-arranged news conference in a hotel off the M6 motorway. He knew the fans had suffered too much and it was time somebody said sorry. "For the best part of two decades the fans have put up with a total lack of success culminating in two relegations in three years," he said. "Failure over such a long period is inexcusable and cannot be explained by bad luck, or chance, particularly for a club with our support base and resources."

Kit Symons, Ged Brannan and Martyn Margetson all made their final bows for the club at Stoke. Ian Brightwell, meanwhile, who had played under 13 different managers in 12 years, had been given a free transfer. Uwe Rosler watched the game from the main stand. Next season, he would be playing in the Champions League for Kaiserslautern while his former colleagues adapted to the realities of life in Nationwide League Division Two, with a local derby against Macclesfield.

But it was Kinkladze's imminent departure from his spiritual home which most vexed the supporters. The Georgian was back on the substitute's bench at Stoke after being flown in by private jet from Tunisia, where his country had played a friendly on the previous afternoon. After his farewell appearance, he was soon back on his travels, completing a £5 million move to Ajax. His three-year stay in Manchester was over but at least the fans had their memories. The wonder goals against the likes of Southampton, West Ham and Middlesbrough would never be forgotten. For many of his colleagues, there was nobody better than Georgi.

"When you talk about the marketing and selling of City, he has played a big part in that," says Francis Lee. "He put around three thousand or four thousand on the gate. He's doing the same now at Derby. Jim Smith asked me about him and I said, 'He will win you matches which cannot be won. If you can get two more players who are on the same wavelength, you will have a devastating team.'"

Eddie McGoldrick adds, "For pure ability, Georgi was up there with the best. At Arsenal, I'd played with eleven internationals week in, week out but the first time I played with Georgi my jaw dropped. His ability was unquestionable and he was a fantastic player. He was a cracking little chap and I had a lot of time for him. But a wet

Tuesday night at Reading or Swindon didn't really suit him and he became a little bit of a luxury."

City could no longer afford the luxury. With relegation looming and debts continuing to mount up, the club was dangerously close to bankruptcy. They desperately needed the money from Kinkladze just to survive. "It was critical, life-saving," admits David Bernstein. "We would have been in very serious trouble if we had not sold Gio. I'm not saying we would have gone bankrupt without it, because we would very possibly have found another way round things. But there's no doubt about it, it was crucial, at a time of extreme financial pressures."

It was the ultimate irony. Even though Kinkladze had not been able to save City on the pitch, he had almost certainly saved them off it.

CHAPTER NINE

Bouncing **back**

WILLIE DONACHIE was fuming. His steely blue eyes seemed sharper than ever as he paced restlessly around the Platt Lane dressing room. A quiet and thoughtful man, City's first-team coach had snapped. His temperate Scottish tones quivered with anger as he reeled off a list of match statistics from the previous week's encounter at Darlington. The facts told their own story as far as Donachie was concerned: City had dominated the FA Cup second round tie at Feethams. A late Paul Dickov equaliser had earned a replay, but it was the vitriolic personal attacks from their own fans behind the City dug-out which had left Donachie feeling sickened.

"Why was I, and all the coaching staff, subjected to a torrent of abuse from start to finish from our own fans?" he demanded.

The 46-year-old was dictating his weekly *Manchester Evening News* column; a duty thrust upon him at the start of the season, but one which he had adopted with typical verve and sincerity. Apparently free from the constraints of office or the curse of "football-speak", Donachie spoke his mind. And his thoughts on that cold December morning were dominated by an overwhelming sense of frustration. Manchester City were his club and had been ever since he left his native Scotland as a raw 16-year-old to join the Blues. But now he felt like an outsider, alienated by the tide of pessimism which had engulfed the club in the late 1990s. A studious character who preferred to slip into the background, Donachie felt compelled to step forward. His mild manner gave way to a granite-edged will to succeed as he issued a condemnation of the prevailing mood. On 11 December, his article sent shock-waves through the club.

"It hurts me to say it, but the behaviour of some of our fans at Darlington last week left me feeling sick," he declared. "Myself, the rest of the coaching staff and some of our players were subjected to a torrent of mindless abuse for almost the whole 90 minutes from people who claim to have the good of Manchester City at heart. It was the worst I can ever remember during my career and I can honestly say it left me wondering why I bother...

"The problem is that there is a growing tide of negativity around this club. It is creeping into every area – the media, the board, supporters and even players. I can understand that City fans have suffered more than most in recent years, but it is just too easy to slag off everyone and everything.

"I'm afraid that our supporters are beginning to wallow in City's misfortune. They are getting into a permanently pessimistic state of mind. But there is simply no excuse for singling out individuals for abuse when they are trying their best for the club... It is easy to say that all supporters criticise their teams, but why should they? Ultimately, we all want the same thing, don't we? Mark my words, if the doom merchants at Maine Road become the majority then we are finished. But I am not going to wave the white flag and walk away. I believe in the players and the club and, given time, we will get it right."

Donachie's inclusion of the board for criticism infuriated and shocked City's hierarchy. Chairman David Bernstein wanted to issue an immediate rebuttal, proclaiming his continued faith in the future and support for Joe Royle and Donachie. His mantra of unity and stability suddenly seemed under threat as the stress of life in the Second Division began to tell. Ultimately, Bernstein held off, allowing the dust to settle after the weekend's match against Bristol Rovers.

The fans, though, were not prepared to keep their counsel. After years of broken promises and shattered dreams, many felt this was merely another kick below the belt. Surely it was the team's responsibility to lift the supporters and not the other way around? If any set of fans were more sinned against than sinning, it had to be City's.

"I just felt something needed to be said," admits Donachie. "I never questioned the loyalty of the fans, I just felt there was a tendency to criticise rather than praise. To be honest, if I had not mentioned the board then I don't think there would have been much of a fuss."

There was little to feel positive about as Royle's side lurched to another goalless draw against Bristol Rovers. It was "the worst display of the season" according to the City manager, who had recalled Craig Russell and Paul Dickov in a desperate attempt to inject some width into their attacking play. It didn't work and, after 57 minutes, fellow forward Shaun Goater was substituted – to loud cheers from all around the ground. After a scoring start to the season, his powers in front of goal had deserted him and his confidence was fading away. The statistics, this time, were bleak: City had scored just once in the last six hours of League football and lagged 14 points behind the division's leaders.

"Maine Road is becoming a hard place for us to play," confessed Royle afterwards. "There are a lot of people getting very uptight and the players are aware of that. The fact is this club has been relegated twice in three years and it is no fun for supporters at the moment. Basically, we are on the wrong end of a lot of frustration and the only way out is to win games."

While there was little to excite on the pitch against Rovers, the sparks were flying around the press box. Earlier in the week, City had suffered the embarrassment of defeat in a first round tie of the Auto Windscreen Shield. The match against Third Division Mansfield attracted the lowest attendance in Maine Road's history – a mere 3,007, which was 1,018 fewer than the previous lowest. Joe Royle picked a second string side, yet still containing the likes of Jeff Whitley, Jamie Pollock, Danny Tiatto and Michael Brown. They duly lost 2-1 in a performance which the manager described as "disgusting." But it was the image of rows upon rows of empty seats which most occupied the minds of the press. As if to illustrate the gaping chasm between Manchester's two top clubs, United were due to play Bayern Munich in the Champions League in front of a packed Old Trafford the following night. The *Daily Mirror*'s northern sports editor could not resist the comparison. He printed a half-page photograph of Maine Road's empty seats on the back of the paper. The stinging analogy with United worked perfectly, but left many City fans feeling ridiculed. If there was one thing you could not question about the club's supporters, it was their loyalty. Despite their Second Division status, Maine Road had been packed out for almost every match that season.

Bitterness turned to retribution on that miserable Saturday afternoon as a group of fans attempted to storm the press room. They had singled out the *Mirror*'s freelance reporter at the game, Lindsay Sutton, who in fact had no influence over the paper's editorial policy. But that hardly seemed the point. City's indignant supporters needed to vent their fury on someone and Sutton was the unfortunate recipient. He needed a police escort from the ground and wrote later about how he came "face to face with the mob." Maine Road, so often the centre of disharmony and unrest during the 1990s, seemed to be slipping back into its bad old ways.

Bernstein and his press officer, Chris Bird, decided they could sit back and watch no longer. Although still determined to keep a low profile, City's chairman knew he needed to speak out. He called in the local media and issued a peculiar statement urging them not to criticise the club's fans. Yet it was his other pronouncements which revealed the growing sense of unease behind the scenes. Typically resolute in his support of Joe Royle, Bernstein nevertheless made clear what was expected: "I believe we have made a great deal of progress in the club, but I realise that until progress is reflected on the pitch, it will count for nothing.

"I have noticed a growing sense of disquiet among our supporters and I think they need to be assured that the manager and his team are aware of what we need. We are looking at ways of strengthening the side in a couple of areas which we believe are necessary. Hopefully, we will also soon see some more positive and confident performances out of this squad. We are very focused on getting things right this season and know the consequences of failure."

Bernstein knew the club was reaching a critical juncture; many more defeats and their promotion ambitions would be in ruins. It was a prospect he dared not even contemplate as Christmas approached. Yet the lowest point of his chairmanship was still to come.

City played their next match at York. Royle recalled Ian Bishop and pitched Craig Russell into attack, alongside new signing Gareth Taylor. The shake-up seemed to work as his side produced probably their most fluent display of the season so far. With the match locked at 1-1 in the second half, there seemed only one possible winner as City launched attack after attack. But then two substitutions changed the complexion of the game. Young Australian striker Danny Allsopp replaced Russell, to the consternation of the visiting fans, while 19-year-old local lad Anthony Dawson was brought on for York. Within seconds, Allsopp had spurned a glorious opportunity to grab the winner only to see Dawson go down the other end and score with his first touch as a professional footballer. It was a hammer blow for Royle, who confided his frustrations afterwards.

"It was a match we should have won, but it was just frittered away and we have ended up with nothing," he said. "If this was a one-off, then I could accept it, but it is the same old story. We have been unlucky too often this season and something is obviously not right."

It was a telling admission from the City boss, who knew he was dangerously close to losing the faith of supporters and his employers. City had slumped to twelfth in the table – their lowest League position in history – and were now closer to relegation than to automatic promotion. Looking back, Royle admits it was the lowest ebb of his Maine Road managerial career.

"I remember I could hear the fans chanting behind me. They were shouting that I didn't know what I was doing after taking off Craig Russell, who'd scored with a deflected shot. It wasn't nice and, in all honesty, we were suffering in that division. Willie and I were going to corners of the country which we'd never seen before. There was also the problem that teams were coming to Maine Road and it was a great occasion for them. They were just delighted to draw 0-0. But I remember saying in the first board meeting of the season that we would do better in the second half of the campaign when our superior fitness and size of squad would count. And we hardly lost a game after that one at York."

Bernstein also pinpoints the match at York as a nadir, but maintains the board never lost its confidence in Royle and his players. "Everyone was getting a bit nervous about that time," he recounts. "We were beginning to wonder what we had to do. We seemed to be doing everything right, but we were stuck in mid-table. But I didn't feel any pressure to act. I honestly felt if we showed a bit of patience, then things would work out. It was just a question of keeping our nerve."

Despite their demotion to the Second Division, City's supporters had not abandoned hope. At the start of the campaign, season ticket sales had already topped the 14,000-mark and their opening-day fixture against Blackpool attracted a heaving 32,134 crowd – the largest for more than two years. The loyalty was staggering as players who had heaped humiliation on Maine Road only months earlier were now treated like returning heroes. A new chairman and a new manager offered the hope of redemption for Manchester's fallen giants and there was no lack of belief as the Blues cruised to a 3-0 victory.

The high turnout was particularly heartening with the impending announcement of a move to a new £90 million stadium in east Manchester. After 75 years, the Blues were planning to leave Maine Road and take up residence at a 48,000-seater ground to be built for the 2002 Commonwealth Games. It was a heaven-sent opportunity, with City not having to pay a penny. The venue, to be called The City of Manchester Stadium, would be funded through public money.

There was another encouraging sign for the future at the start of the season when Royle and his trusted deputy, Donachie, signed extensions to their contracts. Both were now tied to the club until the end of the 2000-1 campaign. One of their key players, Richard Edghill, also committed himself, agreeing a four-year deal.

"I am very impressed with the club's ambitions and I honestly think we have the basis of a decent side here," vouched Royle. "Our immediate aim now is to get back into the First Division but the long-term plan is still to battle back into the Premiership."

For Royle, it was a chance to start from scratch and build a young side which could fight its way out of the Second Division and then punch its weight in the First. Nicky Weaver, Gary Mason and Nick Fenton were all plucked from the obscurity of City's youth team and thrust into the front-line. Royle had flirted with the idea of playing Weaver in the previous season and regretted his decision not to. Now he had no doubts that the 19-year-old was ready to step up a grade. In fact, it was effectively two steps up the ladder as six months previously, Weaver had been playing in the club's third team, behind Martyn Margetson and Tommy Wright. The likeable lad from Sheffield had been spotted playing for Mansfield's reserves early in 1997 and, on the recommendation of goalkeeping coach Alex Stepney, the then-manager Frank Clark had agreed a deal to buy him. Under the schooling of Stepney and his other senior colleagues, Weaver had begun to blossom into an outstanding talent. Yet it was still an almighty gamble as Royle penned the youngster's name on his first team-sheet of the new season.

"I'm sure Nick's surprised everyone with the progress he's made over the past two years," says Royle. "Don't forget, he's still very young for a goalkeeper. Of course, it was a gamble to pitch him into the first-team but I can honestly say that I never had any real doubts.

"In my quieter moments, I sometimes reflect on what would have happened if I had played Nick at the end of our relegation season. I could see how he was developing in training and his potential was obvious. But it would have been a very risky move to make. It's very easy to look back and wonder what might have been, but you live and die by your decisions."

Weaver was not the only fresh face to emerge into the limelight as the new season got underway. Scottish midfielder Gary Mason, a svelte 18-year-old with tremendous athleticism, was surprisingly selected ahead of more experienced counterparts Michael Brown and brothers Jeff and Jim Whitley. The Edinburgh-born playmaker was a favourite with Royle, who was already touting him as a future international player. Initially, Mason slipped into the first-team picture with disarming ease and, on a wave of enthusiasm, was handed a lucrative four-year contract. It would not last. Following City's desperate goalless draw against Bristol Rovers at the start of December, the youngster made only one more appearance. In the following season, he was sent out on loan to Hartlepool but otherwise languished in the reserves. After failing to even scratch the surface of the first-team in 1999-2000, Mason's future seemed in serious doubt. According to Royle, he had "hit the wall."

The wheel of fortune also turned full circle for Mason's young colleague Nick Fenton. Laudably compared to Alan Hansen on his introduction early in the 1998-99 campaign, the young centre-back soon found the rigours of Second Division life too much. After bursting on to the scene, making 13 consecutive appearances and signing a new contract, the Preston-born defender slipped back into the wings. He was nearly sold to Notts County on transfer deadline day in March 2000, but a deal could not be agreed.

Aside from the injection of youth, Royle made only two summer signings ahead of his first full season in charge. Both were Australians: wing-back Danny Tiatto, recruited from Swiss club FC Baden for £300,000, and striker Danny Allsopp, a £10,000 capture from Port Melbourne Sharks. Neither made the starting line-up in any of City's opening four matches and by the end of the season they had made only 11 full League appearances between them. Allsopp's early promise had dissolved as the campaign reached its critical stage, while Tiatto could not curb his tendency to collect red and yellow cards.

Royle instead turned to a man who had been put up for sale only weeks earlier. Kakhaber Tskhadadze, a tall and rangy centre-half, was one of Frank Clark's final signings as City manager. Another Georgian international, Tskhadadze joined Murtaz Shelia and Georgi Kinkladze as former chairman Francis Lee utilised his contacts in Tbilisi. But Royle was notoriously suspicious of imported players. At his first board meeting as manager, he had openly declared, "We won't be signing any more non-EC players." Tskhadadze was transfer-listed at the start of the summer but fought his way back into the reckoning. He lined up in a five-man defence, including Gerard Wiekens as a sweeper, for the opening match against Blackpool but after scoring twice in the first two games, he twisted his knee and ruptured his cruciate ligaments in City's third game, a demoralising 3-0 defeat at Fulham. He never played again and, after numerous unsuccessful attempts at a comeback, retired from the game.

Also retiring from the front-line were two of City's stalwarts from a bygone era. Freddie Pye, the former vice-chairman and loyal ally of Peter Swales, stepped down as the club's honorary president to concentrate his interests on Sheffield United, where he was also a director, while Ian Niven, City's longest-serving director, left the board and became an honorary president. The changes might have seemed cosmetic but they were just the start of David Bernstein's behind-the-scenes revolution. Members of the backroom staff, including publicity officer John Clay, programme editor Joanne Parker and long-serving accounts office worker Ian Niven Jnr, were axed. But it was the resignation of chief executive Mike Turner later in the season which truly signalled a sea-change in the club's operation. Turner, a Francis Lee appointee who earned more than £100,000 a year, reportedly left to "pursue other interests." Significantly he also departed with an undisclosed pay-off package. The suspicion was that Turner had been squeezed out as the club looked to slash its running costs and revamp its management structure.

Speaking for the first time since his departure, Turner says, "I could feel the vibes. They had got their own agendas and it certainly didn't include me and my agenda didn't include them. I have been in football for longer than Dennis Tueart, David Bernstein and Chris

Bird. At the end of the day, I had gone as far as I could at City and it was time to move on. I should stress it was an amicable parting of the ways.

"I had to carry out some unpopular decisions that summer. I delivered all the hammer blows – getting rid of staff, going to tribunals and dealing with claims for unfair dismissals. No-one else wanted to be around at this time. I think they thought I took it all too much to heart, but I knew they were strict business decisions which had to be made. City were still operating with a Premier League-sized staff of around 150 full-time employees whereas Macclesfield, in the same division, had only 12 people on the payroll.

"It's been suggested that my departure had something to do with Alastair Mackintosh's arrival as financial controller, but I was one of the driving forces behind his appointment. To say I was against the guy is totally incorrect. I had just come to the end of the road at City. Two weeks before I went, I said to Bernard Halford that this was going to be my last few days at the club and he couldn't believe it. I didn't feel the confidence was there between certain people on the board and myself."

Because of a confidentiality clause in Turner's contract, he has remained silent until now. It was left to Bernstein to explain the reasons for his departure. Typically, he sought to finesse the continuing cull in staff. "We must treat this as an opportunity. Nobody is indispensable and this will enable us to run the club with a lower level of costs," he said.

The club's press officer, Chris Bird, was duly promoted to the position of chairman's assistant. The 35-year-old, who also ran his own Manchester-based PR company, had been taken on towards the end of the previous season on the recommendation of major shareholder John Wardle. A lifelong City fan, he offered to work free of charge as he sought to impress his new bosses. The gamble paid off, with Bird quickly establishing himself as a key figure in the Bernstein regime. A renowned workaholic, he somehow managed to combine his outside business interests with a growing portfolio of responsibilities at Maine Road. For many, he was seen as Bernstein's henchman, a diminutive, yet dynamic, personality who openly compared himself to Joe Pesci's character from the film *Goodfellas*. At the end of the season, he was appointed the club's chief operating officer, while new financial controller Alistair Mackintosh joined the board.

"I think the relegation to the Second Division helped us in a sense," admits Bernstein, looking back. "I could now clear the place out without any opposition. We had fallen so low that nobody could argue. We had to move very quickly and relegation gave it all an edge of desperation. The board needed to be re-restructured and the management set-up re-energised. Sacred cows were slaughtered. Things that people said could not be changed, were changed. We needed financial discipline, a strong budget and big cost-cutting measures. There were salary reductions as well and people hate that."

The City chairman wonders now why his predecessor did not do the same. Perhaps, he muses, Lee was just too loyal.

"Look, I'm a different sort of person to David Bernstein," counters Lee. "My ability is to motivate people, I enthuse them and try to lead from the front. In the end, I could not convert all these people on the periphery of the club and that was part of the reason why I left. Anyway, if I had got rid of everyone, I would have ended up with six or eight enemies from day one, trying to pull me down. Maybe I am too loyal to people, but that's just my style."

The relics of City's past were slowly being dismantled, both on and off the pitch. Lee Bradbury was the club's record signing, but his £3.25 million move from Portsmouth in the summer of 1997 continued to be shrouded in controversy. The 23-year-old had managed only seven League goals in the previous season and there was precious little to suggest his fortunes would change in a lower division. With the season only days old, Royle issued a warning to Bradbury, urging him to "buck up" his game.

"I have had a chat with Lee and made it clear that we have not lost faith in him," said Royle. "But I also stressed that he has to get his game together. It has been a little bit loose recently. I felt the time was right to leave him out against Fulham (City's third match of the season) and that might just be the jolt he needs."

Yet, despite Royle's public declarations of support, the City manager was secretly paving the way to sell Bradbury. A story in the *Sunday People* stated the Blues were ready to let their costliest signing leave. Although officially denied, the story had been floated from within the club. Bradbury's unhappy stay in Manchester was nearing its end. By late October, City had agreed a £1.5 million deal with

Crystal Palace which would free up a limited amount of funds for Royle to spend. As for Bradbury, he had ultimately been sunk by a chronic lack of goals.

"Basically, my spell at City was a nightmare from start to finish," admits Bradbury. "The transfer fee they paid for me was really over the top and I think the fans expected me to be some sort of Ronaldo when I arrived. But the football just didn't flow and to be honest, I was relieved when Palace found a way out for me. I was also beset by injuries. I did my back in and then, when I started playing again, my confidence had gone. The side was struggling and the fans were not happy which just added to my problems. It was terrible."

Bradbury's last goal for City had been at Millwall late in September. His injury-time equaliser threatened to spark a riot as home supporters spilled on to the pitch seeking retribution. Moments later, the City striker could have snatched victory but missed when clean through. Afterwards, Royle reacted furiously, while outside, Millwall fans fought running battles with riot police.

"We could have won the match, but it's probably just as well that we didn't. I doubt we'd have got out alive," fumed the City boss. "I didn't know supporters were allowed to run on to the pitch and threaten and spit at players. Still, the crowd refereed the game very well. They appealed for everything and got most of it. I am very angry about what I have seen. It was a disgrace."

But perhaps even more surprising than the behaviour of the Millwall fans was the reaction of their chairman, Theo Paphitis. After a public slanging match with Royle outside the ground, he accused the City manager of being drugged up. Royle was due to have a hip replacement operation days later and would be relinquishing his managerial duties for two or three weeks. Paphitis suggested Royle's medication was interfering with his mind and branded the Blues as the "dirtiest side to have played at Millwall this season." It was an unseemly outburst which only served to fuel resentment between the two sets of supporters before their next encounter later in the season. Unsurprisingly, their re-match the following February sparked some of the worst scenes of violence ever witnessed in the ground as away fans once again clashed with police.

For Royle, his enforced absence from the manager's seat at the start of October could hardly have come at a worse time. He had known for some years that his arthritic right hip would need replacing but had hoped to delay the operation until the end of the season. The condition, though, deteriorated alarmingly as he became riddled with excruciating pain. Royle was not only struggling to walk and drive his car, he was also finding it more and more difficult to dress in the morning. For a proud and active man, it was an intolerable situation.

Willie Donachie took over on a temporary basis as City approached a critical early stage in their promotion campaign. After dropping six points in their previous three matches, the Blues took on Preston at home. Michael Brown was recalled to the line-up for his first start of the season. It was not to be a happy return. City were woeful as the visitors ran out deserved 1-0 winners in front of a restless crowd. None of the players covered themselves in glory but it was Brown who was singled out for criticism afterwards.

"Michael has been telling us how good he is and he had a chance to prove it tonight," lamented Donachie. The barbed comments left Brown feeling victimised. The young midfielder, a favourite with the crowd, had won the previous season's Player of the Year award but it was becoming obvious that City's management did not rate him. "I felt let down by Willie's comments because I'd never boasted about being a great player or anything like that," recalls Brown. "It almost seemed like they wanted me to fail, which I couldn't understand."

Within days of his operation, Royle discharged himself from the Alexandra Hospital in Cheadle, south Manchester, after a remarkably quick recovery. For the first time in years, the pain had gone and City's boss could begin to walk freely again. "Even immediately after the surgery, I was in less pain than I was before the operation so that probably shows what condition the joint was in. There is no doubt that I couldn't have delayed the operation any longer."

Royle's first public appearance after the operation came at the club's annual general meeting at the Bridgewater Hall in Manchester. There was uncertainty in the air after the recent death of City's largest shareholder, Stephen Boler. He had died suddenly of a heart attack after returning by private jet to his South African retreat. Ashley Lewis, who represented his interests on the board, had eaten lunch with Boler the day before. "He seemed fine, his usual self," recalls Lewis. "So, it came as a terrible shock when we heard the news that

Stephen had died." His 26 per cent shareholding was bequeathed to his family, with Lewis instructed to continue on the board.

Royle, meanwhile, received a warm reception from shareholders, but there was no disguising the tense atmosphere. The City manager was questioned about his team's formation and its apparent lack of firepower. Typically, he fended off the criticism with panache, but admits now that it began to rankle. "Around that time, somebody described us as the worst team in City's history. I felt that was unfair and untrue. We were going through a bad patch and I knew we needed to bring in one or two new players. But I used that criticism to motivate the squad. I told them that we had a great chance to prove people wrong. That is still one of the most satisfying things in life – proving people wrong. We developed a kind of siege mentality, it was us against them, and I think that became very important as the season progressed and we improved."

At the hub of City's revival was a man with a distinctly chequered history in the game. To many, Andy Morrison spelled trouble. With his cropped fair hair and meaty physique, the strapping central defender looked more like one of the Bash Street Kids than a professional footballer. He was undergoing anger management classes to curb his volatile, and sometimes violent, temper. They had not prevented him from falling out with his manager at Huddersfield, Peter Jackson. When relieved of the captaincy, Morrison reportedly threatened to hurl a desk in Jackson's direction. Not surprisingly, the incident signalled the beginning of the end of his career at the McAlpine Stadium. But while the rest of football steered clear, City decided to take a gamble on the 28-year-old. It was the club's kit manager, Les Chapman, who vouched for his character. Chapman, who had spent a short time coaching at Huddersfield, had been impressed with Morrison's inspirational influence in the dressing room. Now Royle was hoping he could do the same at Maine Road.

Morrison declared, "I am a good talker and like to get people going around me. It's never easy to impose your character upon everyone else when you come straight into a club, but I'll be doing my best."

Built like a heavyweight boxer and, according to Donachie, resembling a "pub player," Morrison made an immediate impact on his home debut against Colchester. His bullet header early in the second half clinched the three points for City as they ran out 2-1 winners. Young Everton striker Michael Branch was also making his first appearance after Royle had signed both on loan earlier in the week. But while Branch only lasted four games, Morrison was signed in an £80,000 deal which Royle described as "an absolute bargain."

Looking back, the City manager is no less enthusiastic: "He has played a major part in the tapestry of our success. We needed a leader and a talker and that's what Andy provided. Of course, we all knew about his history in the game but I think he saw this as a fresh challenge and a new start."

So City had their brawn but there was still a distinct lack of craft. Nigel Clough had been bought to supply just that two and a half years before. A £1.5 million signing from Liverpool, he was Alan Ball's last throw of the dice in the relegation season from the Premiership, but the 32-year-old famous son was an unmitigated disaster. In 38 senior appearances, he scored just five goals. With an estimated salary of £250,000, Clough reportedly cost around £50,000 a game. Now he was ready to admit defeat and retire with nine months left on his contract. City knew they could not afford to make the same mistake again.

Royle was chasing Aberdeen's unsettled midfielder Craig Hignett who was keen on a move back to his native North West to be near his two young children, who lived in Warrington. But the City manager was reluctant to meet the high cost of bringing him to Maine Road. Michael Brown and Neil Heaney were both offered in part-exchange, but the Scottish club was not interested. After three weeks of bargaining, the Blues eventually missed out as First Division Barnsley agreed to meet Aberdeen's asking price of £500,000. It was a humbling episode for City's fans, who were quickly realising that their club could no longer splash out millions on a whim.

Chairman Bernstein had announced a £400,000 loss for the six months up until 30 November. It was a considerable improvement on the previous year's results but had only been made possible by a £1.9 million reduction in running costs. More worryingly still, the club's turnover had plummeted by £2.1 million since their drop into Division Two while they continued to shell out £1 million a year in interest charges. Clearly, promotion was a financial imperative.

As the Christmas period approached, Royle and Bernstein knew results had to improve quickly as the club languished in mid-table.

But the relationship between manager and chairman remained a source of strength.

"I am very fortunate really because I speak to Joe every day, sometimes three or four times a day. He is very open and runs ideas off me all the time. We talk a lot, but there is no interference. I am keen not to take advantage of my position as a chairman-supporter. I would never tell Joe what I thought about the team or that this player should be playing here or whatever," says Berstein.

"I am very firm on that. I will not say a word when I sit next to Joe during matches. I have too much respect for him. To my mind, it would be extremely disrespectful for me to say anything during the pressure of a match. I have my area of expertise and he has his. I wouldn't expect Joe to start telling me about financial matters, so there is no way I'm going to bother him with my opinions about football. I think that has helped us to remain strong partners at the club, even during the more difficult times."

On a windswept Boxing Day, City travelled to Wrexham. It would prove to be a seminal game in their season. Despite being battered for almost the entire 90 minutes, City somehow managed to steal three points. Gerard Wiekens's goal at the start of the second half and Nicky Weaver's heroics at the other end of the pitch frustrated the home side. Meanwhile, in midfield, Michael Brown began a renaissance in form which would have a major impact in City's second half of the season.

"It was Michael's best game since I have been here," said Royle afterwards. "I have been accused of bias against him, but that has never been true. I have just wanted him to do what he does best. Otherwise, it was one of our worst performances of the season. We rode our luck and one way or another, my players just didn't look fit and healthy out there. Nevertheless, it could turn out to be a massive three points for us."

It did. Two days later, the division's early pacesetters, Stoke, were the visitors. As the half-time whistle went, a familiar groan of despondency filled the air. Royle's men were 1-0 down and another opportunity for a home win was slipping away.

"I don't get angry very often in the dressing room, but I remember blowing my top with the players at half-time," recalls Royle. "For one of the few times since taking over at City, I had a real ruck with them. I had to get about them and tell them it just wasn't good enough. We ended up winning 2-1 and people were racking their brains to remember when we last came back from a goal down. Now, it is a regular part of our make-up. It was a major turning-point in the season."

As so often before, it was the infectious influence of Paul Dickov which seemed to turn the tide. The ebullient Scot equalised in the 48th minute and then proceeded to chase every lost cause and strain every sinew in City's cause. His team-mates and the 30,478 crowd responded as Stoke were blown away by a unity of purpose and belief rarely seen at Maine Road during 1998. With five minutes left, Gareth Taylor, a recent £400,000 signing from Sheffield United, headed the winner and the ground erupted in delight. After a miserable 12 months, City had rediscovered themselves.

A little over a week later, Royle also finally discovered the finishing touch to his promotion masterplan. His team of honest artisans still desperately lacked a touch of artistry. It arrived in the shape of 22-year-old Terry Cooke, a 5ft 7ins right winger from the other side of town. The Birmingham-born youngster was another product of Manchester United's youth policy but a serious knee injury had drilled a hole in his development just as he was beginning to threaten Alex Ferguson's first-team. He moved across town on a three-month loan and with a point to prove. It didn't take him long to do it.

The Blues embarked on a nine-match unbeaten run, despatching fellow promotion hopefuls Fulham and Stoke along the way. Cooke was at the centre of it all, his ingenuity and invention setting him apart. If there were any fears about how his Old Trafford connections would be received, they were quickly dispelled. The fans loved him and he seemed equally smitten with his new club. But not everyone was swept along by the euphoria. Donachie, a renowned tough task-master, sounded a cautionary note.

"Terry has the ability to be a Premiership star or he could just end up a decent Second Division player," wrote City's chief coach in his weekly newspaper column. "He needs to dig deep and ask himself where he wants to go. There is no doubt that he has all the right attributes to be a top-class player, but it is just that extra five per cent which is required."

Cooke's application and attitude would be questioned again in the following season. For the moment, most were content to ignore

Donachie's warnings and instead revel in Cooke's uninhibited approach to the game. There was only one problem looming – his three-month loan spell was due to end with three games of the season left. If City wanted to keep him, they would have to sign him. Royle knew it and so did Alex Ferguson. The Old Trafford manager could afford to sit and wait; it was up to his counterpart to strike a deal. However, with Cooke out of contract at the end of the season, the Blues were determined not to be held to ransom.

Royle adopted a softly-softly approach, rarely discussing the issue in public and even, on one occasion, visiting Ferguson to explain a newspaper story which claimed the influence of City fans could help secure Cooke's move. With Bradford also reportedly interested in the United winger, it was clear City would need to find the money from somewhere. David Bernstein was in advanced talks with the Glasgow-based investment house Murray Johnstone about buying Boler's 26 per cent shareholding for £5 million and making a £10m cash injection into the club. Gary Tipper, a City fan and director at the firm, was earmarked to join the Maine Road board.

"The deal would have given Joe Royle money to buy players before the deadline," says Tipper. "City decided to gamble that they would go up with what they already had. Our deal valued the club at £30 million which they obviously felt was too low. We made a formal offer, but it was rejected in April. It was all very amicable. I have the utmost respect for the board and what they have done."

The following season, Bernstein would strike a deal with broadcasters BSkyB, which bought 9.9 per cent of the shares for £5.5 million to price the club at around £50 million. City's market value was going up in line with their surge in fortunes on the field. "I must have spoken to a dozen, maybe more, potential investors during our time in the Second Division," says Bernstein. "There were media companies, individuals, investment companies, but none seemed right for the club. We did speak to Murray Johnstone, but there was another offer which came closer to a deal. It is very easy to snap someone's hand off at the first offer, but we decided to wait. Once again, it was a question of holding our nerve."

Bernstein would now have to find the money for Cooke from existing resources. With one game left of his loan spell, City faced Luton at Maine Road in midweek. The home fans chanted, "We want Terry Cooke," and cheered his every touch of the ball. Little did they realise that a deal had already been struck with United. The Blues had agreed to pay £600,000, rising to £1 million "depending on his success with the club." After all the intrigue and behind-the-scenes manoeuvring, Royle had got his man.

For Cooke, it was a whirlwind experience as his fiancée, Nadine, gave birth to their first baby – a boy named Charlie – just hours before his move was completed. It was, according to City's new signing, "the most unbelievable twenty-four hours" of his life. "To become a dad is a dream come true and to sign for City as well is the icing on the cake. I loved it at Old Trafford and it was always going to be a wrench to leave. But City are another big club and they are so friendly as well. The fans have been wonderful to me. They were chanting my name on Wednesday and I knew I was going to sign but I couldn't let on."

Bernstein, meanwhile, believed the deal was a signal of the club's intent. The chairman had promised they would not be found wanting in the transfer market and he had proved his word. "This is a clear statement to our supporters that we are deadly serious about improving the playing squad and achieving success. Obviously we listen to the fans and I knew they were desperate for us to sign Terry. But I think they also understand that we must get the balance right between keeping the club on a stable financial footing and making the correct investment on players."

While Bernstein continued to preach prudence and responsibility, Royle was still searching for the final explosive element to add to his squad. Loan moves for the Wimbledon winger Mark Kennedy and Tottenham's Andy Sinton both fell through. Stan Lazaridis, meanwhile, agreed to move from West Ham, but then changed his mind overnight. Royle was unperturbed and switched his sights instead to another Premiership player. It was a startlingly audacious bid which has never been revealed before.

Steve McManaman was nearing the end of his Liverpool career. A local lad, he had supported Everton as a boy but joined Anfield's highly-regarded youth academy straight from school. By the early 1990s, his languid and fluent style had earmarked him as a future star. When John Barnes was injured at the start of the 1991-92 season, new boss Graeme Souness pitched the lanky youngster straight into the action. Within months, he was an integral part of their team. Eight years later and after almost 400 games in Liverpool colours,

McManaman had decided to move on. A pre-contract agreement had been reached with Real Madrid and he was destined to become the highest-paid English footballer in the world.

Now, though, McManaman had another offer on the table. Joe Royle had decided to make a bold attempt to sign the England winger on loan until the end of the season. The odds were stacked against him, but City's manager reasoned he had nothing to lose. Liverpool had little intention of playing the Spanish-bound winger much before the end of the season and the prospect of City paying his wages certainly appealed. Suddenly, Royle was within touching distance of pulling off the transfer coup of the season. It would have been front and back page news. But at the eleventh hour, Liverpool dropped out of the deal stating it was too much of a risk.

"Liverpool kept me waiting for an answer for about two days and I genuinely began to believe it might happen," says Royle. "But looking back, I think Liverpool just decided they could not justify allowing McManaman to play in the Second Division." A year on, the Scouse winger lifted the Champions League trophy after his goal helped secure a 3-0 victory over Valencia.

Ever resourceful, the Maine Road boss had another option. With the transfer deadline looming, he made a last-ditch attempt to persuade the former United winger Lee Sharpe to join City. The 27-year-old, now with Leeds, had already agreed a loan move to Bradford but broke off the negotiations to meet Royle at Manchester's Midland Hotel. City's manager knew he would need to use all his powers of persuasion to clinch the deal. Sharpe, though, was not for turning and, after listening to Royle's case, decided to stick with his original intention and moved to Valley Parade.

Royle was now left with just hours to seal a signing before the deadline. With his options rapidly diminishing, he turned to another former Red, Mark Robins, who was playing for Greek club AEK Panionios. The 29-year-old was a boyhood City fan and a proven striker, whom Royle reasoned might just be able to poach a couple of crucial goals in the final weeks of the season. Perhaps even more importantly, he was also a target for City's promotion rivals Walsall. Royle, who was determined to make a late charge for automatic promotion, decided to scupper their plans and managed to persuade Robins to move to Maine Road instead.

There were nine games left of the ordinary season and City were just seven points adrift of second-placed Preston. The next few weeks would be critical as they faced four of their promotion adversaries within a month: Reading, Wigan, Preston and Gillingham. Michael Brown had signed a new three-year contract, rubber-stamping his revival in fortune, while Andy Morrison had been appointed the club's captain, taking over from Jamie Pollock, whose lack of discipline on the pitch and straight-talking off it had forced Royle to act. Pollock was stripped of the captaincy on his twenty-fifth birthday and remained at odds with the City management for much of the rest of the season. But if he was in the doghouse, there was no doubting City's golden boy: Nicky Weaver. The young, blond-haired keeper had signed a four-year contract and was now chasing a club record of clean sheets.

"This club has given me a chance and I want to repay them," he said. "My aim this season is to get promotion and hopefully in a couple of years we will be pushing for the Premiership. I have read speculation linking me to other clubs, but it has never bothered me. I've said before that I'm happy at City and don't want to play anywhere else."

With Ian Bishop also back in the fold, Royle seemed to have found a winning formula as his side surged up the table. Reading, Wigan and Gillingham were all comfortably dispatched as the Blues completed a thrilling eight-match unbeaten run (including seven victories). But just as it seemed they might pull off the impossible and pip Walsall for second place, Royle's side suffered a familiar attack of the jitters at home to Wycombe. The City boss had ended his programme notes with a confident clarion call. "We feel we have succeeded in changing the perception, both in the dressing room and among our supporters, that we are unreliable." They proved to be famous last words as Wycombe punctured City's automatic promotion hopes with a 2-1 victory. Any chance of avoiding the end-of-the-season play-offs had now gone.

The Blues finished third in the table, behind Walsall and Fulham, following a final day 4-0 victory over York. It was Weaver's twenty-second clean sheet of the season and beat the previous record held by Alex Williams. Jeff Whitley also made his return to first-team action, replacing the injured Ian Bishop and scoring the third goal. Whitley had been transfer-listed earlier in the season and farmed out on loan to Wrexham, but now had a chance to resurrect his City career at the most crucial stage of the season.

"It's been a really weird season for me," confessed the Zambian-born midfielder. "I have not played at all and then all of a sudden I am thrown in at the deep end. I felt I deserved a chance after playing well in the reserves and working hard. Going to Wrexham was a great experience for me. I wasn't match fit or confident when I signed for them on loan, but my family live over there and they helped me regain my confidence. I have never wanted to leave City. In fact, I would love to end my career here."

Seven days later, Whitley was taken off the transfer-list and selected in the starting line-up to face Wigan in the play-offs. The Lancashire club had sneaked into sixth place after a late spurt of form. They were now determined to exact revenge for two slender defeats against City earlier in the season. After 20 seconds of the first leg at Springfield Park, it seemed they would not have much trouble. A calamitous mix-up between two of City's most consistent performers, Gerard Wiekens and Nicky Weaver, allowed Stuart Barlow to nip in and give the home side an early lead. According to Royle, David Bernstein turned white as he watched from the stands. But his side fought back and in the 77th minute Paul Dickov swept home the equaliser and a priceless away goal.

So City had the slightest advantage to take into their return leg four days later. An expectant capacity crowd gathered at Maine Road on a sultry summer's evening. The noise was ear-splitting and the atmosphere vibrant as thousands of flag-waving fans urged their side on to Wembley. It was a night of raw emotion, with City's future in the balance. The all-important goal came midway through the first-half when Shaun Goater bundled Michael Brown's cross into the net. Wigan manager Ray Mathias claimed it was a handball, but referee Terry Heilbron ignored his appeals. The incident proved decisive as City survived a late surge of Wigan pressure to win the game. Two days later, Mathias was sacked.

The tribulations of their opponents mattered not a jot to City; they had been through it all before themselves. This was their turn to celebrate and thousands of fans poured on to the pitch at the final whistle to eulogise their side and herald their return to Wembley. Royle, who was afforded a hero's reception, felt the adulation was barely warranted.

"This was for the fans," he maintained afterwards. "Too often in the past we have set ourselves up for the big game and then let everyone down. But we are resolute now and I felt there was never any sign of us buckling. To be honest, we don't deserve that sort of frenzy and acclaim from the crowd. When you think about it, we have only reached what is effectively a Third Division play-off final and nothing more. I want to give these fans something to really cheer about."

After 48 arduous games, City's Nationwide nightmare was finally nearing its conclusion. Their date with destiny was set. The only problem now was getting a ticket. Gillingham, with an average fan base of around 8,000, were their opponents in the Wembley play-off final. Yet, despite the obvious disparity in support, the FA inexplicably opted to allocate both clubs an equal share of the ground. The decision left thousands of City fans scrambling desperately for a ticket. It quickly turned into a fiasco.

Fans – including an 82-year-old season ticket holder – had to queue for more than 12 hours just to get their hands on a ticket. In the days before their most important match of the season, City's supporters were becoming embroiled in an ugly, and at times bitter, dispute with their club. It was secretary Bernard Halford who took most of the flak. He gamely defended his corner, but admitted the Maine Road ticket office was struggling to cope. "I can understand people being upset about queuing for so many hours, but there is not a lot I can do," he countered. "Our ticket office only has 10 windows and it is not equipped to deal with thousands of people at once."

The fans's mood was hardly helped days later when their neighbours won the Champions League in dramatic style to complete a historic Treble. As the Reds mounted delirious victory parades along the streets of Manchester, City's supporters could only shrink into the background again, waiting for their own chance of glory.

Sunday, May 30, was an unseasonably drab day in London. Steady rain had been falling for most of the morning as City's supporters made a half-forgotten pilgrimage to the Twin Towers. It had been 13 years (18, if you discount the Full Members Cup) since their last visit. There was an air of anticipation, tinged with apprehension, as they converged on the decaying old stadium. Suddenly, City seemed to have everything to lose. Their neighbours were European and domestic champions; their opponents were merely eager underdogs. After a remarkable run of form (only two defeats in the last 26 games), City's fate rested on one game – one unpredictable and impassioned occasion.

Joe Royle, a "big-game manager" according to his chairman, told the players to relax. If they believed, and kept on believing, it would be their day. With 20 seconds left of normal time, that self-belief was being stretched to the limit. City were trailing 2-0 and thousands of their supporters were drifting disconsolately out of the ground. Some had already boarded their trains home. The day of hope was turning into a day of disaster for City as they stared into the abyss of another season in Division Two.

Ian Bishop had joined the action as a second-half substitute. "I looked around and could see all the Gillingham flags waving and it literally made me feel physically sick. After all our efforts and belief, it seemed like we were going to end up with nothing. It was almost too much to take."

Michael Brown had been replaced and was watching dumbfounded from the substitute's bench. "I remember Chris Bird coming down and saying he didn't know what would happen if we didn't go up – and he's one of the directors," says Brown. "Everyone was just stunned. I honestly felt numb."

Royle could just sit, watch, wait and hope that his side could find salvation from somewhere. "I had watched Scunthorpe win the Third Division play-offs the day before and was starting to think, 'It looks like we'll be on our way to Scunny next season'. But, in all honesty, I never gave up hope. I knew my side had great resilience and would keep battling until the end."

With precisely 17 seconds left of normal time, Goater's blocked shot rebounded to Kevin Horlock who coolly side-footed City back into the game. Moments later, referee Mark Halsey signalled an additional five minutes of stoppage time. It was a contentious, and critical, decision. As Gillingham's players began to wilt under the pressure, a surge of belief was coursing through City veins. With four and a half minutes of injury time gone, a loose ball dropped to Dickov on the right-hand edge of Gillingham's penalty area. He did not have time to steady himself, he did not even have time to think, City's irrepressible striker simply launched an unstoppable shot into the top corner. Some things are just meant to be.

Royle thought his side would win it in extra-time, but they seemed determined to squeeze every last drop of drama out of the season. With the score still locked at 2-2 after 120 energy-sapping minutes, a penalty shoot-out loomed. Stepping up in front of their own rejuvenated fans, Kevin Horlock, Terry Cooke and Richard Edghill converted from the spot. Weaver needed to save from Guy Butters to secure promotion and he was not about to spurn the opportunity to be a hero. His 6ft 4ins frame blocked Butters's tame effort and then proceeded to perform a manic victory dance around Wembley. Arms flailing uncontrollably and legs with a life of their own, the floppy-fringed goalkeeper galloped off on a wild run of celebration. Only the considerable frame of Andy Morrison was able to bring him to a standstill.

"We knew we had to win after United did so well in Europe," admitted Weaver. "At the end, I was just trying to run as far as I could before anyone could catch me. I was just delirious."

For long-serving defender Richard Edghill, the victory offered a chance for more considered contemplation. "I have been at City for 12 years and this is one of the best days of my career. To be relegated twice was absolutely devastating, but hopefully we are going back in the other direction now. It was particularly poignant for me to play at Wembley as I thought my career was over a few years ago as I struggled to overcome a knee injury. It took me 21 months to get fit again and, in all honesty, just to be playing professional football is a bonus."

The afternoon ended with the City players on their knees on the Wembley turf, paying homage to their fans. It was a genuine gesture of their admiration for the abiding loyalty of their support. Royle, meanwhile, was soon predicting that his side could "do a Watford" and clinch back-to-back promotions into the Premiership. Few believed him.

CHAPTER TEN

Diary **1999**/2000

Sunday August 8: Nationwide League Division One
Manchester City 0 Wolves 1

EXACTLY ten weeks after their Wembley play-off victory, the Blues
are back in the First Division. Two new players are on parade, Mark
Kennedy from Wimbledon and Danny Granville, signed on loan from
Leeds United for three months. It is Kennedy's arrival, in a £1.5
million deal, which really excites the fans. The Irish international, a
long-term target for Joe Royle, provides a new dimension to City's
play down the left-hand side. An inventive and charismatic figure,
Kennedy is set to form an exciting two-winged attack with Terry
Cooke on the right.

It is a throwback to the manager's days at Oldham and Everton.
He had always liked wingers, whether it was Andrei Kanchelskis or
Rick Holden, Anders Limpar or Neil Adams. For Kennedy, it is a
fresh start. A career which had blossomed under Mick McCarthy at
Millwall had stagnated in recent years at Liverpool and Wimbledon.
"I know Joe tried to get me on loan last season so I watched the play-
off final and it's nice to see a big club back where they belong and
not in Division Two. Hopefully things will improve even more and
we can get to the Premiership," says the Irishman.

Royle strikes an optimistic note on the eve of the season after a
pre-season win over Liverpool. "I would be disappointed if we are
not in the play-offs at least and I think that is a feasible, reasonable
target for us. I have seen half a dozen sides up to now and without
kidding myself I have seen no-one better than us. We have no fears
at all and we go into it expecting to do well."

After the hype, the opening game falls flat as Robbie Keane
scores the winner for Wolves, a parting gift to the club before his £6
million move to Coventry. Danny Granville damages his hamstring,
an injury which will keep him out for six weeks.

Wednesday August 11: Worthington Cup 1st round, 1st leg
Manchester City 5 Burnley 0

TEN MONTHS earlier, Burnley had held City to a draw at Maine Road. Times are changing quickly as Royle's side continue their march onwards and upwards. City cruise to victory following Shaun Goater's goal before half-time. Mark Kennedy scores twice, Gareth Taylor adds another and Kevin Horlock completes the rout with a penalty. Afterwards Paul Dickov, a player immortalised for his deed at Wembley, is rewarded with a three-year contract.

Saturday August 14: Nationwide League Division One
Fulham 0 Manchester City 0

ANDY MORRISON'S loose tongue gets him in trouble after a spat with Stan Collymore. The City skipper shackles Colly for most of the game at Craven Cottage, but just when he thinks he has got him licked, Morrison sticks out his tongue at the former Aston Villa striker and gets a red card after a previous booking for a challenge on Geoff Horsfield. Joe Royle, never a fan of referees in the Second Division, cannot believe it. "I've never heard of someone getting sent off for kissing one of the opposition!" is his stunned response. The incident overshadows a determined defensive display as City register their first point of the season. Interestingly, Terry Cooke is left out. Royle opts instead for Ian Bishop in a three-man midfield.

Saturday August 21: Nationwide League Division One
Manchester City 6 Sheffield United 0

COOKE IS BACK for the visit of the Blades as Royle sets all his big guns blazing but it is their midfield firecracker Jeff Whitley who sparkles in an all-action display. His career has been turned on its head following a month's loan spell at Wrexham earlier in the year. "Without any disrespect to them, Jeff came back from there having realised what he was missing at Maine Road," says Royle. Whitley's workrate sets the tone as Kevin Horlock scores two penalties late in the first half. Goalkeeper Simon Tracey is sent off for bringing down Shaun Goater for the second spot kick and ten-men United, managed by former Blue Adrian Heath, succumb in the final half-hour with Kennedy, Goater, Dickov and Gareth Taylor inflicting the damage.

Tuesday August 24: Worthington Cup 1st round, 2nd leg
Burnley 0 Manchester City 1

A TEDIOUS AFFAIR with the Burnley public boycotting a meaningless tie after their side's five-goal deficit from the first leg. Almost half the crowd of 3,647 are at the City end of the ground, all of them anxious for a glimpse of Ian Wright's son Shaun Wright-Phillips who comes on for goalscorer Terry Cooke with 20 minutes of the match remaining. Michael Brown and Jamie Pollock are given run-outs, while Richard Jobson is exceptional on his comeback after a 16-month absence through injury. He will not miss another game during the season.

Saturday August 28: Nationwide League Division One
Bolton Wanderers 0 Manchester City 1

MARK KENNEDY must like the Reebok Stadium. It may be City's first visit to Bolton's space-age ground, but Kennedy scored there for Wimbledon in last season's FA Cup and he repeats the trick. Collecting the ball from deep, Kennedy runs at the heart of the Wanderers' defence before unleashing an unstoppable shot past Keith Branagan. It is his fourth goal in six days and he will cap a memorable week by scoring with a virtually identical strike for the Republic of Ireland in a European Championship qualifier against Yugoslavia in Dublin. Kennedy is rapidly becoming a firm favourite on the terraces – and in the dressing room. He is an entertainer, whose cheeky grin and lyrical Irish voice add to his appeal off the pitch.

Monday August 30: Nationwide League Division One
Manchester City 1 Nottingham Forest 0

NICKY WEAVER'S sixth clean sheet in a row ensures City continue to climb the table. The England under-21 keeper is rarely troubled on a quiet afternoon but shows his class with a fine fingertip save from Ian Wright, on loan from West Ham. Wright senior does not face his son, who is now pushing for a place in Joe Royle's first-team. After the final whistle, the former Arsenal striker remains on the pitch to applaud the home crowd in recognition of their support for his teenage lad. Shaun Goater grabs the winner but reports continue to suggest Royle is searching for another striker to bolster his attack.

Nationwide League Division One *End of August*

	P	W	D	L	F	A	Pts
Ipswich	5	4	1	0	16	5	13
Manchester City	5	3	1	1	8	1	10
Birmingham	5	3	1	1	12	7	10
West Bromwich	5	2	3	0	6	4	9
Stockport	4	3	0	1	5	3	9
QPR	5	2	2	1	9	7	8
Portsmouth	5	2	2	1	5	7	8
Huddersfield Town	5	2	1	2	11	7	7
Fulham	5	1	4	0	5	4	7
Charlton	3	2	0	1	5	3	6
Barnsley	5	2	0	3	12	13	6
Walsall	5	1	3	1	6	8	6
Wolves	4	1	2	1	4	4	5
Crewe	4	1	2	1	7	8	5
Grimsby	5	1	2	2	4	5	5
Nottingham Forest	5	1	2	2	5	7	5
Sheffield United	5	1	2	2	6	12	5
Blackburn	4	1	1	2	5	5	4
Bolton	4	1	1	2	2	3	4
Port Vale	5	1	1	3	6	9	4
Tranmere	5	1	1	3	3	6	4
Swindon	5	1	1	3	4	8	4
Crystal Palace	4	1	1	2	6	12	4
Norwich	5	0	2	3	3	7	2

Saturday September 11: Nationwide League Division One
Manchester City 2 Crystal Palace 1

STEVE COPPELL returns to the scene of his worst moment in football for the first time since his abrupt departure in the winter of 1996. At the time, he cited the strain on his personal life. He does not elaborate on his return three years later. "I think it was in the best interests of myself and Manchester City that I left before I did any long-term damage," remarks the Palace boss on the eve of the game. "It's best just to say I left and my reasons for going were private. I would be the first to say I shouldn't have taken the job. It would have been the easiest thing in the world to sit there and take the money and do so many things but I thought I should go and let someone new come in and impose themselves on the job." In the event, the City fans greet Coppell's comeback with indifference. An undistinguished game ends with the Blues coming from behind with goals from Richard Jobson and Gareth Taylor.

Wednesday September 15: Worthington Cup 2nd round, first leg
Manchester City 0 Southampton 0

A FEW MONTHS AGO, Danny Tiatto was more like 'Desperate Dan' than 'Dan the Man' as he struggled to rescue his City career. His aggressive temperament had led to two red cards and a batch of bookings in the previous season. But a summer of soul-searching and two morale-boosting displays for Australia in pre-season friendlies against Manchester United have revived his fortunes. Tiatto is now proving an able replacement for Danny Granville and catches the eye in this competent team performance against Premiership opponents.

Saturday September 18: Nationwide League Division One
Walsall 0 Manchester City 1

CITY TAKE OVER TOP SPOT in the First Division for the first time after the leaders Ipswich lose at home to Birmingham. City drew 1-1 at the Bescot Stadium earlier in the year, a result which hampered their chances of overhauling Walsall to claim runners-up spot in the Second Division. The roles are now very different as City's fans celebrate their lofty status, leaving their opponents still searching for a first home victory. It is now five successive victories in the League for the Blues, their best run since the start of 1989 when six straight wins set Mel Machin's side on the way to promotion.

Tuesday September 21: Worthington Cup 2nd round, 2nd leg
Southampton 4 Manchester City 3 *after extra time*

TERRY COOKE misses the team coach to the south coast as he is forced to stay behind in Manchester to take part in a random drugs test administered by the Football Association. Cooke works up such a sweat on the training field the day before the game that he is unable to provide a sample of urine and is left with stomach cramps. Joe Royle criticises the timing of the visit by the FA officials and Cooke and the club are later cleared of any wrongdoing.

While Cooke is late arriving, Richard Edghill is delayed returning from Southampton after a stray elbow from Mark Hughes leaves him with concussion. Edghill is detained in hospital overnight, while Hughes receives a red card for his reckless challenge. The match is a topsy-turvy affair, with Paul Dickov putting City ahead before Dave Jones's men hit back and forge into a 3-1 lead. Two late Shaun Goater goals take the tie to extra-time but Dean Richards slots home the decider and knocks City out of the cup.

Sunday September 26: Nationwide League Division One
Ipswich Town 2 Manchester City 1

THE FIRST LEG of an East Anglian double header takes the Blues to one of their bogey grounds and they duly suffer their first away defeat in the League for nine months (their last was a depressing 2-1 reverse at York in the midst of their Second Division season). David Johnson, a one-time City target, opens the scoring for Ipswich but Goater equalises with his third goal in four games. A draw seems a fair outcome, but luck is against the Blues as a shot from debutant Gary Croft deflects off Richard Jobson for the winner.

Tuesday September 28: Nationwide League Division One
Norwich City 1 Manchester City 0

A DECISION TO re-arrange the Norwich game seems to make sense. It allows City the opportunity of 48 hours rest and relaxation at the lavish Sprowston Manor Hotel near Carrow Road. But the energy-sapping extra time in City's cup tie at Southampton has taken its toll. It is their fourth away trip in the space of 11 days. There is no sign of fatigue early on as the visitors rip into Norwich but Jeff Whitley and Shaun Goater have goals disallowed. A punched clearance from Nicky Weaver literally rebounds on him as the ball is knocked forward swiftly to Iwan Roberts, who cashes in on the goalkeeper's error. "We coped well enough with the eleven men in yellow but were never able to come to terms with the three men in black," complains Joe Royle, annoyed at the two disallowed goals.

Nationwide League Division One *End of September*

	P	W	D	L	F	A	Pts
Birmingham	9	5	3	1	19	11	18
Ipswich	8	5	2	1	19	8	17
Charlton	7	5	1	1	15	7	16
Manchester City	**9**	**5**	**1**	**3**	**12**	**5**	**16**
Fulham	8	4	4	0	11	4	16
Barnsley	9	5	1	3	23	16	16
Huddersfield Town	8	4	1	3	15	11	13
Stockport	8	4	1	3	9	11	13
West Bromwich	8	2	6	0	9	7	12
Portsmouth	8	3	3	2	11	12	12
Blackburn	8	3	2	3	12	9	11

Saturday October 2: Nationwide League Division One
Manchester City 2 Port Vale 1

BISH BASHES in a couple of goals and even starts dreaming of a hat-trick. Those who think they are Ian Bishop's first League goals for City since the legendary 5-1 win over United are quickly put straight. "I scored in the following game against Luton," says Bishop, remembering back to his first spell at Maine Road a decade earlier.

"To be honest, I didn't know what to do when I scored today – it's been such a long time! After playing in all the tough away games it's nice to be picked for a home match. I was thinking about the dreams of the hat-trick and what I might do if I did score again but I didn't manage to get close enough to the goal."

Saturday October 16: Nationwide League Division One
Tranmere Rovers 1 Manchester City 1

THE BOSS IS BACK on his native Merseyside and offers some words of comfort to bottom-of-the-table Tranmere. "They won't be there long," he predicts. But Royle does not envisage that his side will help give them a leg up. Mind you, City's boss is far from happy with the performance of referee, Dermot Gallagher. There are no complaints when he awards a penalty which Kevin Horlock converts. Later on, though, Royle's fury begins to mount as a Tranmere defender appears to punch the ball over his crossbar, but nothing is awarded. Moments later, it is the home side which gets a spot-kick when Horlock hauls down Wayne Allison. Rovers equalise, while Horlock receives his marching orders for a second bookable offence.

Tuesday October 19: Nationwide League Division One
Birmingham City 0 Manchester City 1

ROYLE BRINGS out his crystal ball as City go back to the top of the table on the night Charlton lose 4-2 at Ipswich. "I told the chairman at lunchtime we'd win 1-0," claims Royle, who rips into his players at half time after a woeful display in which only the defiance of Nicky Weaver prevents Birmingham from taking command. Richard Jobson is the match winner with a header early in the second half. City agree a fee of £1 million with Leeds for Danny Granville.

Saturday October 23: Nationwide League Division One
Manchester City 2 Blackburn Rovers 0

TEN MONTHS after leaving his job as assistant manager at Manchester United, Brian Kidd is feeling the strain at Blackburn Rovers. His expensive side are languishing in sixteenth place and failing to live up to their pre-season billing as promotion favourites. Early arrivals in the bumper crowd of 33,027 witness an unedifying spectacle in the main stand. Kidd abandons his pre-match preparations and makes his way towards Wilf McGuinness, working as a commentator for BBC *GMR*. The Blackburn boss appears to berate McGuinness in a public exhibition of his emotions. In fact, he is giving his side of the story after recently being criticised in Alex Ferguson's autobiography. But with kick-off less than an hour away, Kidd's timing is unfortunate – to say the least! McGuinness offers a sympathetic ear but Kidd's animated expressions suggest he would have been better off discussing the matter in private rather than in public.

The match is remembered for Richard Edghill's first goal for the club as he becomes the latest player to profit from the excellent service supplied by the scintillating Mark Kennedy. "Usually when I go on a run I'd have stopped and cursed somebody for not passing to me, but I kept going and it's reaped its rewards," grins Edghill, at 25 the club's longest servant. Jeff Whitley rounds off a rousing contest with the second goal ensuring that Kevin Horlock's missed penalty does not matter.

"I think fans in Manchester call it lording it or large-ing it," says Royle. "It's great to be top and it's good for the supporters because they've seen lots of the other side. But I know it's early in the season and we're not getting carried away."

Wednesday October 27: Nationwide League Division One
Manchester City 1 Ipswich Town 0

A NIGHT that belongs to Nicky Weaver, who eclipses his heroics at Wembley with a performance he describes as the greatest of his fledgling career. His stunning saves thwart an impressive Ipswich side. "It was just Roy of the Rovers stuff for me and I don't know how I made a couple of saves towards the end. I suppose it was a reflex reaction," says Weaver. Goalscorer Kevin Horlock describes it as possibly the greatest display he has seen from any goalkeeper and Joe Royle joins in the praise. "I've got to be careful here because he'll be after a pay rise but the kid has been outstanding," says the boss. "He has the ideal temperament. He is almost arrogant on the pitch and very humble off it. He is a smashing keeper and I think that within the next twelve or eighteen months he has got to be pressing the national side."

Weaver celebrates his wonder show with cartwheels at the end of the game but his acrobatics are later banned by the manager, who fears the risk of injury. The only blemish is a knee injury to Paul Dickov forcing him on to the sidelines for the rest of the year.

Saturday October 30: Nationwide League Division One
Port Vale 1 Manchester City 2

CITY END the month as they began it with a 2-1 victory over their old boss Brian Horton. A new main stand at Vale Park is only half built so a hut is used as a temporary dressing room by the visitors. Hardly the sumptuous surroundings Shaun Wright-Phillips might have anticipated for his League debut. He comes on as a second-half substitute, with the Blues trailing. The minuscule striker immediately enlivens a lacklustre City performance and pressurises Mark Snijders into conceding an own goal.

Danny Granville scores the winner but the victory is marred as skipper Andy Morrison twists awkwardly and sustains a knee injury. Wright-Phillips is chaperoned to the post-match news conference by Shaun Goater who was absent through injury. On the same day as his father Ian scores on his debut for Celtic, Wright-Phillips tries to claim the first strike against Vale but Joe Royle decides it goes down as an own goal. "I don't talk about my dad's career and what he does. I will talk to him on the telephone tonight and tell him what happened," says Wright-Phillips, who at 5ft 3ins is dwarfed by his marker, the 6ft 5ins tall Anthony Gardner. "I wanted to get someone smaller on the pitch," jokes Royle. "He's no inhibitions and went to find the biggest man on the pitch, if not the country, and started taking him on."

Nationwide League Division One *End of October*

	P	W	D	L	F	A	Pts
Manchester City	**15**	**10**	**2**	**3**	**21**	**8**	**32**
Ipswich	14	8	2	4	28	17	26
Charlton	13	8	2	3	23	14	26
Birmingham	16	7	5	4	25	17	26
Huddersfield Town	15	7	4	4	26	18	25
Fulham	14	6	7	1	17	9	25
Barnsley	15	8	1	6	28	25	25
QPR	14	6	5	3	20	14	23
Stockport	15	6	5	4	17	19	23
Wolves	15	5	7	3	15	15	22
Bolton	15	5	5	5	22	18	20
Norwich	15	5	5	5	15	15	20
Portsmouth	14	5	4	5	19	21	19
Grimsby	15	5	4	6	15	20	19
Nottingham Forest	15	4	6	5	20	17	18
West Bromwich	14	3	9	2	13	11	18
Tranmere	16	4	4	8	20	27	16
Sheffield United	15	4	4	7	18	25	16
Blackburn	14	3	6	5	15	16	15
Crystal Palace	15	3	5	7	20	28	14
Walsall	16	3	5	8	13	26	14
Crewe	14	3	4	7	15	24	13
Swindon	16	3	4	9	12	25	13
Port Vale	16	3	3	10	18	26	12

Wednesday November 3: Nationwide League Division One

Manchester City 4 Portsmouth 2

AS THE GAME MOVES into injury time the Portsmouth manager bows his head and sportingly doffs his trademark flat cap from the directors' box in response to the crowd's taunt of "Are you watching Alan Ball?" Jamie Pollock has just notched the fourth goal and Ball shows dignity in defeat on his highly publicised return to the scene of his greatest managerial failure. The attendance at the news conference is larger than normal. Among the press ranks is the *Manchester Evening News* reporter Paul Hince, the man Ball blamed for his demise at Maine Road. There are no fireworks, just a polite exchange between the pair. As Hince wrote afterwards: "Alan Ball 1 Her Majesty's Press 0."

Ball is admirably self-effacing. "I came to this club and tried my best but it wasn't good enough. Sometimes it works and sometimes it doesn't. I have no axe to grind. I was treated well when I was here and you expect a bit of stick when you come back. It doesn't change in football. I'm glad City are doing well and I have a lot of friends here. It's good to see the buzz back in the place."

The queue for places in the City forward line is getting longer. Lee Peacock has been signed for £500,000 from Mansfield Town and a bid has been made for Gillingham's Robert Taylor. Gareth Taylor adds further spice to the striker issue by scoring twice against Pompey, Jeff Whitley getting the other goal to make it five victories in a row for the Blues.

Saturday November 6: Nationwide League Division One

Queens Park Rangers 1 Manchester City 1

RANGERS' BLUE AND WHITE hoops mean City must switch to their new third choice kit of red and black stripes for the first time. But all the talk is of the colour of BSkyB's money. The satellite broadcasters have bought a 9.9 per cent stake in the club for £5.5 million. They also pay a further £2 million to become City's exclusive media agents, a figure which could rise to £5.5 million depending on the club's success. Significantly, debts will be reduced as shareholders John Wardle and David Makin convert £4.8 million of loans into shares. A new rights issue also enables fans to buy shares for 90p each, considerably below the market value of £1.25.

David Bernstein pledges that some of the cash will be used to buy players and describes it as a historic day for the club. "This partnership puts us in an elite of top clubs in British football who have done these deals. The fact that a powerful partner like Sky have wanted this deal indicates the potential of Manchester City." On the field, Peacock makes his debut and Mark Kennedy pulls his hamstring, forcing him out of the Republic of Ireland's Euro 2000 play-off against Turkey. Kevin Horlock scores the City goal.

Saturday November 20: Nationwide League Division One
Charlton Athletic 0 Manchester City 1

MARK KENNEDY is ruled out, so a jet-lagged Danny Tiatto is surprised to learn he is playing just hours after returning from Australia's match against Brazil. Joe Royle's faith in Shaun Goater has never wavered, even during the Bermudan striker's three-month lean spell last season. His loyalty is repaid again as "The Goat" plunders the winning goal on his return from injury to make it seven wins out of nine for the Blues. "He's not always the most obvious favourite for our fans but he's got eight goals before Christmas and if he plays enough games he'll get his twenty this season, " says Royle, whose side are now 11 points clear of seventh-placed Queens Park Rangers. "It's great being at the top and we're loving it. You see what a spirit these lads have got and a determination not to be beaten. There is a togetherness on and off the field and they deserve their success." It is a big week with fellow promotion challengers Barnsley and Huddersfield Town visiting Maine Road but the mood in the camp is buoyant.

Wednesday November 24: Nationwide League Division One
Manchester City 3 Barnsley 1

CITY OPEN UP A FOUR-POINT GAP at the top but Joe Royle dismisses talk that his side can emulate Sunderland's runaway success of the year before. "I'll settle for going up by one point or one goal but I can't see anyone going that far clear this year. We are in pole position and there is no reason why we can't keep it up. The problem here is keeping the supporters' feet on the floor – I'll keep the players down." Barnsley are brushed aside with goals from Shaun Goater, Gareth Taylor and Kevin Horlock, as a rejuvenated Jamie Pollock stars in midfield. Skipper Andy Morrison can only watch from the sidelines after undergoing a knee operation described by his manager as a 100,000 mile service. "I've had a similar injury before and quite frankly I'll be glad if I am back in six weeks," says the burly Scot.

Saturday November 27: Nationwide League Division One
Manchester City 0 Huddersfield Town 1

ROBERT TAYLOR watches from the stands after Gillingham accept City's offer of £1.5 million for the striker who almost condemned them to another season in the Second Division. "Quite simply Robert is the hottest goalscorer in the divisions at the moment and I'd like him on our books. He can score goals and has improved with age and is in the best form of his career," says Royle. Taylor, scorer of 18 goals this season, resists overtures from Watford, Spurs and Hearts to sign a four-year contract. "City broke my heart at Wembley last May – I have only been able to bring myself to watch a video of the match in the last two weeks – but all that is forgotten now," he says. A part-exchange deal involving Danny Allsopp falls through. The young Aussie does not want to uproot to Kent.

Nationwide League Division One *End of November*

	P	W	D	L	F	A	Pts
Manchester City	**20**	**13**	**3**	**4**	**30**	**13**	**42**
Huddersfield Town	21	12	4	5	38	22	40
Charlton	20	12	3	5	37	23	39
Ipswich	20	10	5	5	34	23	35
Barnsley	20	11	2	7	38	32	35
Fulham	20	8	8	4	24	18	32
QPR	21	8	8	5	32	27	32
Birmingham	20	8	7	5	32	23	31
Bolton	20	8	7	5	29	20	31
Stockport	20	7	7	6	23	28	28

Friday December 3: Nationwide League Division One
Wolverhampton Wanderers 4 Manchester City 1

CITY CONCEDE FOUR GOALS in a League game for the first time since they were beaten 4-2 at West Ham on their way down from the Premiership in March 1996. Robert Taylor plays alongside Shaun Goater, who scores the consolation effort, but Joe Royle offers an incentive to the men left out. "It's not a case of having a first choice partnership up front. Because of injuries and the amount of games, I'm going to be needing more than two strikers. United wouldn't have won the European Cup with their first choice strikers," says Royle (a reference to the fact that substitutes Ole Gunnar Solskjaer and Teddy Sheringham scored the winning goals against Bayern Munich in the final). However, it's the pacey Wolves duo of Michael Branch and Ade Akinbiyi who come out on top at Molineux as the City defence is run ragged.

Tuesday December 7: Nationwide League Division One
Manchester City 1 Stockport County 2

THE YOUNGEST MANAGER in the Football League offers to resign after this result. At the age of 33, Stockport boss Andy Kilner enjoys the highlight of his short managerial career. "Our captain Mike Flynn says it doesn't get any better than this so he said I may as well quit now… I'll think about it overnight," quips Kilner.

It is no laughing matter for Nicky Weaver. The City keeper's confidence spills over as he is caught in possession on the edge of the area, trying to dribble around former team-mate Alan Bailey. Danny Granville is forced to give away a penalty which Tony Dinning promptly dispatches. Dinning then mocks Weaver's famous Wembley celebration in front of the Stockport supporters. "I've always said that the great goalkeepers don't make mistakes so that is something I will try to rectify," says Weaver, who refuses to hide from the waiting media.

Joe Royle shrugs off a third successive defeat. "It's called football. I seem to remember Manchester United suffering three defeats in a row and leaking goals left, right and centre and they won the Double. You don't sail through forty-six games without a blip. It was disappointing to hear the boos but the crowd will have their say. Three games ago, it would seem I was making a lot of right decisions and if I listen to the people behind me now in the stand I haven't got a clue." Gerard Wiekens scores his first goal of the season.

Sunday December 12: FA Cup 3rd round
Chester City 1 Manchester City 4

CITY TAKE ON the bottom club in the Football League and by the time they return along the M56 they are anticipating a meeting with the side at the other end of the soccer ladder. The players tune into the radio on the way back, to hear they have drawn Premiership leaders Leeds United in the next round. A late rally seals victory at the Deva Stadium in Chester. The North West had witnessed two notable cup upsets on the previous day when Wrexham knocked out Middlesbrough and Tranmere saw off West Ham. "You can tell by looking at the presence of Her Majesty's Press here today that they were coming looking for a shock so it's nice to disappoint them," says Royle. The Football Association had rejected Chester's plea to switch the tie to Manchester in order to make more revenue. A rare headed goal from Ian Bishop, two Shaun Goater strikes and a Matt Doughty own goal light up a dreary day.

Saturday December 18: Nationwide League Division One
Manchester City 3 Swindon 0

A NEWSPAPER HEADLINE on the eve of the game asks whether Robert Taylor is set become the next Rodney Marsh. Marsh's controversial signing in the early 1970s cost City the Championship as the balance of their team was disrupted. Comparisons with Taylor seem a trifle hasty after only his second appearance in a blue shirt. Suffice to say, Royle is not amused. Taylor has the last laugh as he poaches his first goal for the club early in the second half – even if there is a slice of good fortune about it as the Swindon goalkeeper Frank Talia allows a tame shot to slip from his grasp. With his wife about to give birth, Taylor misses the players' Christmas party in Dublin that night, leaving his team-mates to toast his first goal and other scoring efforts from Shaun Goater and Jamie Pollock.

WBA 0 Manchester City 2

ANOTHER NEWCOMER arrives as Tony Grant takes a place on the substitute's bench following a £450,000 move from Everton two days before Christmas. Joe Royle has been tracking the Liverpudlian ever since he took over at Maine Road, remembering his performances for him at Goodison Park. "It was a sad day when Joe left Everton but it has been Manchester City's gain and I am happy to be here now," says Grant, who played against City while on loan for Tranmere earlier in the season. Danny Granville and Shaun Goater are second half goalscorers but the man of the match is Richard Jobson.

Manchester City 2 Grimsby 1

KEVIN HORLOCK is emerging as Manchester City's lucky charm. Incredibly, they have never lost when the Northern Ireland international has scored, a sequence that now stretches for 26 matches, including the last-gasp play-off thriller at Wembley. With another two goals under his belt, the classy midfielder takes his season's tally to nine, leaving him just one goal short of the double figure target he sets every year. Yet an hour before kick-off, he is not even in the team. Joe Royle plans to stick with the same side which won at West Bromwich, but has a last-minute change of heart. Horlock, who missed the last game through suspension, can always grab you a goal, reasons the City boss.

Earlier in the day, Charlton win at Huddersfield Town and Royle has a dig at the Sky TV pundits who describe those two clubs as the "best passing teams" in the First Division. "I'd like to point out that we're four points clear in the table and in a marvellous position. All I can say is pass that," he says. But his mood lightens as he looks back on 1999 with fondness: "It's been a marvellous twelve months. When you look back to the defeat at York a year ago people were talking about this as the worst team in City's history but we've had a Wembley appearance and we have a cup tie to come in the New Year against the Premiership leaders. It hasn't been a bad twelve months at Maine Road."

Nationwide League Division One *End of December*

	P	W	D	L	F	A	Pts
Manchester City	**25**	**16**	**3**	**6**	**39**	**20**	**51**
Huddersfield Town	25	14	5	6	44	26	47
Charlton	24	14	5	5	42	26	47
Ipswich	25	13	7	5	41	26	46
Barnsley	24	14	3	7	48	36	45
Stockport	25	11	7	7	31	33	40
Blackburn	24	9	9	6	31	24	36
QPR	25	9	9	7	34	30	36
Fulham	25	8	12	5	24	20	36
Wolves	24	9	8	7	28	24	35
Tranmere	25	10	5	10	37	36	35
Norwich	24	9	7	8	23	22	34
Birmingham	24	8	8	8	33	28	32
Bolton	24	8	8	8	33	28	32
Sheffield United	25	8	6	11	31	39	30
Crystal Palace	25	7	8	10	34	40	29
Nottingham Forest	25	7	7	11	26	29	28
West Bromwich	25	5	12	8	24	30	27
Crewe	25	7	6	12	24	32	27
Grimsby	25	7	5	13	25	43	26
Port Vale	24	5	8	11	27	34	23
Portsmouth	25	5	8	12	27	39	23
Walsall	25	4	7	14	24	42	19
Swindon	25	3	9	13	18	41	18

CHAPTER ELEVEN

Diary 1999/**2000**

Monday January 3 2000: Nationwide League Division One
Crewe Alexandra 1 Manchester City 1

CREWE FORWARD Colin Little has supported Manchester City all his life – and he has got the scars to prove it. Wythenshawe-born Little has a tattoo of the new City crest on his leg and was even christened after Colin Bell. "My dad, who is City mad, decided to name me after whoever scored the week before I was born. Belly came up with the golden goal and I'm just glad Francis Lee didn't score it because I would have hated going through life being called Francis!" Little promises to show off his badge of honour if he scores, but the only lasting image from this game is Lee Crooks's lone goal of the season. Deputising for 'flu victim Richard Edghill, he steers City into an early lead before a blunder by Gerard Wiekens presents Rodney Jack with an equaliser. Ian Bishop captains the side for the first time and enjoys a touch of nostalgia. It was at Crewe, under the stewardship of Dario Gradi, that he made his League debut 16 years earlier while on a loan spell from Everton. The crowd of 10,066 is the highest at Gresty Road for 33 years but a Charlton victory on the same day halves City's lead at the top of the table to two points.

Sunday January 9: FA Cup 4th round
Manchester City 2 Leeds United 5

CITY MIGHT BE TOP of the First Division, but the Premiership still seems a long way off. David O'Leary's bright and breezy Leeds side blow City away in a fascinating duel at Maine Road. "Leeds are a team of internationals and looked it. They were much sharper than us and we fell down on soccer intelligence," concedes Joe Royle, after one of the most enthralling ties of the competition. City lead 2-1 early on after goals from Shaun Goater and Ian Bishop but once Leeds ease into top gear their incisive passing destroys the Blues, with only Nicky Weaver preventing a much heavier defeat. Golden boy Harry Kewell, who had just broken into the Leeds side when Richard Jobson was at Elland Road, leads the way with two goals. Eirik Bakke, Lee Bowyer and Alan Smith grab the others to cheer up a flu-ridden David O'Leary. "The tie didn't tell me anything I didn't already know," insists Royle. "I already knew we weren't capable of challenging teams at the top of the Premiership. We're not ready to go top of the Premiership at the moment but rest assured we will be."

Sunday January 16: Nationwide League Division One
Manchester City 4 Fulham 0

FEED THE GOAT is the new motto at Maine Road as Shaun Goater bags a hat-trick to take his tally for the season to 18, including 11 in the last 12 matches. He has won over even the most sceptical fans and his name is chanted around the ground as City condemn last season's Second Division champions to another defeat. And Joe Royle confirms Goater will stay in his side even if they make it into the top flight. "Shaun has scored goals against Premiership sides this year. He got two at Southampton and one against Leeds last week. If we get promoted, I have no doubts at all that he'll score goals in the Premiership," says the manager. Goater is just delighted to keep his name on the scoresheet: "As a striker, I like to score at least one hat-trick a season and it was just one of those games where the ball seemed to be following me around. Some days, it's the opposite – you're never going to score whatever you do."

Goater passes up the chance of a fourth goal, allowing Kevin Horlock to score a penalty – his tenth strike of the season. The result, though, is hard on Fulham with the Blues scoring three times in the final 13 minutes. Stand-in skipper Richard Edghill continues to bear the brunt of criticism from some sections of the crowd. "It's never nice to see the supporters picking on one of their own, particularly when the club are having such a good time, but that will always happen and I still maintain that Richard reminds too many people of the bad times here," says Royle. "I know what a good defender he is and have every faith in him. He is a model professional and is seldom beaten as a defender but the public will have their say." Two days before the Fulham game, City beat Bradford 6-0 in the FA Youth Cup with a hat-trick from New Zealander Chris Killen.

Saturday January 22: Nationwide League Division One
Sheffield United 1 Manchester City 0

MICHAEL BROWN dare not show his face in Manchester after scoring the winning goal, just days after his £425,000 move from Maine Road. The Sheffield United midfielder opts instead for a quiet celebration ahead of his twenty-third birthday. "I think I'll keep my head down when I go out tonight," admits Brown. "I know I probably upset a few people with that goal, but that's the nature of football." Brown, who still shares a house with former City team-mate Jeff Whitley, now accepts he never figured in Joe Royle's long-term plans. "I don't think he ever rated me and just wanted to get rid of me," he claims. "I felt very let down, because I'd played a big part in ensuring City's promotion to the First Division. I deserved the chance to start the season and never wanted to leave the club. That's the truth. I don't think Joe Royle ever told me the truth and that is very disappointing."

According to Royle, the defeat at Bramall Lane is his side's "worst display of the season," but there is soon some light relief. Days later, he and his side jet off for a mid-winter break in the sun. With their next match against Bolton postponed, City enjoy a well-earned rest in Lanzarote. "Four days at a warm weather training camp, with some rest and relaxation, will freshen one or two minds as well as bodies," says Royle. One player who remains behind as he continues his long struggle for fitness is skipper Andy Morrison, who has now been out for three months with his knee problem. He makes two trips to Lilleshall as part of his rehabilitation.

Nationwide League Division One End of January

	P	W	D	L	F	A	Pts
Charlton	28	18	5	5	52	28	59
Manchester City	**28**	**17**	**4**	**7**	**44**	**22**	**55**
Barnsley	29	17	4	8	59	42	55
Ipswich	29	15	9	5	48	29	54
Huddersfield Town	29	15	6	8	47	31	51
Wolves	29	11	10	8	38	33	43
Stockport	29	11	9	9	34	38	42
Birmingham	28	11	8	9	39	32	41
Blackburn	27	10	10	7	35	30	40
QPR	29	10	10	9	38	35	40
Fulham	28	9	12	7	25	25	39
Norwich	28	10	8	10	27	30	38
Bolton	27	9	9	9	35	31	36
Tranmere	28	10	6	12	37	38	36
Crystal Palace	29	9	9	11	42	47	36
Sheffield United	29	9	8	12	36	44	35
Grimsby	29	9	7	13	33	49	34
Nottingham Forest	29	7	9	13	30	37	30
West Bromwich	29	5	15	9	25	33	30
Crewe	29	7	8	14	28	38	29
Walsall	29	7	8	14	32	46	29
Port Vale	27	6	9	12	31	37	27
Portsmouth	29	6	9	14	34	45	27
Swindon	29	3	10	16	21	50	19

Saturday February 5: Nationwide League Division One
Nottingham Forest 1 Manchester City 3

JOE ROYLE had been sipping pina coladas in the Spanish sunshine a week earlier and after this victory at a shivering City Ground he recommends to the chairman that his players go back for more. Paul Dickov has recovered from the knee injury that kept him out for more than two months but is struggling to get further than the substitute's bench and makes a late appearance as replacement for goalscorer Robert Taylor. Wigan Athletic move in with a £500,000 offer for Dickov, which is flatly rejected. "I love it here and I have a great relationship with the fans but I want to be playing first-team football," says the frustrated player.

At the same time, evergreen Richard Jobson signs a new one-year contract which will take him up to his thirty-eighth birthday in 2001. Jobson is commanding alongside Gerard Wiekens as they repel a struggling Forest side. The future of Ian Bishop and Tommy Wright, both out of contract in the summer, is less certain as they reject new pay deals. City take 6,500 fans to Nottingham and the trip is well worthwhile with City collecting another three points and Shaun Goater grabbing another two goals.

Saturday Feb 12: Nationwide League Division One
Manchester City 3 Norwich City 1

TERRY COOKE goes on the transfer list and Joe Royle gets on his soapbox. The City manager causes a stir with an attack on women officials in his programme notes. "I am NOT sexist but I do not approve of female officials in professional football. How can they make accurate decisions if they've never been tackled from behind by a fourteen-stone centre half, or elbowed in the ribs or even caught offside?" he writes. "In my opinion there is only one sport in which men and women compete equally against each other and that is equestrianism, and I'm afraid the performances of female officials that I have seen thus far have done nothing to change my opinion. Yet we are now going to have one officiating at the Worthington Cup Final (Wendy Toms); how must many of the long-serving officials feel who have never had such a big game? I know I am going to be accused of being sexist but too many people are trying to be politically correct and no-one is prepared to voice the other opinion. I have."

Royle had decided to speak out after a recent incident which cost his club a place in the FA Youth Cup. City lost 1-0 at Derby County, the goal scored from a free kick awarded after goalkeeper Steve Hodgson gestured at a lineswoman.

On the eve of the Norwich match, Terry Cooke asks to leave after failing to force his way into a squad weakened by injury. "I'm fed up with playing reserve team football and my patience has worn thin," he snaps after only one full appearance in five months. "I've put my views very strongly and I'm not going to put up with it any longer. There's been no bust up or bad words and I've done everything I've been asked but I can't see any rewards." The Norwich match is won, with yet another Shaun Goater goal and two from Mark Kennedy, who ends a five-month absence from the scoresheet.

Friday February 18: Nationwide League Division One
Huddersfield Town 1 Manchester City 1

AMBITIOUS WIGAN ATHLETIC are back again, this time with a £1 million offer for Jamie Pollock. City accept the bid but Pollock is reluctant to drop down into the Second Division, recalling painful memories of last season when he struggled to adapt at that level and was sent off three times. Pollock prefers to wait until the end of the season rather than rushing into a move. Joe Royle is far from happy – the cash would have been useful to fund his efforts to strengthen City's squad. With skipper Andy Morrison still toiling to regain fitness, the Blues are again linked with Alfie Haaland of Leeds. Meanwhile, the contest for midfield places is getting hotter with Jeff Whitley rejuvenated after a break, keeping Tony Grant out of the side.

City suffer an off night in West Yorkshire, despite Shaun Goater's twenty-second goal of the season. In the end, they are grateful for the heroics of goalkeeper Nicky Weaver who keeps them in the game. The England under-21 international is attracting interest from Premiership clubs but pledges his future to the Blues. "I want to play at the top level and I want to play there next year but if we don't go up this time I'm sure we'll go up next season. I know that to fulfil my ambitions I don't need to leave City because it's a big enough club. A lot of people with experience in the game have advised me not to leave because you never know how quickly things might change. I'm playing well here so there's no reason to change it," he says.

It is two years to the day since Joe Royle took charge and his success in revitalising the club has not gone unnoticed in the boardroom. "We are more than happy with Joe. He has done a fantastic job in two years," comments David Bernstein. "He took over in extremely difficult circumstances and has worked miracles. The first six months of his reign weren't easy but since Christmas last year the results speak for themselves. To have won a final at Wembley and reached where we are in the league is a tremendous tribute to Joe and Willie Donachie and all the staff and players."

Saturday February 26: Nationwide League Division One
Manchester City 1 Walsall 1

IAN BRIGHTWELL admits the worst thing about his sentimental return is having to wear a red shirt for Walsall. The 31-year-old defender was a true blue during 12 years with City and still supports his old club. "It was strange coming back to play against City but I didn't like pulling on a red shirt. I never wear red, even when I go out socially," admits Brightwell, who is given a warm reception by the crowd. "I was pleased with my performance and thought I did well marking Mark Kennedy but I hope the result doesn't stop City from getting automatic promotion. They have been a big part of my life since I was a boy and I watched them in the play-off final at Wembley last season."

The manner of City's performance raises doubts about their ability to finish in the top two after less than impressive displays against Norwich, Huddersfield Town and now Walsall. "We were awful. Our performance at Sheffield United was poor but that easily beats it. At the moment we're scraping through," admits Joe Royle, maintaining that 92 points is the target for automatic promotion. "I've said all along that's the number of points needed and I don't see any reason to change my opinion."

A suspended Danny Tiatto is glad of a day off after an exhausting schedule which has taken him to Chile and Hungary playing for his country. Next month he is off to the Czech Republic. Yet again, Shaun Goater's goal saves City but one of his former strike partners is unable to find a settled home. A transfer-listed Gareth Taylor returns from a loan spell with Port Vale and is soon off to join QPR on a similar basis. Meanwhile, the broadcaster BSkyB have still not taken up the option of a place on the board four months after buying a 9.9 per cent stake.

Top of Nationwide League Division One *End of February*

	P	W	D	L	F	A	Pts
Charlton	32	22	5	5	59	29	71
Ipswich	33	18	10	5	55	32	64
Manchester City	**32**	**19**	**6**	**7**	**52**	**26**	**63**
Barnsley	33	17	7	9	63	48	58
Birmingham	33	15	9	9	50	37	54
Huddersfield Town	33	15	8	10	50	36	53

Saturday March 4: Nationwide League Division One
Crystal Palace 1 Manchester City 1

SHAUN GOATER listens to the game over a special radio link-up from the British Virgin Islands where he is preparing for Bermuda's World Cup qualifying campaign. City had wanted to fly their ace marksman from Heathrow on Concorde after the game at Selhurst Park to join up with his international squad. The £7,000 fare is not the problem but a lack of available flights scuppers the plan. Goater scores a hat-trick in a 5-1 win for Bermuda, but the Blues miss his prowess in front of goal against Palace. Lee Peacock takes his place in attack alongside Robert Taylor. The partnership starts well, with Taylor hitting an early goal as Palace fail to cope with Mark Kennedy who is switched to the right-wing. The ever-improving Danny Tiatto and Jamie Pollock return, with Kevin Horlock and Ian Bishop rested because of fatigue. But City have to settle for a third successive 1-1 scoreline, an attack of "draw-itis" as Joe Royle calls it. City drew on only three occasions in the entire first half of the season. On the same day, Ipswich are beaten by Portsmouth, bringing to an end their 18-match unbeaten run. It means City's point at Palace takes them into second place on 64 points, above Ipswich on goal difference and with a game in hand. They are ten points behind Charlton, who have won 11 League games in a row.

Wednesday March 8: Nationwide League Division One
Manchester City 1 QPR 3

NICKY WEAVER is forgiven by the fans for two first-half blunders that gift QPR goals and lead to City's first home defeat for three months. He is applauded off the field and then gets a vote of confidence from his manager. "His performance doesn't alter the fact that, in my opinion, he is the best in the country by a mile. There's not another goalkeeper I would take before him," claims Royle. "He'll get over it very quickly. He's had two magnificent years but tonight he had a mad twenty minutes." It is also a miserable night for Robert Taylor, whose Maine Road career continues to be jinxed. He is ruled out with a groin injury and a virus and has made only eight full appearances in over three months since his move. The prospects of a return at Barnsley at the weekend do not look good. "There's time for him to get swamp fever and cholera by then," quips an exasperated Royle.

The day before the game, Wigan Athletic take Terry Cooke on a month's loan. Cooke had recently issued a statement through his solicitor denying rumours he is a drug taker. "I've been alarmed at the number of people who've approached me and advised me they've heard Terry's problems involve him leading a less than desirable lifestyle," says David Chapman in a statement. "One particular, disturbing rumour is that Terry has been taking drugs, which is totally without foundation and no doubt originates from an occasion last year when Terry was physically unable to provide a urine sample following a random drugs test at Platt Lane. The rumours are at best mischievous, and at worst defamatory, and totally untrue." The Cooke issue will not go away and, some time later, City deny rumours that there is a clause in his contract which requires them to pay his old club Manchester United £400,000 on completion of 40 appearances. When Cooke leaves, he is two games short of that total.

Saturday March 11: Nationwide League Division One
Barnsley 2 Manchester City 1

LEE MILLS makes his debut in his native Yorkshire following a loan move from Bradford City until the end of the season. City have to pay more than £100,000 to clinch the deal but Mills knows what it takes to get into the Premiership, having scored 23 League goals for

Bradford in their promotion season. "Last year at Bradford we pipped Ipswich so hopefully it'll be a case of déjà vu," says Mills, who becomes the seventh player to lead the attack during the campaign, joining Shaun Goater, Paul Dickov, Gareth Taylor, Lee Peacock, Robert Taylor and Danny Allsopp. However, a rib injury ruins Mills's afternoon and he makes only two further appearances as a substitute during the last few weeks of the season. In fact, almost all of City's strikers are becoming plagued by injuries, with Allsopp and Peacock ruled out for the season. Thankfully, Shaun Goater is fit, although showing signs of weariness, as his whistlestop trip with Bermuda takes its toll. His late scrambled goal is not enough and City end up with nothing. To make matters worse, there is an ugly incident involving police and fans at a catering stall at half time, with South Yorkshire officers accused of baton-charging supporters.

City have gone five games without a win, their worst run this season and have picked up three points out of the last 15. "We've been written off now for a number of weeks but we're not writing ourselves off," says a defiant Royle. Barnsley steal a march, becoming the only team in the top six to win and overtake City in the process. The Blues are down to fourth for the first time in five months but still have a game in hand. Ipswich go down 2-1 at Wolves and, in one of the surprises of the season, Charlton are beaten at home to bottom club Swindon. It ends a run of 12 wins in a row which has given the Londoners a 12-point cushion at the top.

Sunday March 19: Nationwide League Division One

Manchester City 1 Charlton Athletic 1

THE BBC *Radio 5 Live* commentary team of Alan Green and summariser David Fairclough are unimpressed by City and question how many of their players would be good enough for the Premiership. Robert Taylor is even described as "like a pub player." The comments infuriate Joe Royle, whose feud with the outspoken Green goes back to his Everton days. Green later calls the City boss a "big baby" accusing him of being far too sensitive. Royle responds by claiming that Green is "universally disliked and distrusted" throughout soccer. A diverting interlude as the season reaches such a tense climax.

The Charlton boss Alan Curbishley does not need to worry about criticism – he is looking down on the rest with his side 13 points clear. It's a dramatic turnaround since the start of the year when City held a four-point advantage. Now City are second on 65 points – the same as Ipswich and Barnsley – courtesy of their superior goal difference. Birmingham are also mounting a concerted challenge and are two points further back. "It's hotting up behind and the chasing pack have all got it within them to clinch the second place. I think any of the teams can do it," says a cagey Curbishley. "Birmingham look very strong and are having a great run. I know City are playing better than their results suggest. Barnsley are capable of scoring goals and Ipswich have had a wobble but they are one of the better sides in this League. I've been around the First Division a long time and I think this year it is the strongest it has ever been." Shaun Goater scores one of his luckier goals as the ball bounces off his shin past Dean Kiely but City show signs of regaining their earlier season form.

Tuesday March 21: Nationwide League Division One
Stockport County 2 Manchester City 2

THE PROLONGED ABSENCE of skipper Andy Morrison has left the Blues without a leader and the breakdown in communication on the field is proving a headache. With the defence starting to creak, it is more than two months since a clean sheet. In the last seven games, City have collected five 1-1 draws and two defeats. It is hardly promotion form and the pressure is beginning to mount. At half-time at Edgeley Park, Joe Royle reads his players the riot act as they trail 2-1 despite taking an early lead through Jamie Pollock. "We've got nine games left and if we win them all we go up. I fancy us to win them all and I'm always puzzled when we don't win," says Royle, after watching Richard Jobson grab a late equaliser to leave Stockport without a win this year. Their manager, Andy Kilner, expects City to make the Premiership but thinks it will be via the play-offs. Royle admits he is taking steps to tighten up the back four and tells the fans he is set to make a signing before the transfer deadline later in the week. A crowd of 3,412 turn up at Maine Road to watch the match on a giant screen.

Saturday March 25: Nationwide League Division One
Manchester City 2 West Bromwich 1

CITY BUY Spencer Prior for £500,000 from Derby County. The 28-year-old makes his debut on a day which proves to be a turning point in the season. "I'll help out as much as I can and try to talk to the other players. It's probably going to be a bit easier to communicate here than at Derby because there's a few more English players," says Prior. City had inquired about Aston Villa's Colin Calderwood before moving for Prior. Meanwhile, Tony Vaughan joins Nottingam Forest for £350,000.

City win in dramatic fashion with two goals in the final 13 minutes. After Lee Hughes gives West Bromwich the lead, the mood darkens around Maine Road. It seems City's miserable run is going to continue. But Royle's men summon up all their strength of character to fight back. Mark Kennedy equalises to restore belief, but it is Shaun Goater's stoppage-time winner which prompts scenes of unbridled celebration among the home fans.

"Before the game I could sense the fans were starting to doubt again," admits Joe Royle, reflecting after the season is over. "If any set of fans has a right to be suspicious and cynical it's these ones. They have taken so much crap over the years and last-minute horrors. You could sense they were thinking 'Oh Christ they've taken us to the brink again, I always knew this team wasn't good enough and why isn't Terry Cooke playing?' But I never stopped believing and I still believe now."

Top of Nationwide League Division One *End of March*

	P	W	D	L	F	A	Pts
Charlton	39	27	6	6	73	34	87
Ipswich	39	20	11	8	59	37	71
Barnsley	39	21	8	10	76	56	71
Manchester City	**38**	**20**	**9**	**9**	**60**	**36**	**69**
Huddersfield Town	39	19	9	11	59	40	66
Birmingham	39	19	9	11	60	42	66

Saturday April 1: Nationwide League Division One
Swindon Town 0 Manchester City 2

HARD-UP SWINDON roll out the welcome mat, giving City fans both ends of the ground to cash in on the huge demand for tickets in Manchester. Blues' supporters make up almost half the 12,397 crowd but witness a drab encounter which City win at a canter. There is a rare outing for Tony Grant who has hardly figured in the side following his mid-season move. His misfortune continues as he is replaced early in the second half. "I've been dying to play and not being in the side has got me down," confesses Grant. Paul Dickov makes a statement to his manager by setting up goals for Mark Kennedy and Shaun Goater.

Wednesday April 5: Nationwide League Division One
Manchester City 2 Bolton Wanderers 0

A CUNNING PLAN fools Bolton as Gerard Wiekens adopts an anchor role in midfield, a position he filled when he first came to the club. "I've had it in my mind for some time to use Gerard that way. It's nice to have someone who can defend in front of the back four and sometimes we've looked vulnerable there lately," says Royle. It is the ideal time to play Bolton, only three days after their stamina-sapping two hours at Wembley where they lost to Aston Villa in a penalty shoot-out in the FA Cup semi final. The weary Wanderers are subjected to an early attacking blitz and full back John O'Kane is substituted after 25 minutes, with his side two goals down, after being tormented by a dynamic Mark Kennedy. Kevin Horlock is back after a rest and pops up with a goal but the biggest celebration comes when the hard-working Paul Dickov scores his first goal for more than six months. Bolton are in danger of becoming the nearly men, losing semi-finalists in both major cup competitions and now seven points adrift of the play-off places. In contrast, City have won three in a row and, with six games left, are a point clear of Barnsley and three ahead of Ipswich.

Saturday April 8: Nationwide League Division One
Manchester City 4 Crewe Alexandra 0

IT'S THE PERFECT fifty-first birthday present for Joe Royle as his team chalk up their fourth straight win to pile the pressure on their rivals. "We're not making wild predictions. We're just going to enjoy the victory," says the boss, who goes out for an Indian meal with his wife, Janet, afterwards. Spencer Prior, meanwhile, is proving a powerful influence; every game has been won since his arrival. He even scores, along with Shaun Goater and Paul Dickov, who bags a brace. "Paul is like a crocus – he seems to bloom in spring," adds Royle, poetically referring to the Scot's influential role at the same time last year. Goater gets the all-clear from Bermuda to stay with his club until the end of the season. Fellow promotion rivals Ipswich beat Port Vale and Barnsley grab a last minute winner against West Bromwich. The final sprint is on – with City second by a neck.

Top of Nationwide League Division One *5 games to go*

	P	W	D	L	F	A	Pts
Charlton	41	27	8	6	76	37	89
Manchester City	**41**	**23**	**9**	**9**	**68**	**36**	**78**
Ipswich	41	21	12	8	63	38	75
Barnsley	41	22	9	10	82	59	75
Birmingham	41	20	10	11	61	42	70
Huddersfield Town	41	19	11	11	59	40	68

Sat April 15: Nationwide League Division One
Grimsby Town 1 Manchester City 1

GRIMSBY set a quiz game to weed out away fans trying to purchase a ticket from Blundell Park. "Is the Grimsby mascot called Harry the Haddock?" is one of the questions to test supporters' local knowledge. (Answer: No, it's the Mighty Mariner). Demand is high for tickets with the Blues only allocated 2,200 seats. Some fans, who fail the authenticity test, resort to bribing local residents to buy them a ticket.

With the fear of trouble in the nearby resort of Cleethorpes, security is stepped up, but a cold wind and rain offer little incentive to stick around after the match. It is fish and chips all round for the players on the coach after the game – and an extra portion for Spencer Prior, whose goal gives City an early lead before Alan Powton scores Grimsby's first goal in more than ten hours of football. Ipswich take advantage of City's draw by winning 1-0 at Stockport but Barnsley are held at Port Vale. Two days before the match, Andy Morrison finally makes his comeback from injury in a reserve game.

Top of Nationwide League Division One *4 games to go*

	P	W	D	L	F	A	Pts
Charlton	42	27	8	7	76	38	89
Manchester City	42	23	10	9	69	37	79
Ipswich	42	22	12	8	64	38	78
Barnsley	42	22	10	10	84	61	76
Huddersfield Town	42	20	11	11	60	40	71
Birmingham	41	20	10	11	61	42	70

Saturday April 22: Nationwide League Division One
Manchester City 2 Tranmere Rovers 0

THE PENDULUM SWINGS dramatically towards City who surge four points clear of the pack with three games remaining. Ipswich lose 3-1 at QPR and Barnsley slump 2-0 at Wolves. When the results are flashed up at Maine Road the roar is almost as loud as for the goals scored by Shaun Goater – his twenty-eighth of the season – and Jeff Whitley. It is Goater's one hundredth game in a blue shirt and his fifty-second goal for the club but there is no time for celebration as the players are whisked off to their south coast hideaway straight afterwards in readiness for the match at Portsmouth 48 hours later. Off the pitch, the Blues push their advertising hoardings together to prevent long throw specialist Dave Challinor from getting a run up, but it hardly matters. Tranmere rarely threaten the City goal. Wins over Pompey and Birmingham will take City up.

"There's still a job to do and without being daft or blasé we can't afford to switch off," warns Royle. "You don't have to be a genius to work out how many points we need so that no-one can catch us but we have to concentrate on Portsmouth because it's a hard game. We've seen it before at Manchester City where we get ahead of ourselves but a lot of those demons are behind us now."

Top of Nationwide League Division One *3 games to go*

	P	W	D	L	F	A	Pts
Charlton	43	27	9	7	77	39	90
Manchester City	**43**	**24**	**10**	**9**	**71**	**37**	**82**
Ipswich	43	22	12	9	65	41	78
Barnsley	43	22	10	11	84	63	76
Birmingham	43	21	10	12	63	43	73
Huddersfield Town	43	20	11	12	60	43	71

Monday April 24: Nationwide League Division One
Portsmouth 2 Manchester City 2

FIRST IT WAS Michael Brown, now Lee Bradbury. City's old boys seem determined to come back and haunt the club. Bradbury's two goals will hardly boost his popularity in Manchester, where he endured an unhappy 18 months as City's record signing. He has invited a number of his old team-mates to his wedding in the summer and must be hoping they still turn up. Joe Royle is more concerned with referee Paul Alcock, whose harsh penalty award against Robert Taylor offers Portsmouth a lifeline. Taylor is adjudged to have handled in the area, just as the Blues are coasting at 2-0. For the former Gillingham man, it is cruel luck after his goal and another from Spencer Prior set the visitors on course for victory. "One incident changed the game," complains Royle, who stays behind on the pitch at the end to shake the hand of referee's assistant Wendy Toms, burying the hatchet over his comments on women officials. "I told her it wasn't personal. I have an opinion of women officials and it wasn't directed particularly at her." Barnsley beat Norwich and the following night Ipswich overcome Crystal Palace 1-0 to leave them two points behind the Blues with two games to play.

Top of Nationwide League Division One *2 games to go*

	P	W	D	L	F	A	Pts
Charlton	44	27	10	7	78	40	91
Manchester City	**44**	**24**	**11**	**9**	**73**	**39**	**83**
Ipswich	44	23	12	9	66	41	81
Barnsley	44	23	10	11	86	64	79
Birmingham	44	22	10	12	65	43	76
Huddersfield Town	44	21	11	12	62	44	74

Friday April 28: Nationwide League Division One
Manchester City 1 Birmingham City 0

THOUSANDS of fans swarm on to the pitch at the final whistle. The last player to leave the field is goalkeeper Nicky Weaver, who is carried aloft to the tunnel. Blue and white flags are waved in the air and the players take a bow from the directors' box. The party atmosphere brings down the curtain on a fabulous season as City move within touching distance of the Premiership. "Tomorrow could be a great day but equally it could be another seven days of nail-biting," warns Joe Royle, aware that his side are up if Ipswich fail to win at champions Charlton. "Five years of relief and emotion spilled out on the pitch at the end. This club has been the butt of all the music hall jokes in the past but now the fans can be proud."

The match-winner is Robert Taylor, who hates play-offs, having failed in the end of season shoot-outs in three of the last four years, twice with Brentford and, most notably, with Gillingham in the previous season. Weaver is another player who has tasted the lower leagues, having made one appearance for Mansfield before his £100,000 move to City. "It'd be a dream come true to play in the Premiership. It'd be my fifth season in football and I'll have played in every division if we get up, so that would be something to be proud of," he says.

Royle spends the following day watching his son Darren play for Ashton United in the Unibond League and by the time he leaves the ground Ipswich are on their way to a 3-1 win to take the shine off Charlton's Championship party. City deny claims that the Birmingham celebrations were premature but promotion is put on hold and a long, nervous countdown is under way towards the final game at Blackburn. Mark Kennedy is the only City player named in the Professional Footballers' Association all-star team. But there is no doubt which team has the star supporters in the First Division. City's average attendance at Maine Road for the season is 32,088 – over 10,000 more than Birmingham, the next best.

Top of Nationwide League Division One *last game to go*

	P	W	D	L	F	A	Pts
Charlton	45	27	10	8	79	43	91
Manchester City	**45**	**25**	**11**	**9**	**74**	**39**	**86**
Ipswich	45	24	12	9	69	42	84
Barnsley	45	24	10	11	88	65	82
Birmingham	45	22	10	13	65	44	76
Huddersfield Town	45	21	11	13	62	46	74

Sunday May 7: Nationwide League Division One
Blackburn Rovers 1 Manchester City 4

IT IS THE enduring image of the day – the most treasured memory in a glorious season. Mark Kennedy, such a vibrant force in City's campaign, sprints exuberantly towards his mentor. Joe Royle, swelling with pride and delight on the touchline, stretches out his arms to embrace his star player. Within an instant, the Manchester City manager is submerged in a sea of bodies as the rest of his players come tumbling on top of him. The team which Joe built is paying its own tribute to the boss.

"That goal was the highlight of the season for me. I know that's not original but that's when I knew we were up," says the manager. "It was a marvellous gesture of Mark to run towards me – it certainly made a nice picture, if not a particularly flattering one of me. Kennedy has made a massive impact for us this season and I think he just saw me on the touch-line. I wasn't waiting for him, that's for certain." For Kennedy, it is a symbolic 'thank you' to the man who has rescued his career – and saved his club.

City are back in the Premiership after another unforgettable afternoon in their epic adventure. After Matt Jansen opens the scoring for Blackburn, it seems there might be one last twist in the tale. His side flow forward in wave upon wave of attacks as the Blues struggled to survive. With Ipswich winning against Walsall, after an hour of the game City are heading for the play-offs. Nicky Weaver's woodwork is struck four times but the ball will not go in. Somewhere along the way, City's luck has changed. The club which suffered almost every sling and arrow of outrageous fortune during the 1990s can suddenly do no wrong. They cruise to victory with four goals in 20 minutes – courtesy of Kennedy, Shaun Goater, Paul Dickov and a Christian Dailly own goal. As the final whistle sounds, thousands of fans swarm on to the pitch while the streets of Manchester begin to fill with joyous Blues. After falling so far, the rise seems even sweeter. After the ignominy of Macclesfield, Colchester and Lincoln, they can now look forward to Anfield, Old Trafford and Highbury.

Nationwide League Division One *Final table 1999/2000*

	P	W	D	L	F	A	Pts
Charlton	46	27	10	9	79	45	91
Manchester City	**46**	**26**	**11**	**9**	**78**	**40**	**89**
Ipswich	46	25	12	9	71	42	87
Barnsley	46	24	10	12	88	67	82
Birmingham	46	22	11	13	65	44	77
Bolton	46	21	13	12	69	50	76
Wolves	46	21	11	14	64	48	74
Huddersfield Town	46	21	11	14	62	49	74
Fulham	46	17	16	13	49	41	67
QPR	46	16	18	12	62	53	66
Blackburn	46	15	17	14	55	51	62
Norwich	46	14	15	17	45	50	57
Tranmere	46	15	12	19	57	68	57
Nottingham Forest	46	14	14	18	53	55	56
Crystal Palace	46	13	15	18	57	67	54
Sheffield United	46	13	15	18	59	71	54
Stockport	46	13	15	18	55	67	54
Portsmouth	46	13	12	21	55	66	51
Crewe	46	14	9	23	46	67	51
Grimsby	46	13	12	21	41	67	51
West Bromwich	46	10	19	17	43	60	49
Walsall	46	11	13	22	52	77	46
Port Vale	46	7	15	24	48	69	36
Swindon	46	8	12	26	38	77	36

DAVID BERNSTEIN only addresses his players once in a blue moon. The chairman, determined not to impinge upon his manager's territory, keeps a discreet distance from the dressing room. Yet, as the clock ticked down to his club's final game of the season, Bernstein decided it was time to step forward once more. For only the fourth time during his tenure as chairman, Bernstein spoke directly to the players.

His first address had been delivered almost two years earlier after the Blues had sunk to their lowest ebb. In the summer of 1998, they were about to embark on their first season in English football's third tier. It was a humbling experience for one of the game's greatest clubs – but Bernstein saw an opportunity for the future. A chance for the players to become heroes and for the club to rise again.

"I told them they had an opportunity to make history – genuine sporting history," says Bernstein. "We had fallen so far. I said if we could get back quickly, they would have a permanent place in the affections of our supporters.

"It was a wonderful opportunity. Nobody wanted the fall to happen, but it created this opportunity to rise again. Fate seems to have played a part when you look back at things. When you watch back those final seconds at Wembley on the tape, some very strange things happen. If there is a football spirit, it was definitely on our side that day. But I honestly believe, and I know it is a cliché, but the harder you work and the more professional you are, the more luck comes your way."

There was certainly plenty of luck on City's side as they completed the final leg of their journey back to the top at Ewood Park. Bernstein watched from the directors' box as the fate of his club was resolved in front of his eyes. Just years earlier, he would not have been able to look. The lifelong City fan had a habit of retreating to "the sanctuary of the boardroom or anywhere"; just to escape the anguish of watching his side. The tension was too much – anything could go wrong and so often did for City.

Now it had all changed. Bernstein was confident, "supremely confident" in fact, that the Blues would go up. Sporting the same lucky blue socks as he wore at Wembley a year before, City's chairman felt an inner strength – a genuine belief that things would go right.

"I must admit I was sure we would win it," he says. "We had been on such a long and exciting journey and I knew we wouldn't fall at the final hurdle. There is a new confidence about the club, a good feeling which has got through to the fans. It was marvellous to see them celebrate in the last 10 minutes. It was magic. That was payback for the suffering they've had."

THE DAY HAD STARTED well for Francis Lee. City's former chairman spent the morning watching his son Jonathan play rugby in a Cheshire Cup final. The 13-year-old, evidently inheriting his father's sporting prowess, finished on the winning side. It would, Franny hoped, be a prelude of things to come.

After rushing home, the Lee family gathered around the television. It was a beautiful day and Gill Lee was planning a barbecue for later in the afternoon. But for now, there was only one thing on everyone's mind – a football match in Blackburn. Francis Lee watched in hope and then disbelief as Rovers bombarded City's goal.

"They should have been 5-0 up, it was incredible," he remembers. "When the ball hit the post in the second-half and went straight back into Weaver's arms, I said to my wife, 'This is our day.' That really is one of the great things about the last two seasons. The club's luck has totally turned around. For the previous nine years, we had nothing but pig-bad luck. Mind you, I do believe you make your own luck and Joe Royle does deserve a great deal of credit for what he has done."

As City equalised, Lee's mood began to relax. He could sense the tide had turned. When Christian Dailly scored an own goal to put the visitors ahead, he knew there was something special in the air. "Christian nearly signed for us before he went to Derby. My wife and I went out for a meal with him to the local Chinese and we got on really well. He's a lovely lad and he was keen to come to City. When he scored, Gill turned to me and said, 'Do you think he was thinking about us then?'"

As City clinched their place back in the Premiership, Lee cracked open some bottles of "the bubbly stuff" to celebrate. There was not a tinge of regret, he insists, just pleasure and pride that his club was back in the big time.

"I have been associated with City for 33 years, since 1967. I played during the most successful period in its history. They bought me for £60,000 and sold me for £120,000 – not bad is it? I was deeply honoured to be the club's chairman. I invested a lot of money and I did my best. But, regardless of anything which happened, I love the club. City is my club and it always will be."

BRENDA SWALES SAT QUIETLY on her own. She had not invited her daughters or grandchildren around to her house in south Manchester. For once, she wanted to be alone. Brenda knew this was going to be a special day, a day to spend with her memories of the man she loved.

With the countdown to City's big game at Ewood Park underway, she sat in her husband's favourite chair. She felt a tingle of emotion, almost as if Peter was there with her. "I sat in Peter's favourite room, surrounded by all the photographs of him. I felt very close to him and it brought back so many happy memories."

As the match unfolded, Brenda watched transfixed as her husband's beloved Blues clawed their way back into the Premiership. The faces may have changed, the kit may look slightly different, but this was still City, the club which dominated her life for 20 years. She felt a warm glow, a heady surge of nostalgia. Peter may have gone, but his club was still there.

"It was a great game and it brought so many memories flooding back for me. I thought back to the match at Bradford when we went back up to the First Division. Peter was so happy that day. "He never stopped caring about City, even after he had left the club. If he was watching down, he would have loved the Blackburn game. He would have loved to have seen his club get back where they belong."